# Dispatches from

## Homelessness in Fresno 2002 - 2015

Mike Rhodes

Every reasonable effort has been made to obtain permission for copyrighted material included in this work, and to ensure accuracy at the time of publication, but prices, locations, etc., can change. Any errors that may have occurred are inadvertent and will be corrected in subsequent editions, provided notification is sent to the publisher. The author does not accept and herby disclaims any liability to any party for any loss or damage caused by errors, omissions, or any potential disruption or problem due to application of information contained in this book, whether such incidences result from misuse, negligence, accident, or any other cause.

**ISBN-13:**
**978-1519608024**

**ISBN-10:**
**1519608020**

Special thanks to Michael Evans for copy editing this book.

Mike Rhodes
P.O. Box 5706
Fresno Ca 93755
(559) 978-4502
mikerhodes@comcast.net

# Chapters:

1. Preface..................................................................1

2. How I Got Involved in the Homeless Issue.............3

3. Bulldozing Homeless Encampments...................8

4. The Rescue Mission.......................................17

5. Dispatches from the War Zone........................24

6. The Lawsuit Against the City of Fresno..............31

7. The Disturbing and Tragic Death of Pam Kincaid.....53

8. Mayor Alan Autry Reacts to the Settlement...........64

9. Poor People Gonna Rise Up!..........................71

10. Monitoring City Compliance.........................109

11. Homeless Man Beaten by Police Officers...........122

12. A New Mayor, a Homeless Czar and theWeaving of an Illusion................................................128

13. Maintaining the Status Quo...........................144

14. Alternatives to the Dominant Paradigm............149

15. The Big picture.....................................160

16. The War Against the Poor Goes into Hyper drive..169

17. More Lawsuits Filed Against the City of Fresno...187

18. What is Motivating the City of Fresno?.............197

19. A New Homeless Policy Emerges in Fresno........207

20. What have we learned? ...............................217

# Chapter 1

# Preface

Did the City of Fresno really use federal money intended to help the poor and bulldoze homeless shelters with it? Why was it necessary for a federal judge to order the city to stop violating homeless people's constitutional rights? And how many homeless people have died prematurely as a result of government officials' violent, corrupt and illegal conduct?

What emerges in these pages will disturb and incite you to take action. The stories represent more than a decade of my writing about and investigating homeless issues for the *Community Alliance* newspaper, KFCF 88.1 FM and Indymedia. Much of the information comes from articles previously published, but a significant amount is new and is from California Public Records Act requests, recent interviews and research.

The perspective in *Dispatches from the War Zone: Homelessness in Fresno 2002–2015* comes from my experience as an independent investigative journalist. I make no apologies for standing with the homeless, who are probably the most discriminated group of people in this city, state and country.

My bias on behalf of the homeless is obvious and has often put me in conflict with government officials, the police and many of the social service agencies that maintain business as usual. Unlike the mainstream media, this reporting does not depend on developing and nurturing good relations with the power brokers in this community. Many of the articles written have angered the power elite and because of that, getting information from them has been challenging.

If you are a reporter for the mainstream media and you don't tell the story the ruling elite in Fresno wants you to tell, they will cut off your access. If your job depends on access to high government officials and business leaders and they black-list you, then you are out of a job. This has happened to more than one aspiring journalist in this town.

If you are going to write and publish a book like this you have to have indepen-dence. That independence gives you the freedom to tell the truth that some people don't want you to know about. Being an independent journalist doesn't have a lot of perks, but you are able to tell the truth and make the powerful uncomfortable.

I have also been an activist in support of homeless people's rights. This too makes my perspective in telling the story about the homeless in Fresno different from just about anything else you are likely to read. Actually, there are no other com-prehensive books about the homeless in Fresno during this time period, so this account is definitely unique. Being a supporter of homeless people's rights and working within numerous groups to defend those rights brings an inside view of what this grassroots struggle looks like. It is an honor and a privilege to share that perspective with you.

Getting to know homeless people as co-workers, friends and allies has been one of the most rewarding parts of the experience. Although I have never been home-less myself, I did get to know many homeless people well. There is a collective and collaborative nature that comes with living on the street. People share what they have. They know and talk to their neighbors every day. My hope is that by giving homeless people a voice in this book, readers will get to know and under-stand that they are someone's mother, father, brother or sister.

Somewhere in the back of our minds we all know that if circumstances had been different, if we had a serious health problem, a job loss, mental illness or an untreated addiction, that we too could be homeless. We need to treat the homeless like we would like to be treated if we found ourselves on the street with nowhere to sleep.

It is clear to me that homelessness is a manifestation of a political and economic system that is not meeting people's needs. Understanding that landscape of the shredded social fabric of this city will make you better prepared to envision and implement the changes needed to transform Fresno into the great city it can be. A city where all people are treated with the dignity and respect they deserve.

My greatest hope is that this book will encourage you to join the movement to fight for the resources and political will necessary to end homelessness.

# Chapter 2

# How I Got Involved in the Homeless Issue

I could hear voices in the back of my print shop in downtown Fresno getting louder. The yelling was coming from the alley, and with the roll-up door open I could see a homeless man trying to escape the taunting coming from a police officer who was still on his bike. The officer was calling the homeless man a "human cockroach," telling him to get a job and that his girlfriend was a whore.

When this incident took place in the summer of 2002, I was not a homeless advocate. In fact, I was generally annoyed with having to clean the trash, urine and human feces from the alley so that customers and delivery people could get to our shop. But I was disturbed by this affront to common decency and soon headed to the alley to see what the hell was going on.

The officer was now off his bike and in the homeless man's face, continuing to insult him. The homeless guy was trying to evade the officer, but he could not get away. Finally, I stepped into the middle of the scene and asked if the homeless guy (his name is Dave Ritter) would like to come in and recycle some paper and aluminum plates. He was more than happy to get out of his current circumstance, which probably was not going to end well.

After getting Dave settled into his work, I returned to the alley where Officer Mike Smith was pacing back and forth. The officer stated to me that Dave is a worthless drain on society and that he intended to arrest Dave for an alleged incident that had taken place earlier at the market on Ventura Street and Van Ness Avenue. No doubt, the officer expected me to sympathize with his efforts because

I was a White middle-aged business owner who (like many others) was fed up with the homeless.

Instead, I asked for his name and badge number and filed a complaint with Internal Affairs. In the complaint, I wrote "that the behavior exhibited by Officer Smith was unprofessional and demeaning, the officer appeared to be provoking a confrontation, and that police officers have a duty to protect not harass the public." I waited for a response from Internal Affairs and even called them a few times, but I was never informed of an outcome in the case. A year or so later, in an informal setting, I asked Fresno Police Department (FPD) Chief Jerry Dyer about what had happened. He assured me that the incident had been taken care of, although he did not say exactly how it had been resolved. Although I never found out what (if anything) happened to Officer Smith, I do know that he continued to work with the homeless in downtown Fresno for many years after that incident.

At the time this happened, I was the editor of the *Community Alliance* newspaper, a monthly alternative/independent newspaper in Fresno. The paper is the voice of the progressive movement and supports peace, social and economic justice. My curiosity was aroused by this incident, and I wanted to know more about what was going on with the homeless in downtown Fresno.

Dave, who I had not met before the confrontation with Officer Smith, said that the police were always harassing the homeless when they were north of Ventura Street in downtown Fresno.

South of Ventura Street is the old industrial section of downtown Fresno. There are some warehouses, light manufacturing and many abandoned buildings in that part of downtown. Not too many Fresnans visit the area or even know it exists. On the other hand, the area north of Ventura Street was being developed with the new Fresno Grizzlies baseball stadium having been built that year. Optimism about downtown Fresno (north of Ventura Street) was up, and developers and builders did not want the homeless giving potential investors a bad impression.

The Poverello House and the Rescue Mission, the two largest social service agencies in town that focus on the needs of the homeless, are both located south of Ventura Street, which gave powerful and influential forces an argument for why people like Dave should not be wandering around in the business district of downtown Fresno.

The Poverello House was established in 1973 by Mike McGarvin, who started out by giving away food to the poor and homeless. The project grew and today takes up an entire city block, where the homeless can receive food, clothing, dental care, live in a tool shed and sometimes find a pathway out of homelessness.

The Poverello House, which will be discussed throughout this book, is not going to end homelessness in Fresno, but it does try to make people's lives a little easier by providing essential services. On the other hand, it has been the moving force behind the destruction of homeless encampments that have emerged in areas around its facility. Spokespersons and staff at the Poverello House often talk to the media about how dangerous and violent the homeless are who live outside on the street.

Whatever issues I have with the Poverello House are minor compared to the problems at the Rescue Mission. For years, you would have to attend a religious service to sleep at the Rescue Mission. Now, even that is not enough. If you are not in a recovery program, you can't sleep at the Rescue Mission. In other words, they have more than 100 beds available, but most of them are empty each night because the homeless do not abide by the Rescue Mission's right-wing conservative religious doctrine. The Rescue Mission has even sent its "disciples" (men enrolled in a program at the Rescue Mission, sometimes ordered to be there by the court) into the homeless encampments and destroyed homeless people's property. More about that later.

In 2002, friends of mine who work in grassroots groups like Food Not Bombs (FNB) told me about their experiences in working with the homeless. The FNB operates under the assumption that it does not need government permission to feed the hungry and gives food to anyone who shows up. The FNB folks are amazingly committed—showing up on the same day, week after week, sharing what they have with the poor.

FNB activists such as Dallas Blanchard and Kelly Borkert shared their knowledge and introduced me to more homeless people. There emerged a pattern of stories about homeless people in the downtown area (north of Ventura Street) being woken up, harassed and told to move on. Homeless people living south of Ventura Street, as long as they kept themselves out of site, were largely left alone.

My assumption, when I first started getting involved with this issue, was that this was mostly about economic development. The builders and developers had a financial interest in keeping the homeless out of parts of downtown where redevelopment was taking place. The elected officials at City Hall were directing the police to push the homeless out of downtown because their presence there was not good for business. The mayor and the City Council did that because builders and developers are major contributors to their political campaigns and are a major factor in getting them elected. The homeless had no political power and were therefore being pushed around by forces outside of their control.

I was about to find out that it was a lot more complicated than that.

Dave Ritter was taunted by Fresno police officer Mike Smith who called him a "human cockroach," told him to get a job and said that his girlfriend was a whore.

Many people in the community believe that the Rescue Mission helps the home-less, serves them meals and is the place of last resort where anyone can go to get off the mean streets of Fresno. You are about to learn that there is a whole lot more to the story.

# Chapter 3

# Bulldozing Homeless Encampments

The raid on the first homeless encampment I saw destroyed started shortly after dawn on a cold morning in February 2004. The encampment, which included tents, plastic tarps and some wooden structures, was on Santa Clara Street, directly in front of the Poverello House. The location made sense to the 100-plus people living there because they could stay warm in the Poverello House's day room, eat and use the restrooms. The shelters kept them dry at night.

Days before the police, fire and sanitation departments showed up, notices had been posted announcing the eviction. You could smell the wood burning in the 55-gallon barrels and small cook stoves as city workers arrived. The fire department moved in first and used large hoses to extinguish the fires, removing what little heat the homeless residents had.

The mainstream media started arriving and were directed to a spokesperson from the Poverello House. He explained that this "cleanup" was necessary because of the drugs and violence taking place in the encampment.

I remember thinking (maybe I even said it out loud to the media) that there are drugs and violence all over Fresno. People use drugs, they hurt each other all over town (even in north Fresno), but I don't recall anybody suggesting we bulldoze the Bluffs or River Park. Just because these people are poor and politically powerless, why is the city about to bulldoze their shelters?

Most of the homeless stood by watching as the bulldozing began. There were a few who resisted, saying they had nowhere else to go and that they wanted to stay where they were. When someone resisted, Poverello staff, undercover police and negotiators would quickly surround that person. Nobody was going to be allowed to sleep on Santa Clara Street that night.

It was during the demolition of the Santa Clara Street encampment that the Poverello House established a tent city on its property. The purpose of this experiment was to provide homeless people a place where they could live in a tent, but in a controlled environment. Poverello staff would be in charge of who stayed in the tents, which were behind a chain link fence and on top of pallets. Residents would have to pass by a guard as they came and went; you could not arrive until 5 p.m. and you had to leave by 8 a.m. every morning. No drugs or alcohol were permitted. Some homeless people described it to me as a concentration camp. Others were glad they had a safe place to sleep at night.

As the morning of the homeless encampment demolition progressed, the police came on bicycles, in cars and on foot. There were uniformed officers and undercover police. The police presence was large enough that the homeless got the message that resistance was futile.

After the fire department had thoroughly extinguished all fires, the police moved in to force everyone out of their shelters. Moving tent to tent, they made it clear that it was time to move on and with the bulldozers and garbage trucks moving into position, it was obvious that the demolition of the encampment was about to begin.

The orange-vested City of Fresno sanitation workers, under the protection of the police, started at the western end of Santa Clara Street (near E Street). They dismantled the shelters (tents, tarps and wood structures) and pushed everything onto the street where the bulldozer was waiting. Whatever the homeless were not able to carry away was put on Santa Clara Street and destroyed.

The structures being bulldozed contained everything that some people owned. Maybe they were not around because they were staying with a family member during the time of the demolition. Perhaps they were in the hospital or had spent the night in jail. Whatever the reason, many homeless people lost everything they had that day. Even those who were there that morning could only escape with what they could carry away.

You could see the sanitation workers moving valuable personal property into the street, where it was about to be destroyed. There were the obvious things you would expect: clothes, sleeping bags, tents and food. But, as I would later find out, many people lost items that might affect their health such as their heart, diabetes or asthma medicine. Other homeless people lost their ID, what little money they had, wedding photos and contact information of family members and friends —items that might have helped them get off the streets.

Once the city sanitation workers had pushed everything off the parking strip and over the curb, the bulldozers moved into action. They were brutally efficient, scooping up an enormous pile of homeless people's property and sticking it into the waiting garbage truck. The property was crushed and compressed into the garbage truck. When one truck was filled, it would go to the dump and another garbage truck would take its place.

Several hours later, all that was left was compacted earth and a few scrapes on the ground where the bulldozer had left marks. The mainstream media had done interviews with Poverello House and City of Fresno spokespersons who assured the community that the city had done the right thing by cleaning up the streets. They said that the violence, drug use and other illegal activity could not be tolerated and that the homeless, if they wanted to get off the streets, had places to go. There were programs the homeless could participate in, shelters where they could sleep or they could choose another way of life. The Poverello House and City Hall spun what had happened as a positive development. It was clear that they had coordinated their messages and were working hand-in-hand to force the homeless out of this area.

Meanwhile, Caltrans, the state agency responsible for highway, bridge and rail transportation planning, construction and maintenance, was busy destroying an encampment on the other side of the railroad tracks, this one on H Street (south of Ventura Street) inhabited by about 50 people. The group in this encampment had built their community out of wood shipping crates, the area was clean and there were no reports of violence or criminal activity. Residents in this encampment said it was a model homeless community that provided safety and security for its members. Erick Grove, a spokesperson for the encampment, said that the place was so well run that the new (tent city) facility at the Poverello House was modeled after their organization. No drugs, illegal activity or violence were allowed.

Grove said that "we are dealing with homelessness. We've got people looking for jobs. We've put people in programs. We're taking all the stuff—they can't get into the mission after 7 o'clock, can't get into the Poverello House at all; there's no place for them. We see an old man freezing on the street, we take him in."

Grove had some concrete ideas about what needed to be done. "We can actually build another organization to take care of all the extras and give the people something they need," he said. "Some need mental health resources, some need a program, some just need housing. As families, we're sticking together to make it happen, the city has recognized it. They say they are coming down here to help, but they do the opposite. We've taken care of crime. We've stopped a lot of crime in this area, it's about taking care of our brothers and sisters. We're here and we're making the best with what we got. It's a God blessing that they feed people, but they can't do the housing part. This cold is killing people right now; the cold is very dangerous."

Dontae Johnson, another H Street encampment spokesperson, said, "We're not blaming anybody; we're just asking for health access and to let us have our freedom." Speaking about the restrictions at the Poverello House, he said, "You can't get anything going, you have to be in by 5 p.m. and out by 8 a.m. I think it's a control issue. They know that it scares you, you may have done time, had warrants, and they use that against you. For instance, I was riding my bike and they pulled me over. They put me on the ground and searched me, then they found out I was in the Marines; they were like 'oh you just got back, I'm sorry. Well, you shouldn't be in this area at this time.' I told them 'hey, I gotta be here to get dinner at Poverello at 5 o'clock.'"

Johnson added that "the solution is to get some of these warehouses and get us somewhere to stay. Everybody here, we have trades, we can work here, we can do it. And we have been doing it. The City Councilmen, they get in your face and look at you like there is going to be some hope and then when stuff like this happens they're nowhere to be found. That's some cold business, City Council, it's messed up. So I'm like, what do we have to fall back on? We look to the authorities, and they're like go where ever you're gonna go. But then we go somewhere and we get in trouble for going there. They are trying to clean up the streets; granted, I get that, that's cool. But you can't bunch everybody together, criminals, prostitution, crack. It's not like that though. There are people out here that are truly trying to get on their feet, and we need the help."

The destruction of the H Street encampment appeared to contradict the stated goals that both the City of Fresno and Poverello House gave to the media as the reason for clearing the homeless off of Santa Clara Street. H Street was a well-functioning encampment run by and for the homeless.

The *Fresno Bee* newspaper claimed that "the shantytown sprang up last fall (in 2003) when a few people with good intentions donated tents and sleeping bags to Fresno's homeless." Jean Chipp, director of the Sleeping Bag Project and a member of Food Not Bombs, took exception with that statement. She said that "most bags I've given away have been at Roeding Park at the Food Not Bombs meals on Saturdays. As for the 'people with good intentions' quote, I don't see it that way. I feel there is room for help at many different levels. For the most part, the Sleeping Bag Project is there to help at the lowest of those levels. No matter what, these people are still people, and the weather is still cold and wet and they are outside day and night in that weather...Along with giving bags away, we do donate to various social service groups that work with this population so we do work at different levels. I try not to judge these people—it's not my role."

At the time of this homeless eviction in February 2004, there were maybe 250 shelter beds in Fresno, mostly at the Rescue Mission, which was for men only and required participation in religious ceremonies as a prerequisite for a bed at night.

Although it is impossible to determine how many homeless people there are in Fresno on any given day, everyone agrees that it was more than 250. Perhaps the best estimate at the time came from a 2002 Continuum of Care report that said there were about 19,000 homeless people in Fresno and Madera counties, with about 16,000 in Fresno. Mike Purtell, who worked at the Poverello House in 2004, told me that at the time of the evictions there were about 1,500 homeless people in downtown Fresno, but he added that "nobody really knows how many homeless there are in Fresno."

One thing that was clear to me after observing the demolition of the Santa Clara Street and H Street homeless encampments was that the City of Fresno, the Poverello House and Caltrans did not have a viable plan for improving homeless people's lives, let alone ending homelessness in Fresno.

How could millions of dollars be coming into Fresno to address the homeless issue and the end result is that next to nothing was reaching the homeless who are actually living on the street? Instead, city and state resources were being used to bulldoze and destroy their belongings, with representatives from the Poverello House playing the role of cheerleaders in this macabre drama.

In January 2004, homeless people had established shelters on Santa Clara Street. There were 50–100 people living there before being evicted on February 2.

These police officers, arriving on bicycles, had come to evict the homeless on Santa Clara Street.

The sanitation workers would move through a section of the homeless encampment, throwing personal property into the street, where it was picked up by a bulldozer and destroyed.

The bulldozers put load after load of homeless people's property into the back of a garbage truck where it was crushed and taken to the dump.

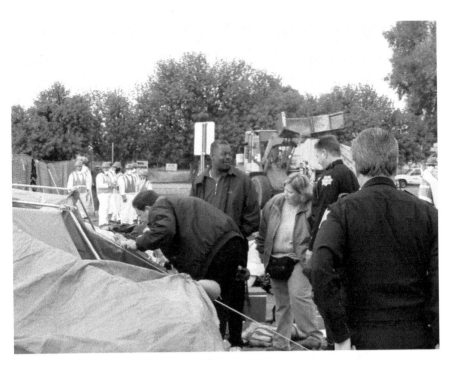

Sometimes a homeless person would refuse to leave. When that happened, the police would move in and force that person to "move on."

Erick Grove was part of a homeless encampment on H Street that was destroyed by Caltrans on the same day the City of Fresno destroyed the Santa Clara Street encampment.

# Map of Downtown Fresno showing the location of homeless encampments

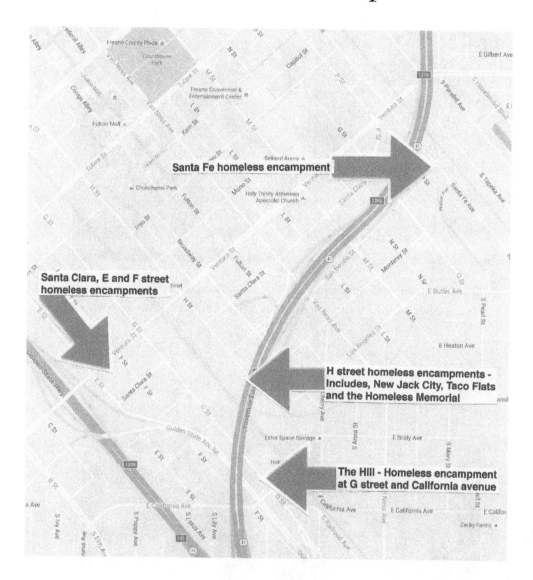

Santa Fe homeless encampment

Santa Clara, E and F street homeless encampments

H street homeless encampments - Includes, New Jack City, Taco Flats and the Homeless Memorial

The Hill - Homeless encampment at G street and California avenue

# Chapter 4

# The Rescue Mission

Just down the street from the Poverello House is an agency that has a disturbing and controversial relationship with Fresno's homeless. The Rescue Mission is a faith-based, conservative, Christian, nonprofit that has been in Fresno since 1949. This long-established group owns the strip of land south of Ventura Street along the east side of G Street.

You will see no homeless encampments on the land owned by the Rescue Mission next to the railroad tracks. You will not see homeless people living in any permanent structures on the public sidewalks near the Rescue Mission either. CEO Larry Arce used to tell people that he had police authorization to keep the sidewalks and streets in front of the Rescue Mission free of homeless people's property. He even admitted in federal court that he would direct his staff to throw away homeless people's property if it was on the sidewalk in front of the Mission.

Here is how that conversation went:

> Attorney for the homeless: So let the word go forth from the Fresno Rescue Mission that any cart that you have, if you leave it anywhere near the Fresno Rescue Mission, it will be thrown away? That's true; isn't it?

> Arce's response: If the individual doesn't have enough sense to realize that if it has value to that individual, and if he leaves it out there, yes, we will throw it away.

> Attorney for the homeless: You will throw it away?

Arce: Yes, sir.

Arce and the Rescue Mission took the position that if any property was left near its buildings, even if the property was owned by someone eating a meal in the Rescue Mission, it would be considered abandoned and thrown away.

There were times when Arce would direct his "disciples" to raid nearby homeless encampments and destroy their property. Arce and his disciples were considered by many of the homeless as the terror of G Street, and they seemed to have police protection, even if city officials would not acknowledge it.

Lori, a homeless woman, told me that "we were at the doctor's office over at the Poverello House when someone came in and said the 'disciples' from the Rescue Mission were throwing our stuff away." She said her husband immediately went to the Mission to ask Arce for his property back. Included in the property taken was Lori's husband's heart medicine. "Arce told my husband, 'Oh well, the city told me to do that,' and that there was nothing we could do about it," Lori said.

In an incident that happened in the summer of 2006, Rescue Mission disciples directed by Arce targeted an area known as The Hill, which is a homeless encampment just south of the Rescue Mission. It is public property. Using a forklift and a dumpster, Rescue Mission crews moved through the area throwing away everything in their path. Bryan Apper, who works with St. Benedict Catholic Worker, said he tried later that day to recover one homeless woman's property. Apper said, "We were concerned for Peggy because they had taken her new red tent that a church group had just given her. Peggy is barred from staying at Naomi House (a nearby homeless shelter for women) and would literally have no place to sleep that night."

Apper, his wife Liza, who also works with St. Benedict Catholic Worker, and Ashley Fairburn from Food Not Bombs decided to go and retrieve Peggy's property from the Rescue Mission dumpster. They found the tent and Peggy's other property in the dumpster. As they were driving away, they were stopped by the police. Arce had called the police to complain that they were trespassing on his property and stealing items from the Mission dumpster.

The Rescue Mission "cleanup" crews struck again in early 2007. Big Sue, who lived on The Hill, said the homeless people in that encampment had set up Christmas ornaments over the holidays. The *Fresno Bee* even ran a nice feel-good story with a photo about how the homeless had set up the display. Big Sue said that Rescue Mission disciples came out a couple of days after Christmas and stole the display. Big Sue said, "After that I put up a sign of a big heart on the fence and the words 'love each other' and 'forgive,' but they came out and stole those too." She said the big heart symbolized how her heart had been broken when they stole the ornaments.

Arce, at that time, repeatedly told anyone who questioned his actions that he had an agreement with the police and the City of Fresno to keep G Street clean. Curious about this agreement, I submitted a California Public Records Act request to the City of Fresno and the FPD asking for a copy of the document authorizing the Rescue Mission to take and destroy homeless people's property. City officials told me, after a thorough search of their records, that no such document existed. The City of Fresno Public Information Office asked Arce if such a document existed. Patti Miller, public affairs administrator, wrote in an e-mail, "Rev. Arce assured me as well that to his knowledge, no such document exists."

In 2009, a lawsuit was filed against the Rescue Mission, alleging that it took personal belongings critical to homeless people's survival such as clothing, medication, tents and blankets, as well as irreplaceable personal possessions such as family photographs, identification, personal records and documents. The lawsuit was settled out of court for an undisclosed amount of money. After the lawsuit, the Rescue Mission seemed more restrained in its attacks on the homeless.

In 2004, the Rescue Mission established what was perhaps the only outdoor drunk tank in the country at its facility. The idea was to save the City of Fresno money on booking expenses, but there were other motivating factors behind the operation. Arce said one of the reasons he wanted to oversee the drunk tank was to provide "spiritual counseling for addiction."

The idea, as it was explained to me, was that the plan would save the city money by gathering up inebriated homeless people, putting them in the drunk tank and allowing right-wing religious fanatics to rant at them. What could go wrong?

Arce told me that nobody was going to be locked up in the drunk tank. He said that there would be a guard house and that there were plans to install video surveillance cameras but that anyone brought to the facility would be free to go. Of course, he added, the police would be called and persons leaving the drunk tank would be taken to jail if they left before Rescue Mission staff said they could go. When asked about the razor wire around the perimeter of the planned outdoor drunk tank, Arce smiled and said that it was there to keep people from breaking into the drunk tank.

During my interview with Arce, the location seemed less than ideal. True, the razor wire and bare ground was protected from the rain by the freeway overpass. But the weather—it gets below freezing in the winter and the heat of summer can surpass 110 degrees—might not be the ideal environment for sleeping off a hangover.

Were Rescue Mission staff properly trained in the event that someone suffered from a medical emergency? Was it legal to only give men the option of avoiding jail by going to the drunk tank? Women did not have the option of going to the drunk tank. Did city officials really believe they would save $400,000 a year on booking expenses or was this just another way to humiliate the homeless and support the U.S. version of the Taliban?

Speaking before the Fresno City Council before a vote was taken on this issue, community activist Gloria Hernandez said, "I have a lot of concerns with this proposal. If we have a drunk tank, both rich and poor ought to go in there. I hope that when you look at this, the money is not important; the people are important." Nobody on the City Council jumped up to suggest putting a drunk tank on the parking lot at River Park where north Fresno drunks would be put on display, perhaps counseled by Muslim clerics.

Edie Jessup from the Unitarian Universalist Church of Fresno said that she was concerned about the "20,000-plus homeless in Fresno and Madera who are at risk because of the eroding safety net." Jessup went on to say that "an open air drunk tank is not a solution to the problem and this has a terrible appearance for the city of Fresno. I can only imagine the legal and human rights suits that the establishment of this facility will create."

But these concerns did not deter the enthusiasm for the project by City Council members. Brian Calhoun was almost giddy saying that he was "very intrigued and impressed with this approach. This is a win-win. A thumbs up for a very good way for dealing with this population."

Even liberal City Council Member Tom Boyajian voted to support the proposal. Boyajian dismissed the potential to convert the prisoners to Christianity by saying, "Maybe you will give them handouts and say this is the kind of thing that maybe can help you because you have an issue that you need to take care of. You are trying to bring more humanity to these individuals."

The outdoor drunk tank was not the only attack on this community's homeless population by City Council members. In addition to the bulldozing of homeless encampments, City Hall passed an anti-panhandling ordinance and started a public relations campaign to convince the public not to donate cash to the poor and homeless. The public was told that the homeless would use the money to buy drugs and alcohol.

In recent years, the Rescue Mission made a decision to no longer allow the homeless to sleep in its facility unless they are enrolled in a recovery program approved by the Mission. That has resulted in most of the beds being empty, even as thousands of homeless people sleep outside on the sidewalks and vacant lots.

The Rescue Mission's "tough love" policy is embedded in the right-wing religious doctrine that says helping the homeless without preaching to them and getting them into a program is enabling them to continue down a sinful and self-destructive path. Arce wants the homeless to hit bottom and ask for help and redemption. It is in this spirit that homeless people are refused a place to sleep, why their property is being taken and destroyed, and why people like Arce can sincerely believe that by being cruel, they are being kind.

City Hall, the Poverello House and the Rescue Mission have been in an unholy alliance to demonize the homeless, take their property, destroy their shelters and convince the public that this approach is doing homeless people a favor. For some mysterious reason, that approach has not reduced homelessness or improved the conditions in which they live. On the other hand, it has brought in significant resources to these homeless agencies and has, through the magic of a modern-day advertising campaign, given the city the ability to create the illusion that it is helping the homeless.

Larry Arce, CEO of the Fresno Rescue Mission, sent his "disciples" to take and destroy homeless people's property.

A typical raid by the Fresno Rescue Mission on a homeless encampment, where its "disciples" would come, take property and destroy it.

Bryan Apper with St. Benedict Catholic Worker, commenting on this photo, said, "We not only recovered this woman's quilt, we also recovered a water bottle that was a gift to her from the Mission at their much-publicized 'birthday party for the homeless' the Saturday before. The top brass of the Mission watched as we recovered these items. In our negotiations, Larry Arce said that his crew had just cleaned up trash. We also recovered a brand new Bible, which was also a gift at the birthday party, held it up and asked, 'So this is what you call trash?'"

# Chapter 5

# Dispatches from the War Zone

In the early spring of 2006, I was driving down Ventura Street and passed E Street, noticing that a new homeless encampment had emerged. I stopped to talk to some of the residents to find out what was going on. It was through this contact that I would get to know Cynthia, Dee, Pam and many other homeless people who would be my guides as I continued to learn about this subculture that is sometimes hidden in plain sight.

This homeless encampment was on a small strip of land, next to Highway 99, and near the Poverello House. The homeless people living there had constructed a few tents and temporary shelters that were visible from Ventura Street. I was told that a week before I found out about this encampment Caltrans and the FPD descended on the area with bulldozers, gave residents a couple of minutes to get out and proceeded to destroy everything in their path. One resident told me that when she resisted, an undercover police officer pulled a gun on her.

Dee, one of the women at the encampment, told me that the police and Caltrans workers came at dawn and with little warning began scooping up the tents with the bulldozer and dumping them in garbage trucks. "What these people don't understand," she said, "is that everything we own in the world is right here. All of our clothes, papers, everything is in the tent, and they just threw it away."

Dee said she had been homeless and in this area for about five years. She said that "if you don't have a home and you can't live on public land [in this case, land owned by the State of California], what are you supposed to do?" When Caltrans workers moved in to destroy this homeless encampment, she said she was confronted by an aggressive undercover police officer who told her to get out. She asked the officer how she was doing and was told "better than you! At least I have a home." Dee said the officer was laughing at her and the plight of the homeless as the bulldozers moved in.

I was told by the people living in this encampment that during the last demolition they had to grab their tents and try to get out of the path of the bulldozer. They were largely successful, except for one tent with a large gash. A homeless woman pointed to that tent, saying, "Well, at least it is not raining this time of the year." About a week after the bulldozing, there were 20–30 tents and other structures back on E Street near Santa Clara Street.

Chuck, a homeless man living at this encampment, told me he had been there only four or five days. He said he had applied for disability and while waiting for his claim to get processed he had no income. He said, "People should not judge you by the circumstances you find yourself in." Chuck said he had a job until recently, but with a permanent leg disability, he had no way of making money. He was able to walk over to the Poverello House, with the help of a cane, for three meals a day, but that was about it.

The Poverello House's tent city had become a Village of Hope, consisting of a handful of tool sheds where a couple of dozen people could spend the night. Down the street, the Rescue Mission had beds for a hundred or so homeless people, but only if you are willing to sit through a Christian religious service. That left thousands of homeless on the streets of Fresno each night with nowhere to go.

Gloria Rodriguez, public information officer for Caltrans, told me that the homeless were in violation of Caltrans policy, they were illegal and had to be removed. According to her, it was a public safety issue. Jeff Cardinale, public information officer for the FPD at that time, said his department was just supporting Caltrans.

The real reason for the destruction of homeless people's shelters would not be revealed for a couple of years. For now, all the homeless knew was that the "cleanups" were increasing in frequency and intensity.

Chuck had a simple solution. He said, "Why can't they just provide some temporary shelter while we sort out my disability? There is a huge open field down the street. Why don't they just open that up for the homeless?" To suffer the pain of a debilitating injury, no home to live in and now the prospect of having his tent destroyed, Chuck was more than a little frustrated.

On May 25, 2006, at 7 a.m., Fresno city workers were again sent to destroy the homeless encampment on E Street. Backed up by the police, workers from the sanitation department moved their bulldozer and garbage truck into position. As men in orange vests and face masks moved in, the homeless hurried to disassemble their tents and load their belongings onto shopping carts.

This was the fourth attack on the homeless in the few months, and most of the residents on this small strip of land, under Caltrans management, were used to the routine. A police officer comes by a day or two before the eviction and tells the homeless to move. This is followed by the arrival of the city sanitation crew and the police. The homeless residents know that if they can move their belongings across the street in time, they will be able to move back before the day is over.

I talked to Monte and Will the day before the evictions, and they were mostly philosophical about what was about to happen. "We will just pack up our stuff and wait for them to leave," said Monte, a military veteran. Will is a disabled vet. He was injured in the Korean War and uses a wheelchair. The shrapnel in his spine left him paralyzed. Will was on the street as the eviction began, early in the morning. He wondered out loud why the city has the resources to destroy their community but not to provide a portable toilet or dumpster for the trash that accumulates.

When I arrived, Will was talking to Liza Apper from the St. Benedict Catholic Worker project. Liza and her husband Bryan were there to observe the "cleanup" and try to provide some protection. While Bryan talked to the agencies involved about the law, Liza positioned herself in front of a tent that had been targeted for destruction. The owners of the tent were away when the bulldozer arrived, and Liza was the only thing between the tent and certain destruction. She was told to move but held her ground. Eventually, the bulldozer operator decided to go around Liza and moved further down the strip of land to scoop up blankets, food and other items that had been left behind. About 30 minutes later, the owners of the tent returned. They hurriedly took down their tent and moved across the street.

The attacks against the homeless continued throughout the summer and by August had reached a new level of intensity. On August 26, 2006, barbed wire fences went up on E Street to keep the homeless off a strip of land owned by Caltrans. The homeless were told to move to the Poverello House, which was about one block away. Fresno Assistant City Manager Bruce Rudd said, "We met with the Poverello House yesterday, and they said they could take in anyone who needed a place to stay." Several homeless people I talked to scoffed at this assertion and said the Poverello House doesn't have the facilities to take in the hundreds of people who had just been displaced. Dee, one of the homeless women in the area, told me that the Poverello House closes at 12:30 p.m. on Saturday. "There is no way they are going to let us all in there," Dee said.

I went to the Poverello House and asked for the person in charge. I talked to Paul Stack, who said he was in charge for the day. I asked him if I could see the facilities where the hundreds of homeless people were going to sleep tonight. Stack looked like a deer caught in the headlights of a car and said that he would have to call his boss and have him call me. He confirmed what Dee had said; they start getting people out of the Poverello House at about 12:30 p.m. and everyone is gone by 2 p.m. on Saturday. Nobody from the Poverello House called me back.

Before leaving the Poverello House, I ran into the director of the Naomi House, which is located next to the Poverello House. The Naomi House provides women with a place to sleep. It has room for 25 women, and a lottery system is used to determine who gets to stay the night. When I told her about the "cleanup" on E Street and that the city spokesperson was saying all of the homeless could come to the Poverello House, she just rolled her eyes. She said, "We don't have enough room as it is. How are we going to take more people in?"

With more than 1,000 homeless people in the downtown area at that time, and inadequate shelter space available, what was the city going to do with people who are homeless? I asked that question to Rudd. Rudd said, "We are going to encourage people to avail themselves of the facilities available." I asked if people would be arrested for camping on the street. Rudd said, "I hope it doesn't come to that."

Right after my conversation with Stack and my interview with Rudd, things started getting exciting on the Caltrans strip of land on E Street. Liza Apper had put herself in front of the garbage truck that was being filled with the homeless people's tents, clothing and other possessions. She refused to move saying that "we have got to take a stand for justice." Several FPD officers arrived, and an animated conversation took place. Liza refused to move.

About that time, several activists from the Fresno C.A.F.E./Food Not Bombs collective were starting to position themselves in front of some of the homeless people's possessions. FPD Officer Rey Wallace pushed them toward the street. The activists managed to outmaneuver him and ended up in front of the bulldozer.

The police and city sanitation crew gave up on the strategy of trying to talk those engaged in civil disobedience out of the act and removed both the bulldozer and the garbage truck. This turned out to be only a brief tactical retreat. Most of the homeless and their allies moved down to the other end of the strip of land where there was an African-American man in a wheelchair who was refusing to leave his tent. As everyone went to the other end of the strip of land, the city brought in a crew to start building a fence around the property.

Walter, the guy who was refusing to move, demanded a permanent place for him and his dog. The police negotiated with him for several hours before finally working something out that was acceptable.

As Walter was being led away, I heard City Manager Andy Souza telling a Channel 47 (CBS) reporter about how all these people could go to the Poverello House and they would be given a place to sleep for the night. After the interview, I told him that what he said was a nice story for the TV audience and that it would probably make people feel better knowing that the homeless had a place to stay, but that he and I both knew it was not true. We talked about the lack of shelter beds, and I asked him what short- and long-term plans the city had for eliminating homelessness.

Souza did not have a lot of answers to the question about the city's plan for eliminating homelessness, but we did have a conversation about what short- and long-term solutions might exist. He seemed to think that the crisis precipitated by the day's events might motivate the city to work toward developing a plan to end homelessness. We agreed that pushing people out of one area to another was not a solution. It just displaces the problem. He listened as I told him the homeless in this area need a safe place to stay, trash service, running water and portable toilets. These services would be less expensive than the constant attacks being carried out and would actually help rather than hurt the homeless.

Police Captain Greg Garner and Rudd joined us. Souza said that living conditions like this would never be tolerated in north Fresno by River Park. Garner said that the solution was not always something the City of Fresno could come up with. He asked, "Why don't the churches and other community groups get together to help?" There was agreement that most people in north Fresno don't know that such conditions exist in this community.

While we talked, the bulldozer and cleanup crew were busy filling the garbage truck with the possessions of the homeless. When they were done on E Street, they turned and headed east on Santa Clara Street.

For a while, in early 2006, homeless people would pick up and move their tents and other property from one side of the street to the other to avoid having it destroyed by city sanitation workers and the police.

Officer Rey Wallace (left) tells homeless advocate Liza Apper to allow city sanitation workers to destroy homeless people's property. She refused, later getting into a tug of war with Wallace. Wallace once told me that "the homeless people that live here are the luckiest homeless in Fresno." Surprised by the statement, I asked him what he meant. "They have maid service. We come out and clean up for them about every other week."

City sanitation workers picked up one shopping cart after another (each filled with homeless people's property) and put them into the back of a garbage truck. The carts and property were crushed, compacted and taken to the dump. One cleanup crew supervisor was overheard saying, "I wish I had a nickel for every cart we destroy."

There were many acts of resistance to the demolition of homeless people's property. These two women put their bodies in front of a bulldozer at the E Street encampment and refused to move.

# Chapter 6

# The Lawsuit Against the City of Fresno

It was during one of the attacks on the homeless, like those described in the previous chapter, that I decided to do something more than just report on these gross violations of homeless people's human rights. I was on a phone interview with Robert Norse of Santa Cruz who has a show on a pirate radio station there when he asked me why nobody had sought a temporary restraining order or a preliminary injunction against the City of Fresno. By that time, I was convinced that what the city was doing was immoral and probably illegal.

After calling a few local attorneys, who for a variety of reasons could not take the case, I contacted the American Civil Liberties Union (ACLU) in San Francisco. I described what was happening here and soon they asked me to set up a meeting with some of the homeless people who were, in my opinion, being abused by the city.

The meetings went well, and the ACLU joined together with two law firms: Heller Ehrman, an international law firm with more than 730 attorneys in 15 offices nationwide, and the Lawyers' Committee for Civil Rights (LCCR) of the San Francisco Bay Area.

The attorneys for the homeless reached out to the City of Fresno to try and resolve the alleged violations of their clients' rights out of court. Representatives from the city, believing they were not in violation of the law, rejected those negotiations, which forced the matter before Judge Oliver W. Wanger in the U.S. District Court, Eastern District of California.

On October 19, 2006, the City of Fresno was issued a temporary restraining order

(TRO) that stopped it from taking and immediately destroying homeless people's property. The practice of destroying homeless encampments had been challenged in a lawsuit filed two days earlier.

The lawsuit said that clothing, medication, tents and blankets, as well as irreplaceable personal possessions, such as family photographs, personal records and documents, had been destroyed by the City of Fresno in these raids. Paul Alexander with the Heller Ehrman law firm argued that without a TRO, the City of Fresno would likely continue these attacks that result in the taking and destruction of homeless people's property.

In arguments before the court, Alexander said that the FPD had lined up homeless residents in October 2006 and told them that the city would return and destroy their property. He cited a declaration from FPD Captain Greg Garner stating that there had been complaints about the homeless in that area but that the police had not yet acted on those complaints.

Judge Wanger asked James Betts, the attorney representing the City of Fresno, about the city's "found property procedure." Betts said the city does have a policy but that he did not have it available. Both Judge Wanger and Alexander said it was unlikely that the written policy would allow for the immediate destruction of people's property by the city. Alexander cited the Pottinger case in Miami, which specifically addressed the issue of the confiscation of homeless people's property by the police. A case in Los Angeles was also cited as evidence that the police do not have the right to take and destroy homeless persons' possessions. Alexander said California Civil Code 2080 states that if the police take a citizen's property the owner must be given every opportunity to recover those items. Items must be stored for at least 90 days.

Judge Wanger said that he did not think the police should be put in the position of deciding what was valuable property. He said, "One man's treasure is another man's junk." Betts made two points: These incidents are not happening on city property, and the police are only responding to residents' complaints.

Betts claimed the homeless were illegally camping on private property and that the city had received numerous complaints. He argued that the city always gives written and oral warnings when a "cleanup" is about to take place and that it works with the Poverello House and the Rescue Mission to make sure the homeless know when the next demolition is coming. Betts argued that the city's response was compassionate.

In arguing against the issuance of a TRO, Betts said that it "would unduly burden the city to the point that they would not be able to respond to property owners' complaints." Judge Wanger said that the Fourth and 14th amendments to the U.S. Constitution and state law protect citizens from having their property taken and destroyed without due process and that sometimes those rights will cost the city money, in this case for storing confiscated property. The judge did not say that the city could not take homeless people's property, but rather that the city can't immediately destroy that property. Issuing the TRO, Judge Wanger said, "The court does find that the property rights, shelter, clothing, ID and other items justify the intervention."

Betts then asked the court if the homeless could be made to post a bond to insure against damages incurred by the TRO, if the city ends up winning the case. Judge Wanger pointed out that the homeless have no resources to post a bond and that the public interest would be served by waiving the bond. Wanger said a court date would be set to hear arguments for the preliminary injunction in November 2006.

There were several homeless people in the federal courtroom when the TRO was issued. They were all excited to have won a victory in this struggle for their civil rights. As news of the TRO spread to the homeless encampments in downtown Fresno, it brought hope and encouragement to those who had suffered from the city's relentless raids.

The lawsuit against the City of Fresno changed the discussion about the homeless in this community. The homeless were not looked at as victims but as people who were starting to stand up for their rights. Community activists and the homeless organized a rally at City Hall where Food Not Bombs provided food, sleeping bags were distributed and a large group (both homeless and supporters of the homeless) camped out in front of City Hall.

The lawsuit was the springboard that connected progressive community activists with getting to know the homeless. The *Community Alliance* newspaper played a pivotal role in this effort by printing numerous articles about the homeless. Through these articles, people started to realize how much of the propaganda they were hearing in the mainstream media was just not true.

To illustrate the human element of homeless people's lives, the *Community Alliance* printed the following two articles about a couple of the women in the lawsuit. Their stories, which are in their own words, speak about the challenges of being homeless in Fresno and put a human face on the story. Both of these articles were printed in the November 2006 *Community Alliance* newspaper.

## Charlene Clay

I am 48 years old, and I currently live in Fresno. I have lived in Fresno for 15 years. My husband and I have been homeless for approximately six months. We had to leave our last apartment because the rent was $850 per month, and this was more than we could afford to pay. We do not have enough money for an up-front deposit and first and last month's rent to be able to rent an apartment. I would really like to have housing because I want my grandchildren to be able to visit me. During the time that we have been homeless, I stayed for a little while at the Naomi House for women, but this meant that I could not live with my husband. I have been in several abusive relationships in the past. One of my previous abusers knocked my teeth out. My current husband is not abusive, and it is important for us to stay together. Because my husband and I cannot stay together in shelters, and because space is limited there, we sleep outside in tents.

Sometime during the first two weeks of April 2006, the City of Fresno took almost all of my personal belongings. I do not recall the exact date, but I remember the events well. We were camped on a hill off of G Street. My husband and I were at the Poverello House when we heard that the city was taking people's property. We initially thought that the city was only taking belongings from in front of the Poverello House, but then someone told us the city was going up to the hill where our belongings were. I walked as fast as I could to get there, but I do not walk very fast because I need surgery on my foot, and I have high blood pressure and asthma. By the time I arrived at the site, it was empty, except for the crumpled shell of our tent and a few other stray items. All the tents and items belonging to the Mexican workers we shared the site with were also gone. I could see the tracks in the dirt from where the dump truck had driven.

The city did not give us any notice that it was going to take and destroy our belongings. My husband and I lost almost everything we owned, including my teeth, my medications, a small TV, a laptop computer, a bike, our dog food, blankets, sleeping bags, my husband's weights for lifting and our clothes, including a new pair of shoes I had, and my personal papers. I was extremely upset.

The city came again to our campsite on October 8, 2006. We were camped in a new spot, under the bridge at San Benito and H streets. At 8:30 in the morning, the police came without any warning and started taking shopping carts from people. The police threw everyone's possessions on the ground and then took all the carts and threw them onto a truck. After taking the carts, the police said they would be back for all the rest of our belongings at noon that day, but they have not come yet. I do not know where I could go to be safe from these property seizures.

Based on my experience, wherever I go as a homeless person in the city of Fresno, the City of Fresno workers, accompanied by the Fresno Police Department, will come to take and destroy my personal possessions. This has happened to me twice already, and I believe it will happen again. The city has made it clear to me by destroying my property twice and by the way in which they did that. That because I am a homeless person, I will always be vulnerable to having my property taken and destroyed by City of Fresno workers and the police.

**Pamela Kincaid**
For the last five or six years, I have lived in the area just south of downtown Fresno. I make a little money from recycling and selling crafts but not enough to afford an apartment or other housing. I have occasionally stayed at the Naomi House, which is the one women's shelter in town. However, I am claustrophobic and have had panic attacks when I have stayed there before, so I have not done that for the last two years. Also, I have a dog who stays with me for protection and for company, and he cannot stay with me if I am in a shelter. So most of the time, I live outside.

Approximately one year ago, I had set up a makeshift tent by the railroad tracks, just south of the downtown area of Fresno. I believe that this is the railroad's property. A man who works for the railroad comes through the area every month or so, basically to check on things. He asks for people's names but has never asked me to leave, and I have not heard him ask anyone else to leave. Except for a dock in the back of Wilson's Motorcycle Warehouse, I have never seen any signs in that area telling people they can't be there.

I had also seen Fresno police and sanitation workers come through the area every month or so, taking homeless people's property. I was usually able to keep my belongings from being taken by moving them when the workers came through. Unfortunately, this one time approximately one year ago, I left my property unattended, and when I came back, it was all gone.

Almost all of my possessions were taken, including important documents like my identification, my birth certificate and my telephone/address book, which had important contact information for people I want to keep in touch with. Worst of all, I lost family photos, including the only pictures I had of my sister, my daughter and my deceased mother. Those photos can never be replaced.

No one, either from the city or from anywhere else, told me beforehand that city workers were going to come through that day and take homeless people's property. No one told me any way to get my property back once it was taken. Having previously seen city workers just throw away other people's belongings into a dump truck as if it were trash, I have no doubt that this is what was done to my belongings that day.

Approximately two months ago, I was again staying near the railroad tracks, just south of downtown. Since the previous time that my property was destroyed, I had managed to accumulate a few things that I was keeping with me. I had many of my belongings in a shopping cart, covered by a tarp. This was an old, outdated cart that had been abandoned and I was using it to store my possessions. This is one of the ways I could move my possessions. I left for an hour or two in the middle of the day, and when I returned, the cart had been taken. Items that had been stored in the cart had been dumped onto the ground. Some items, such as clothing, were still there. However, other important items had been taken. These included a toolbox and various tools (screwdriver, wire strippers, flashlight). Those tools were very important to me because I used them to make a little income. For example, I used the wire strippers to take wire off of metal items so they can be recycled. I used my other tools to take apart metal items to sell for scrap. Also, I used these tools to make crafts, such as jewelry and "dreamcatchers," which I was able to sell to make a little bit of money.

Since I knew that city workers often came through the area and took homeless people's belongings, I was sure that this is what had happened that day. I later confirmed with other homeless people in the area that city workers had been in the area that day and that the workers had been particularly focused on taking shopping carts. I never received any notice from the city or from anyone else that people from the city were going to be coming through the area taking carts or anything else, and I was not given any way to get my belongings back after the fact.

I have also personally observed other raids, including one that happened approximately four and a half months ago. In that raid, I saw city workers destroy homeless people's property, even though it was clearly owned. For example, I saw city workers use a bulldozer-type machine with "claws" to scoop up and destroy an eight-man tent that was set up near the railroad tracks. That tent belonged to a homeless man I knew from the area, who was living in the tent but who just happened to be gone when the city people came by. He also had some cats staying with him. I think the cats might have been inside the tent at the time it was destroyed; at any rate, I never saw them again after that. I saw a similar raid about a month earlier. One of the city workers told me at that time that they were doing these raids because local politicians were upset about having seen stories on the news about how homeless people were living on the streets of Fresno.

Before I became homeless, I used to have a house and a job. I lost both when I developed injuries at work that made it impossible for me to keep my job. I hope that someday I will be able to get off the streets and into permanent housing. But the fact that the city keeps taking and destroying my property makes that goal seem that much harder to achieve. I always live with the fear that the city will come and take what few possessions I have left.

\*\*\*

The lawsuits filed against the City of Fresno, based on the information given by homeless people from stories like the ones above, led to hearings in federal court. I attended those hearings and published daily reports about what was happening. The first day of hearings was on November 7, 2006.

The insights I gained from these hearings were invaluable in my understanding the complexities of this issue, the viewpoint of the social service providers and the limitations of the law.

On the first day, the courtroom of Judge Wanger was filled with homeless people and their allies. The first witness was Liza Apper, a homeless advocate who has put herself in front of bulldozers to protect homeless people's property. She spoke about the May 25, 2006, incident when she stopped a bulldozer from destroying a tent. The police ordered Apper to move, but she held her ground. The bulldozer eventually moved around her and destroyed other shelters. After the threat from the bulldozer was gone, Apper said that a man came out of the tent. Twist (the homeless man's street name) had been asleep and unaware of the danger.

Apper said that Fresno was exceptionally hostile to homeless people and on a national scale is probably one of the most unfriendly cities. Betts, the attorney representing the City of Fresno, objected repeatedly and attempted to limit Apper's testimony. Apper said Fresno was in the top 10 of U.S. cities that are hostile to the homeless. She estimated there were 4,000–8,000 homeless on the streets of Fresno and that there are few shelters where a homeless person can find a bed. Apper said the Fresno Rescue Mission has 120–150 beds, the Poverello House had 22 tool sheds that sleep two people each and that the Naomi House had 24 beds.

Because of a scheduling issue, Jim Connell, executive director of the Poverello House, was the next witness. Connell said the Poverello House complained about the homeless encampment on Santa Clara Street in 2003 and 2004 because he believed criminal activity was taking place.

Connell described the period leading up to the raid on the homeless encampment by saying that "the Poverello House was getting complaints. There was verbal harassment of people coming to visit our facility, sanitation problems and needles and syringes on the ground." In late 2003 or early 2004, FPD Captain Garner called a meeting of social service groups. The purpose of the meeting was to come up with a solution to the Santa Clara Street encampment. Connell said that Captain Garner told the group he would not clear the street until someone stepped forward and set up additional housing for the homeless. According to testimony, Connell was the only person at the meeting to agree to set up more shelter space. The agreement was to use a piece of land, recently purchased by the Poverello House, and set up a tent city. This has turned into the Village of Hope, which has 44 beds in 22 tool sheds.

Connell described the Village of Hope as a self-governed community that provides for its own security, has its own city council and members are voted in and out. He complained that the occupancy rate over the summer of 2006 was only 50%–60%. He then used that figure to argue that any homeless person who wants a bed has one available. Connell said the reason homeless people are not staying at the Poverello House is because the Village of Hope has "minimal standards." For example, residents of the Village of Hope are not allowed to bring in drugs or alcohol. Connell did not mention that these tool sheds get extremely hot in the summer or that residents must leave by 8 a.m. and can't come back until late afternoon.

The issue of how many homeless are in Fresno came up several times. Connell challenged the findings of the Continuum of Care report, which concluded that about 1% of the population in Fresno was homeless at any given time. The 1% figure is a national average. Some people think that because of economic conditions the number of homeless in Fresno is higher—perhaps as high as 2%. But Connell argued that the number was far less than the figure cited in the Continuum of Care report. "I don't know how many homeless there are in Fresno. It could be 200 or 2 million."

Connell said that he does not believe any homeless people have ever had their property taken without receiving a notice that a "cleanup" was about to take place. He said that the Poverello House has written, printed and posted many of the notices preceding the raids. But when asked if he has ever seen a notice posted in a homeless encampment he said "no."

When asked how often he has been in the homeless encampments around the Poverello House, Connell said that he has walked through them maybe six times. Connell has worked at the Poverello House 16 years and has only walked outside where the encampments and the homeless are located an estimated six times. The homeless and their allies in the courtroom gasped at the admission. Connell also said he was unaware of current activities in the area because he had just returned from a vacation in Europe.

The level of hostility Connell had against the homeless who refuse to subject themselves to the discipline of his Village of Hope became more apparent as he was challenged on his perception of whether the homeless are being treated in a compassionate manner by the police. Connell said that "Captain Garner has shown compassion and patience in his work with the homeless. Officer [Rey] Wallace is exceptionally compassionate." In testimony before the court, Connell said it is compassionate to throw away homeless people's property if they are not present when it is destroyed. Michael Risher, an attorney with the ACLU, asked Connell if it would be compassionate to throw away a bicycle that was leaning up against a fence. "Yes" was the reply. How about a shopping cart with someone's property inside? "Yes." Connell drew the line at destroying somebody's property if it was clearly identifiable and could be returned to the owner. He said the Poverello House has a program that allows homeless people to store property for 30 days.

Rev. Floyd Harris was the next witness. Harris had participated in a cleanup of the homeless encampment over the summer. He described how it was possible to clean up the homeless encampment without destroying property. Harris said he went to the encampment the day before the cleanup to talk with the residents. The homeless agreed to help, and when Harris brought a youth group they all worked together on the cleanup. Harris disputed Connell's description of the encampments as being covered with human feces and having needles and syringes all over the ground. Harris said, "I've seen more needles north of Shields Avenue than south of Shields." Harris said he and his co-workers did not have to wear biohazard suits to conduct the cleanup. "I wanted to show the youth group that came out that day not to be afraid of the homeless," Harris concluded. "We are all one community."

Apper returned to the stand and described the June 22, 2006, attack on the homeless encampment. Photos were shown of her struggling with Officer Wallace over the possession of a shopping cart. On that day, the police and sanitation had concluded their cleanup on the west side of E Street (south of Ventura Street) and the homeless had removed what they could and put it on the east side of E Street. In a surprise move, the police directed city sanitation workers to start throwing entire tents and shopping carts into the garbage truck and crushing them. What was being destroyed was obviously the property that the homeless people sought to save from destruction.

Apper next described the August 26, 2006, raid that ended with the city constructing a fence around the homeless encampment to keep people from returning.

The hearings continued on November 16 and 17, 2006, as attorneys for the homeless sought a preliminary injunction to prevent the city from taking and immediately destroying homeless people's property during raids carried out by the FPD and the city sanitation department. The City of Fresno did not deny that it had taken homeless people's property and destroyed it. The justification for the practice was that notice was given of the raids and the property taken had been abandoned. The city also argued that it would be burdensome to collect and store homeless people's property.

Larry Arce, CEO of the Fresno Rescue Mission, was called as a witness in support of the city's policy. Arce said that his agency does the same thing. "We clean the street in front of the Rescue Mission every day and throw everything away that is left behind." When asked if they would throw away someone's property if the person had left it in a cart in front of the mission while getting a warm meal, he said, "If someone leaves their property in front of the Fresno Rescue Mission, they have no sense." Arce said they have thrown away many shopping carts full of homeless people's possessions over the past several years.

The three days of hearings effectively positioned the homeless social service providers, such as the Rescue Mission and the Poverello House, as supporters of the city's policy of destroying homeless people's property. Paul Stack, Poverello House facilities manager, said the homeless set up a large encampment on Santa Clara Street (right in front of the Poverello House) in 2003–2004. Stack said the Poverello House received complaints about the encampment from visitors and donors who came to their facility. Rick McNeil, also an employee at the Poverello House, did not have a problem with the destruction of homeless people's property. He said he had never seen anyone's property destroyed if the person was with it. McNeil said the homeless are always given time to move, and they always get a warning before the "cleanups" start.

The testimony by the homeless told a different story. Sandra Thomas said she had her property destroyed on June 22, 2006, after being told it would be safe by Officer Wallace. Thomas said she moved her four shopping carts from the west side of E Street to the east side because of an impending raid. The custom and practice of the FPD had been that it would direct the sanitation department to move down the strip of land on the west side of the street and the homeless people would take whatever possessions they could to the east side of the street and then return when the sweep was over. Thomas asked the homeowner and Officer Wallace if she could safely leave her carts on the public sidewalk in front of a house. She was promised that her carts would be safe. She then left for a short time to take a shower at the Poverello House. When she returned, all but one of her carts were gone, crushed in the back of a garbage truck. Dramatic video of the incident was shown in the courtroom. The video showed Thomas's cart being picked up by sanitation workers and tossed into the garbage truck. Thomas cried as she told the court about what was in the carts. "I lost my ID, my grandmother's diamond wedding ring, Social Security paperwork, clothes and blankets," Thomas said. Afterward, "I had no place to sleep, no blankets and I caught pneumonia."

Doug Deatherage was also affected by the June 22, 2006, attack on the homeless. Deatherage says he was told on the day of the attack that it would take place. He and his fiancée, Pamela Streeter, gathered all they could and took it to the east side of the street. Deatherage went to the grocery store while Streeter stayed with their possessions. When he got back, Streeter was crying and everything was gone. "We lost shoes, clothes, my antique stamp collection, letters and photos from my family, and worst of all, Streeter had an urn with her granddaughter's ashes. We lost everything." Deatherage said the city sanitation workers took their property over Streeter's protest.

One unexpected aspect to the court proceedings was that they showed the practice of destroying homeless people's property is something not limited to the downtown area. Jeanie Nelson testified that she was homeless and living at a church near Millbrook and Shields avenues (north central Fresno). Nelson said she had made arrangements with the church she attends to stay on the property. "At 8 a.m. in June or July of this year (2006), an officer told me to get up and move to the canal bank (near the church)," Nelson testified. "I was told to shut up and sit down on the canal bank." Nelson said that she had met the officer before. "The officer said 'didn't I tell you that I never wanted to see you again?'" Nelson said she tried to show him a paper showing she had the church's approval to be on the property, but he would not look at it. Nelson said that "he then pushed my shopping cart into the canal." She lost her medicine, birth certificate, clothing and bedding. The loss of her medicine resulted in a trip to the emergency room. She said the officer threatened to come back and give the church a citation for allowing a homeless person to stay there.

Alphonso Williams lives near Roeding Park, a couple of miles north of the downtown area. While living there, he said he had seen the FPD destroy homeless people's property seven or eight times. He has had his property destroyed several times. The first time it happened, two FPD officers told him he had one hour to move. Williams managed to find a friend with a truck and they loaded it with everything he and his wife owned. Before they got a block, the police pulled them over and said the truck was going to be towed. Testifying at the hearing, Williams said, "We were told to take our stuff out of the truck and put it on the sidewalk." He went to find other transportation and when he returned 30–45 minutes later, what he saw was a garbage truck driving away. "The officer told us we were too late. They took my wife's wheelchair, her medicines and our wedding pictures," Williams said.

The next time Williams lost his property was when he was living on a lot next to the old Harley-Davidson store on Olive Avenue. Williams said, "We had the owner's permission. We kept the place clean, and everything was fine. I went to get a cup of coffee at McDonald's, and my wife came up and told me that city workers and the police were there and going to destroy our property." Williams said that the shopping cart with his property was even on private land and that the person in the house had given him permission. That did not matter to the FPD, which directed the sanitation department to destroy it. When Williams protested, the FPD pulled out Tasers and threatened to shoot him.

Pam Kincaid said she had been homeless for six years. "They have taken my things six or seven times. They don't give you any notice," Kincaid said. She has had craft tools, tents and clothing taken and been left with just the clothes on her back. "It is devastating when this happens. It is like being raped," Kincaid said.

Betts called FPD Captain Garner to the stand. Garner said the police always notify the homeless in writing and orally before a "cleanup" is about to occur. Garner has never seen an instance when someone who was present or nearby has had property destroyed. Garner said, "We do not have a policy to deprive homeless people of their property or move them out of downtown. We respond to complaints. We have never cleaned up an area without a complaint from the property owner."

Standing Order 3.8.12 was entered into evidence. This code is the protocol for how the FPD handles property. The procedure for what to do with found property, such as bicycles and shopping carts, does not call for their immediate destruction. Found or abandoned property is cataloged and stored for a period of time so the owner can reclaim it. Garner did not have a compelling explanation for the exception when dealing with homeless people's property. He repeatedly called homeless people's property abandoned debris. Even when shown a picture of a nice bicycle being thrown into a garbage truck and crushed, he stuck with his story. Judge Wanger shook his head.

Garner claimed an October 8, 2006, raid when the FPD took numerous shopping carts from an encampment near H Street was within the law because of the new City of Fresno shopping cart ordinance. When it was brought to his attention that the shopping cart ordinance was not effective until October 27, 2006 Garner became defensive and claimed he had the right to do it anyway.

Philip Weathers, with the city sanitation department, testified that he coordinates the "cleanups" with FPD Officer Wallace. Weathers said that his department is entirely dependent on the FPD to determine when and where to go. Weathers said that his crews were not trained to collect and store homeless people's property. According to Weathers, everything that the FPD tells them to clean up is abandoned debris and it is all destroyed. Asked under cross-examination if he has ever found out what the effect is to the people whose property he destroys, Weathers looked confused. After the question was asked several times, with the same response, Weathers' testimony was over.

Fresno City Manager Andrew Souza was the last person on the stand before the weekend break. Souza said the city conducts these "cleanups" because of complaints from the public. He said complaints are received in many different city departments and that the city needs to respond. Souza said he considers city policy to be fair because it has notified the homeless of the "cleanups" and the debris left behind is abandoned. However, he said that because of the current controversy, "my recommendation to the mayor is that we do not do any more sweeps." Souza said that the city has looked into the cost of storing homeless people's property, rather than destroying it, but there are significant problems with a policy that included those elements. Souza said it would cost $50,000 to train sanitation workers in the procedures. In addition, Souza had concerns about liability issues that could result if persons claimed property (taken and stored by the city) that was not theirs.

The final day of the hearings in federal court saw Souza back on the stand. Souza was asked if he had ever called the city managers of other cities to ask how they deal with the homeless. He said "no," that he had never talked to any other city manager about this issue. Alexander, one of the attorneys for the plaintiffs, asked Souza about Community Development Block Grant (CDBG) funding. This is money that the federal government gives to Fresno, some of which is designated for addressing homeless issues. Souza said the City of Fresno gives this CDBG funding to Code Enforcement and the FPD. When asked if the money could have been used to gather and store homeless people's property (rather than destroy it), he said, "yes," but that the city had not designated CDBG money for that purpose. Alexander asked Souza if the homeless have a "safe place" to go. In other words, is there anywhere in Fresno the homeless could go where they would not be subjected to police sweeps? The answer was "no."

Souza had said the City of Fresno only engages in sweeps after receiving complaints from the owner of a property. He was asked if Caltrans, the owner of the property at E Street and Ventura Street where many of the sweeps had taken place, had complained. "Do you have an e-mail or letter regarding complaints from Caltrans," Alexander asked. Souza's response, "no."

City of Fresno Attorney Betts argued that the city receives complaints about the obstruction of city sidewalks, that many of these complaints are received by phone and that the city has to respond. Betts and Souza said that sorting and storing homeless people's possessions would require negotiations with organized labor because it would be an expansion of employees' duties. Souza said that the shopping carts that were destroyed in the sweeps were done so properly and handled according to the city policy.

Officer Wallace was called to the stand. Wallace was a specialist (roughly equivalent to a corporal) in the Southwest Division of the FPD. He described his duties as interacting with the homeless on a daily basis. He said that "every one of them knows my name" and that being on the street regularly builds trust. He says that he "clears encampments because of complaints." He receives all of the complaints. Wallace said that after receiving a complaint, he visits the site. He talks to the residents and asks for their cooperation in cleaning up the area. If things do not improve, "I set up a cleanup." Wallace then described the process: He would coordinate the cleanup date with the city sanitation department. He would then print up a written notice of the cleanup and pass out the notices from one shelter (tent) to another. If someone was not at the shelter, he would post it on the tent. He would tell residents to tell their neighbors about the upcoming cleanup. Then, on the day of the cleanup, he would come by one hour before the event and remind everyone it was about to happen. Wallace said he always gave people time to remove their property. He said he directed the city sanitation workers where to go and that he has never thrown away any person's property if that person was in possession of it. Any unattended carts were considered trash and thrown away.

Wallace discussed the incident (described above) where he attempted to take the shopping cart away from Apper. He said the carts were abandoned and just because there was a homeless advocate trying to save the cart, it did not change the law.

ACLU Attorney Risher asked about the destruction of homeless people's property. Wallace answered that the carts he has ordered destroyed are all abandoned. "They are all abandoned if they are not in someone's possession," Wallace said. He has seen hundreds of shopping carts destroyed over the last two years. Wallace declares that he has "determined that unclaimed property is trash." He says that this was an "out of the box" solution that emerged to deal with the issue of homelessness in Fresno.

The Apper/Wallace video was shown again. This video shows Officer Wallace and Apper in a tug of war with one of the shopping carts on E Street. Wallace claimed that "the carts were not in her possession. She attempted to assert possession...it was trash, there was no owner present." Risher said, "You knew they belonged to somebody?" Wallace's response, "It was trash; it was left abandoned." The video showed neatly stacked possessions stacked in four shopping carts. The police destroyed three of the four carts.

The hearing then moved to closing arguments.

Attorney Alexander, speaking on behalf of the homeless, said that the Fourth Amendment limits government's ability to seize and destroy someone's property. The immediate destruction of homeless people's property violates the Fourth and 14th amendments to the U.S. Constitution and California civil law. Alexander argued that we are a nation of laws and "we can't make up rules as we go." The judge, when issuing a TRO in this case, said, "One man's trash is another man's treasure," and Alexander reminded the court of this fact. The City of Fresno, in a report it issued (Consolidated Plan) says there are 8,824 homeless. There are nowhere near that many homeless shelter beds in this community, therefore it is inevitable that some homeless people will have to sleep outside. The Rescue Mission has beds, but in order to stay, you have to pray. There are a few beds in the tool sheds at the Poverello House, but not everyone wants to stay there, even if they could. The city's policy says you have to be in possession of your property or it will be taken and destroyed. Wallace created this policy and City Manager Souza agreed it was the city policy. They say this policy is fair because they give notice that they are going to come and destroy homeless people's property. And yet, the only notice they could show the court had the wrong date on it! Let's look at the balance of the hardship—the homeless have their shelters destroyed, clothing, tools, an urn, a grandmother's wedding ring, a lock of a son's hair, an ID, a birth certificate and their constitutional rights destroyed. The cost to the city in this balance of hardship—it might cost them $50,000 to train workers in how to handle property and find a place to put it.

Betts, the attorney representing the City of Fresno, said that the homeless could have moved their property to the Poverello House (they have some storage facilities). Betts then asked the court if they could discuss the terms of the Preliminary Injunction (he seemed to assume he was going to lose the case) and the judge said he would be given an opportunity to be heard after his ruling. Betts' summation seemed a little defeatist. From my seat in the courtroom, it looked like he was throwing in the towel and asking for the mercy of the court.

Judge Wanger said the testimony showed there is a lack of available shelter space in this community. But, he said he was not there to force the city to provide more shelter for the homeless. This is a narrowly defined case. The court recognizes that the city has a duty to make calls for service, health and safety issues, and to clear obstructions from the sidewalks. However, he said that "people can't be punished because of their circumstances. They can't be deprived of their constitutional rights."

Wanger said the City of Fresno has no written policy on how to deal with the homeless during these sweeps. He said that specialist Wallace had created the policy out of whole cloth, and his policy had transmogrified homeless people's property into trash. Wanger said the City of Fresno takes property into possession all of the time. Why should the policy on how to deal with homeless people's property be different from that of anyone else? With an $800 million plus budget, the city should be able to do better than this.

The judge said that Officer Wallace has a "woefully mistaken understanding of the law." It is dishonest and demeaning to identify someone's property as trash. The Fourth, Fifth and 14th amendments are being violated because property is being taken without the opportunity to be heard.

Judge Wanger said that the city is being disingenuous when it argues that it can't clean these sites without destroying the property. The city deals with this all the time—crack houses, meth labs, etc. The police and fire department are capable of dealing with hazardous cleanups.

In the end, the judge ruled that the balance does not compute. The Constitution of the United States is on one side, and the City of Fresno's need to clean up a street is on the other. Judge Wanger issued a Preliminary Injunction that stops the City of Fresno from taking and immediately destroying homeless people's property.

What seemed to impress Judge Wanger was the evidence the attorneys for the homeless presented. The attorney representing the City of Fresno would argue that all the city did was to throw away rubbish. The legal representatives for the city would show the court photos of piles of garbage and claim that was all that was thrown away. Then, the court would be shown video of city sanitation workers picking up a 10-speed bicycle and throwing it into the back of a garbage truck, a photo of a carefully packed shopping cart thrown away and a perfectly good tent being destroyed.

My daughter, Simone Cranston-Rhodes, had shot the video that helped make the case, showing that the city was doing way more than cleaning up trash from the encampments. I thought at the time we were taking pictures and shooting the video that it was amazing that the police, city sanitation workers and officials from City Hall acted like they had nothing to hide.

The point that the attorneys for the homeless so effectively made in court was that the City of Fresno can't have one policy for abandoned or lost property for middle-class and affluent citizens and another one for the poor. In other words, if the policy was to recover a lost or stolen bicycle for someone in north Fresno and try to return it to the person who owned it, the city could not have a different policy for people who are poor and/or homeless.

One of the most significant revelations that came out of the hearings in federal court was the origin of the policy that led to the bulldozing of the homeless encampments. Although the city had claimed that it had a written policy regarding what it cheerfully referred to as "cleanups," that policy was never produced. The attorneys for the homeless were pretty sure the city would not produce such a document (if it in fact ever existed) because that would be documenting what they believed was a violation of the law.

Instead, what we learned in court was that Wallace, a specialist with the FPD, came up with the policy himself as a way to address the issue of homelessness in Fresno. Here is the testimony that exposed the origin of the policy:

The Court: In other words, where did you receive, if you will, the directive to treat unclaimed property as trash for immediate destruction? Where does that come from?

Wallace: It was one of the things that, in order to do the cleanups, that as I told you in problem-oriented policing (POP), we have to come with out-of-the-box ideas as to how to take care of things. And it was a way that I was—in order to make the homeless take possession and keep possession of their stuff, instead of having stuff scattered all over the city, where I get complaints that there's abandoned trash or abandoned carts, stuff all over, that this way they take responsibility for their property. And if they didn't take responsibility for their property, when I came through to do my cleanups, we would take it as trash.

The Court: Do I understand, then, that you are the originator of the policy?

Wallace: Yes.

The Court: Thank you.

This was a major revelation that came as a surprise to those of us in court that day. I was not sure if Wallace had been told to fall on his sword or if the City of Fresno was really so foolish as to allow a specialist in the FPD to establish such a significant policy decision—one that could cost the city millions of dollars.

It was also discovered that the FPD was using money designated for code enforcement to fund the "cleanup" of the homeless encampments. The ironic and tragic implication of this revelation was that the city received CDBG funds based on the need to clean up and bring southwest Fresno neighborhoods out of poverty and that money was given to code enforcement, which then used it to bulldoze the homeless encampments.

The city would have gotten away with it, and these facts would never have been discovered if the homeless had not stood up for their rights and filed this class action lawsuit.

A settlement in the case was finally reached on June 6, 2008. Judge Wanger gave preliminary approval to a $2.35 million class-action settlement between a class of hundreds of homeless Fresno residents and the City of Fresno and the California Department of Transportation. The court had already determined that Fresno's practice of immediately seizing and destroying the personal possessions of homeless residents violates the constitutional right of every person to be free from unreasonable search and seizure.

"The Court's ruling and the settlement should send a strong message to other cities throughout our country that if they violate the rights of their most vulnerable residents, they will be held accountable," said ACLU attorney Risher, who worked tirelessly on the case.

Plaintiff Williams said, "I felt like everything was taken away from me, but this settlement gives me hope for the future for myself and all the other people who suffered."

"Many homeless people lost everything they owned to the city's trash compactors and bulldozers. With this settlement, they can access what has always been the solution to homelessness: a safe, clean place to live," said Elisa Della-Piana, an attorney with the Lawyers' Committee.

Funds from the multimillion dollar settlement, which attorneys called "unprecedented," went to individual plaintiffs whose belongings were destroyed in the illegal sweeps, as well as into an account to provide housing and medical care to the approximately 225 class members.

The ACLU and the LCCR used the attorneys' fees awarded in the case for programs to protect the legal rights of poor and homeless people and to oppose the abuse of government power.

Attorney Alexander volunteered more than 1,000 hours on the case. His legal team was recognized in 2007 with the State Bar of California President's Pro Bono Service Award for their "around the clock" efforts. The firm pursued the case on a pro bono basis and will not recover any fees in the settlement.

"For the homeless in Fresno, this case has been a watershed event," said Alexander. "They have stopped the destruction of their property. They have caused new rules on dealing with the homeless to be created. They have gained compensation for the losses they suffered. But most importantly of all, they have shown that in this country, the Constitution applies to everyone and that our federal courts are a place where justice can be found, even if you are homeless and down and out."

The legal struggle was an enormous victory for the homeless in Fresno. Not only would they be compensated for their losses, but the City of Fresno was now restrained and would have to follow the court order to not immediately take and destroy homeless people's property. New procedures would have to be established and all property stored for 90 days.

There were also other major changes taking place regarding the city's policy on the homeless. A 10-Year Plan to End Homelessness was being developed, a Housing First plan was being discussed and Mayor Alan Autry was enraged by his defeat in federal court.

Attorneys representing homeless people filed a lawsuit and held a press conference on the steps of Fresno City Hall. They were seeking to stop the city from taking and immediately destroying homeless people's property.

Pam Kincaid spoke at the press conference announcing the lawsuit against the City of Fresno. Kincaid was the lead plaintiff in the lawsuit.

Liza Apper (left) stood in front of this tent and refused to allow the bulldozer to destroy it. Shortly after the bulldozer left, Twist (a homeless man) emerged from the tent. He had been sleeping and would have been picked up by the bulldozer, put into a garbage truck and taken to the dump if Liza had not held her ground. Nobody knew that Twist was in the tent until after he came out.

The homeless plaintiffs in the lawsuit against the City of Fresno and their attorneys celebrate the $2.3 million settlement in federal court.

# Chapter 7

# The Disturbing and Tragic Death of Pam Kincaid

Pam Kincaid was the lead plaintiff in the class action lawsuit against the City of Fresno. She was also my friend. In the summer of 2007, after the preliminary injunction was issued in federal court but before the settlement was announced, Kincaid was homeless and living in downtown Fresno. She moved around a lot, mostly because the police and the city were still pushing homeless people from one place to another.

In addition, because of her visibility in the lawsuit, she received more than her fair share of unwanted attention. She had been telling me for months that she felt she was being targeted by the police and others because of the lawsuit. She was upset about being arrested and put in jail for several days without charges ever being filed. Kincaid described what happened: "You know why they arrested me, don't you? It was retaliation for the lawsuit."

The arrest occurred when Kincaid was driving around with friends in downtown Fresno. "All of a sudden there was this swarm of cop cars," she said. "They got us all out of the car, but they seemed mostly interested in me. One of the guys I was with had an open can of beer, which they just totally ignored. They arrested me on a probation hold. I'm not on probation and they knew that!"

Kincaid spent the next several days in jail. No charges were ever filed. As she was being released, Kincaid asked one of the sheriff's deputies why she had been in jail. Kincaid told me the officer rolled her eyes and said, "There ought to be an investigation." Kincaid thought she knew exactly why she was arrested and put in jail: She believed it was because she was a high visibility plaintiff in a controversial lawsuit that put the City of Fresno and the FPD in a bad light.

Life on the streets is hard on homeless people. If you are a woman and homeless, you can double or triple the difficulty factor. There are few beds for homeless women in Fresno, and Kincaid had given up trying to find a safe place where she could stay at a shelter. She was streetwise, but living in a tent in downtown Fresno can still be dangerous. She told me that there were people on the street who were upset with her because of the lawsuit. Specifically, she said the drug dealers, who are a small part of the downtown homeless community, were angry with her. They were angry because the lawsuit had increased law enforcement's presence around some homeless encampments, and the drug dealers blamed her.

On one occasion, Kincaid and I talked about the drug situation downtown. She said it was just unexplainable how the police will come in and arrest one person who is dealing drugs and leave everyone else alone. She said, "All they would have to do is to come in here with a drug sniffing dog and it would be all over." She believed there had to be some kind of payoff going on for the police to protect some dealers and arrest others.

Rev. Floyd Harris was at the corner of G and Santa Clara streets talking to homeless people in early 2007. He was surprised at how openly drugs were being bought and sold. He too questioned the motivation of the police to selectively enforce drug laws. The drug wars, as they play out in downtown Fresno, were making some people rich, other people vulnerable and some people ended up dead.

Kincaid usually lived in remote locations in the old industrial section of downtown Fresno (south of Ventura Street). She often lived with other people because that provides a homeless woman with some protection. Kincaid, like many homeless women, also had a dog.

It is notable how often Kincaid, and others in the encampments she lived in, were forced to move. Even after the preliminary injunction and victory in court, homeless people were endlessly harassed and told to "move on." The City of Fresno conducted one of its raids on homeless encampments on Santa Fe Street, just south of Ventura Street, in early July 2007. Kincaid was living there at the time. This was the fourth or fifth time she had been forced to move since the beginning of the year. It did not help that she lived with her boyfriend Steve, who was known to be abusive.

Probably the most psychologically traumatizing thing that happened to Kincaid during this period was being told that her daughter had died in an automobile accident. Someone had gone to a homeless encampment asking for her and when she could not be found several people were asked to tell Kincaid that her daughter had died. When Kincaid heard the news she was devastated.

Although she had held up well under the other pressures in her life, the news about her daughter was different. It was the kind of psychological warfare that traumatized and disturbed her more than anything. Being homeless, getting arrested for no reason, having her property taken and destroyed by the city, even being beaten by her boyfriend was something she could deal with. The news about her daughter broke her heart.

In July 2007, Kincaid was living with Steve in a vacant lot on Mono Street, just east of R Street. According to an interview I had with Steve, the two of them started walking toward a store on Ventura Street when they saw an FPD patrol car cruise by, turn around and pull up beside them. This is not unusual if you are living on the street. The police are always stopping homeless people and asking them for their ID, running their names through the database and seeing what comes up. It is like fishing. Every so often, the police catch someone who is in violation of parole, has an outstanding warrant or for some other reason is being looked for by law enforcement.

Cynthia Greene, who was homeless and who had been another named plaintiff in the lawsuit against the City of Fresno, told me she was stopped four times on one day in mid-July 2007. Greene said, "I was out trying to collect cans for recycling, and the police came up and asked me for my ID. I would get done with one stop and a few minutes later I'd get stopped again. This is unusual even for Fresno." Greene said she felt uncomfortable with all of the stops and was concerned that she was being targeted.

Al Williams, another named plaintiff in the class action lawsuit against the city, was also arrested and released with no charges ever being filed. The day after Williams was put in jail, the encampment he lived in was raided and his disabled wife was forced to move. Later, Sherri (Williams' wife) was arrested for trying to use the restroom at McDonald's (this story will be told in a later chapter).

According to Steve, the police officer checked both his and Kincaid's IDs and let them go. As they were leaving, a group of six or seven people (at least one them Steve identified as being a drug dealer) walked by and went to the police car. Steve said that he looked back and saw the officer pointing at him and Kincaid while the office talked to the group. Kincaid decided to stay at her encampment, and Steve continued on to the store. Feeling something might be wrong, Steve returned (without going to the store) to see four of five women from the group that had approached the police car savagely beating Kincaid.

Steve said, "Pam is on the ground and one of them has these boot heels, you know like these dress boots, you know what I'm talking about? With the big heels? And they are just..." (Steve jumps up and down as if stomping something on the ground.) According to Steve, they were saying, "Drop the suit, drop the suit, you're hurting us, you're hurting them, now we're hurting you."

Steve said that after he stopped the assault on Kincaid he tried to flag down a police patrol car. The first police vehicle that went by on R Street did not stop. Within 15 minutes, another patrol car came by. This time, the officer stopped and Steve explained what had happened. The officer left, saying he was going to find the perpetrators of the crime, but he never came back to follow up on the victim or write a report of the assault.

I talked to Jeff Cardinale, the FPD's public information officer at that time, about police involvement in this incident. Cardinale insisted that there was no record of any contact with Kincaid or Steve on R or Mono streets that day.

Kincaid was admitted to the Community Regional Medical Center (CRMC) on July 13, 2007. The nurse who attended to Kincaid said she was black and blue from the waist up. "It was clear that Pam had been beaten," the nurse told me. The police report issued at the time she was admitted to the CRMC was vague. The police report suggests that Kincaid had a bad sunburn, might have a mental illness and did not want to press charges.

A man with extensive contacts in the homeless community confirmed, at least in part, Steve's version of what happened to Kincaid. He said three young women were bragging about how they had beaten up Kincaid. Fearing retaliation himself, he did not want to identify those involved.

I didn't find out that Kincaid was in the hospital until about a week after she was admitted. She was still black and blue, and it did not look like she had sunburn to me. She was clearly disoriented. Her attending physician, Dr. Arman Ossia, told me that Kincaid did not know what city she was in or what year it was. He explained that she had subdural hematoma, which causes swelling inside the skull, and the pressure can cause the disorientation and delusions she was experiencing. He was cautiously optimistic that she would regain her memory.

After Kincaid was at the CRMC for more than a week, it was agreed that she needed to move to more long-term care. But without insurance or any resources, the options were limited. The University Medical Center (UMC) was one of the few long-term care facilities that would take Kincaid. On the day before she transferred to the UMC, I talked to her nurse again. She told me that Kincaid was starting to remember what had happened and said that the attack had to do with the lawsuit against the City of Fresno.

Kincaid was relocated to the fourth floor of the long-term care facility at the UMC. At about 1:30 a.m. on August 1, 2007, she went through the doors to a balcony and fell four floors to her death. The doors to the balcony, which had alarms that did not go off, were supposed to have alerted staff if anyone opened them. She either went over or under the balcony wall.

This mystery of what happened has never been solved. Did the alarm on the door malfunction? Did Kincaid wander out onto the balcony and have a tragic accident? Perhaps the nurses let her out to smoke a cigarette and get some air, and she went over the edge. It is also possible that somebody pushed or threw her off the balcony. The coroner said it was a suicide.

Several of Pam's friends saw her just before she died. They said she was doing better, she was not suicidal and her nurse said her memory was starting to clear up. Even now, in 2016, we are left with many unanswered questions:
- If what Steve is saying is true, what did the police officer say to the group that attacked Kincaid?
- Why did the police officer who Steve stopped not return to help Kincaid or write an incident report? Why do the police have no record of this contact?
- Why did the police who talked to Kincaid at the CRMC not conclude that a crime had been committed and try to find out who attacked her?
- What went wrong at the UMC? How could a patient who is known to be disoriented walk onto a balcony and fall from the fourth floor?
- Why was a repairperson working on the alarm system leading to the fourth floor balcony the morning after Kincaid fell?
- Why does Fresno not have more shelters for homeless women?

Cardinale told me that the FPD was not investigating either the beating incident or the suspicious circumstances of Kincaid's death. He suggested that I talk with the sheriff's department. After being initially told by the sheriff's department that it did not have an active investigation either, I called back again. This time I was told that it was investigating Kincaid's death. Several months later, the sheriff's department said that it could find nothing out of the ordinary about the circumstances of her death.

Mayor Alan Autry, who was in office when this incident occurred, often talked about Fresno being "a tale of two cities." I can't help but wonder if the mayor had shown up at the CRMC, beaten nearly to death, would the FPD have concluded that he was sunburned, delusional and that no investigation was necessary? Maybe this is a tale of two cities—one where there is justice and fairness if you are well to do, but if you are poor (especially if you are a homeless woman) you can't even get the police to open an investigation after you have been beaten.

Kincaid was a hero. She stood up for her rights and the rights of all homeless people. As the lead plaintiff in the lawsuit against the City of Fresno, she sometimes became a lightning rod and was vilified by those who would continue the system of bigotry and hatred against the homeless. Kincaid took pride in being a recognizable leader of an effort that would result in better conditions for Fresno's homeless. Being a part of the lawsuit was something she did not for herself but for all homeless people.

Kincaid paid the ultimate price for this selflessness. The fallout from the attacks against her also affected her family as they learned of her death. I received a call from the mother of Kincaid's daughter's friend who said she had read my article on the Internet about Kincaid. She said that Kincaid's daughter was in the room with her and wanted to know about the details of her mother's death. I drove out to Coalinga to meet Kincaid's daughter, who had just graduated from high school and had not been in an auto accident.

Kincaid's daughter had been taken from her and placed in a foster home after Kincaid had become homeless. I learned from her daughter that Kincaid had led a relatively normal life, worked, been married, had children and then through a series of incidents ended up homeless. Her daughter was grateful for the closure in knowing about her mother's death, but I could not help but wonder who had spread the rumor about Kincaid's daughter's death. Who would be so cruel to do such a thing? What motivation did they have for that action? Was someone who worked for the City of Fresno capable of such treachery?

There is an alternative narrative that some people believe explains the incident that resulted in Kincaid being beaten and ending up in the hospital. Her partner Steve was abusive, and Kincaid would sometimes escape, calling a friend for help. Once she called me crying and said she had to get away. I put her up in a hotel for a few days, but when I returned Steve was there. It was a complicated and destructive relationship, but one that Kincaid chose to stay with. Did Steve savagely beat her and then tell a story that made many people believe the police and drug dealers were involved? It is hard to answer that question because the police did not conduct a thorough investigation of the crime.

Of course, that still does not explain how she ended up going over the balcony at the long-term care facility. Again, if there had been a thorough investigation of that incident, what happened would not still be a dark, disturbing and troublesome mystery.

A memorial service was held for Kincaid on August 26, 2007. The service was organized by several of her friends. Brian and Liza Apper organized people to bring art, music and stories about Kincaid's life to the event. Everyone was given a box of Crayola markers and asked to create an image that reminded them of Kincaid. Some people wrote words that symbolized some of her qualities such as "kindness, gentle, courageous and brave."

Her partner Steve painted a rainbow and said "she is a rainbow" and that "she wanted dignity and respect for everyone." Randy Johnson, who is one of the named plaintiffs in the lawsuit, said Kincaid told him that she was not in the lawsuit for the money—she was in it because she wanted to help all homeless people. He drew a picture of a tent—one for him and another for her.

Paul Alexander chose the word "courage" to describe Kincaid. He said that "we will always keep Pam in our hearts."

Pieter Moerdyk led participants in several songs with his acoustic guitar, getting good group participation when he sang "Come Out of the Shadows." The chorus went like this:

Come out of the shadows and step into the light
You might have to quarrel
You might have to fight
Mother earth will applaud you and the universe will smile
Come out of the shadows
And stay with us a while.

The memorial service honored Pam for standing up for justice. It gave her friends an opportunity to mourn her death and gave dignity and respect to this homeless woman who made a difference in this community.

Kincaid wrote this poem shortly before she died:

Homeless Dog
By Pam Kincaid

It's Okay to be homeless.

I've been sitting here
askin' my dog what did
he do wrong, is he an
alcoholic, dope fiend dog
or what.
He had to do something
wrong because he's a
homeless, homeless dog.

Give me a break. My
dog doesn't even know he's
homeless. He's fat. He
weighs 80 pounds. Because
I feed him well.

This is family
red and yellow black and white
we are children in His sight
all the children of the world not any
more—and really never was!

Let me tell you
something. Im
sitting here talking to
my dog—storm coming
I told him it's okay
it's okay. He doesn't
really know he's a homeless

homeless dog.

Why do you judge me
you have no right to
judge me or anybody else
God help me because
I don't know if I can go back
return to what you have busted up
you come out here and say you want
to help and save the homeless
when you better start looking
at yourself. Don't pity me
show some compassion
and respect. Your no different
just because you have a roof over
your head doesn't make you
any different—Don't
be little me—look
yourself in the mirror, see
if you like who's looking
back—just because I'm
homeless doesn't mean
I did something
wrong.

I am in some eyes
homeless, it doesn't mean
I did something wrong
I did not do anything
wrong, I worked my
whole life and still
do because to
believe this is not an
easy loafer get
everything free life
like some judge it to
be and those that feel
that way, I dare you
to come and try it.

Pam Kincaid

Pam Kincaid liked to paint her toenails blue.

Paul Alexander, the lead attorney representing the homeless in their lawsuit against the City of Fresno, attended the memorial service. On a card describing how he remembered Kincaid, Alexander wrote: "Courage. We will always keep Pam in our hearts."

Steve drew a rainbow and said that "she is a rainbow."

# Chapter 8

# Mayor Alan Autry Reacts to the Settlement

Fresno Mayor Alan Autry was not happy with the settlement, and his office issued a press release criticizing the agreement. In it, Autry said the "white-collar exploitation of the homeless by the Court and the lawyers is unconscionable."

Judge Oliver Wanger was concerned by the mayor's declaration and invited Autry to his court to discuss the matter. He wrote, "Exploitation means unethical utilization for selfish purposes. The word exploit means to use selfishly for one's own ends. The term exploitation is defined as use or utilization esp. for profit; selfish utilization. Webster's Unabridged Dictionary 2d ed. (1999) p. 682. Exploit means to make unethical use of for one's own advantage or profit; turn selfishly or unfairly to one's own account; hence. Webster's New World Dictionary of the American Language (College Ed. 1957). The publicly issued statements of Defendant Alan Autry, the Mayor and Chief Executive Officer of the City of Fresno, call into question the good faith of the City Defendants in entering into a settlement."

The courtroom was packed with media, the homeless, staff from City Hall and lots of other people interested to see what was going to happen.

As the courtroom session got started, Judge Wanger noted that he had received an electronic communication from Caltrans, which was also a defendant in this case. Legal counsel for Caltrans argued that no one from Caltrans had made any derogatory statement about the settlement and that Caltrans, regardless of what happened with the City of Fresno, would accept the terms of the settlement. Caltrans had agreed to contribute $85,000 in the settlement.

Judge Wanger said that the "court did not negotiate the settlement." He continued, "It is the parties and not the court who agree to the settlement." Judge Wanger reminded the court that the lawsuit is still before the court and that a jury trial could begin as early as next week. He said that it was his understanding that one of the defendants had objected to the settlement.

Speaking about Autry's public statement following the settlement, Judge Wanger said, "You can't accuse the court of committing criminal conduct." Judge Wanger said that everyone has a right to criticize him, "but it is beyond the understanding of this court" what Autry's intent was when he issued his statement. Judge Wanger read the statement, with special emphasis on the section that read "white-collar exploitation of the homeless by the Court and the lawyers is unconscionable." Judge Wanger said, "There is no basis to a settlement if the parties don't agree."

Paul Alexander, legal counsel for the plaintiffs, was asked for his input on the status of the settlement. Alexander said that it is his "position that the plaintiffs have entered into a binding settlement." He said the City of Fresno, Caltrans and the named plaintiffs in the case have come to an agreement and it must be honored.

Judge Wanger asked if Alexander thought that the settlement was an enforceable contract. Alexander said he thought so and that the plaintiff's legal team supports the settlement. Judge Wanger replied, "And what assurance do you have that the city will fulfill the agreement?" Alexander said the city would transfer the money to an administrator, who would then distribute the money, and that the court would hold the city accountable. "If there is any problem, we will be back," Alexander said.

City of Fresno legal counsel James Betts was asked for his position on the settlement. He agreed with the plaintiffs that the settlement should move forward and then disagreed with Judge Wanger's narrative regarding Autry's statement. He disagreed that "any statement made suggests we don't want this settlement. The city wants this settlement to stand."

Judge Wanger asked Betts if there was any basis in the law for his client's (Autry) statement that the court was engaged in "white-collar exploitation of the homeless." Betts replied that "the mayor has the right to make a political comment" and that the line of questioning was a violation of the separation between the judicial and legislative bodies of government. Betts informed Judge Wanger that he would instruct his client (Autry) not to answer the question.

Judge Wanger told Betts that Autry is a defendant in this case and asked him to respond. Autry said, "I would like to respond." Judge Wanger asked him, "What is your basis of the statement about white-collar exploitation?" Betts interrupted and said that his client is speaking against the advice of counsel. "I thought I was in America and not the Soviet Union," Autry said. Judge Wanger reminded Autry that there are political and practical consequences to your words and actions.

Autry: "Am I being held to your definition of exploitation?"

Wanger: "My request to you is that you explain yourself. Yes, there could be consequences."

After a brief huddle between the mayor, Betts and City Attorney Jim Sanchez, Betts returned and said that he objects to the line of inquiry. He said this was an issue of the separation between the legislative body and the court. He instructed his client not to answer.

Judge Wanger said that Autry's earlier comment, after a preliminary injunction was issued to stop the City of Fresno from taking and immediately destroying homeless people's property, was different. In late 2006, Autry said that it "would behoove Judge Wanger and benefit this community greatly, if he wishes to continue to express his personal opinion rather than judge, to venture out of his robe and chamber occasionally, enter the real world and find out the real truth." Judge Wanger said Autry's statement last week was of another nature.

Autry, not taking his legal counsel's advice, began to speak. "We hope we could live in the world we want, but we are in the real world. I love America." Autry said that he felt many court decisions are unfair. With this "so-called settlement, I felt as if the homeless and all the people of Fresno had a gun to their head." Looking at the plaintiff's legal counsel, Autry said he felt the city was up against overwhelming power: "We are up against a group that will stop at nothing to win. These lawyer fees are outrageous." He concluded, "I believe the homeless were being taken advantage of here."

Judge Wanger then asked Autry and each of the defendants in the case if they agreed with the settlement. They were all called upon, one at a time, to stand and say whether they agreed with the settlement. They all did. With that, Wanger said that the settlement is intact and the agreement would proceed.

But Mayor Autry was not ready to let the issue go just yet. A debate between Autry and Judge Wanger was organized at the Downtown Club in October 2008. Attorneys, judges and political junkies filled the venue to watch the fur and feathers fly.

At the debate, Autry was aggressive and defensive of city policy, claiming that nothing but garbage was thrown away and challenged Judge Wanger for not understanding that what the city was trying to do was throw away "mattresses with everything from E-coli to hepatitis" on them and syringes infected with AIDS. Autry claimed that the homeless were having sex and shooting drugs in front of children who live in nearby houses.

Judge Wanger responded:

"The court's description of the facts of the case were based on essentially a procedure that the city had adopted following the recommendations of a corporal who was apparently never vetted by any attorneys or any people higher in authority. That notice would be given, the trucks would move and everything that was on the street would be seized and destroyed in a dumpster. This included the ashes of a person, false teeth, documents and the last lock of hair of a child. What we learned was this: What I said was, the city came in and said 'we followed the law.' That was false. 'We have no resources to deal with their property, we cannot store it, we cannot hold it, we don't have the money, we can't deal with it.' That was false. And the way the homeless were treated in the street by the people who were seizing and destroying their property in front of them was demeaning. And so I simply described what those facts were. My order said don't do it, don't take and immediately destroy property. Enforce the laws...the only entity that wasn't following the law was the city of Fresno."

At the debate, the mayor attempted to blame the lawsuit on greedy attorneys from the Bay Area. He started his attack by saying that "the ACLU has run a reign of terror on American values in this country since 1920." He went on to say that the founder of the ACLU was an agnostic and a socialist who supported homosexuals and child molesters.

"You have an entity called the ACLU with $350 million descending on Fresno saying you had better give us a bunch of money or were going to bust you," Autry said. He added that "the ACLU is, I believe, the enemy of this country...they have caused more damage in this country than you can calculate."

In his concluding remarks, Autry let his acting talents shine (he had been an actor before becoming the mayor of Fresno), saying, "I saw these so-called caring lawyers running from the homeless once this was settled. They couldn't get out of town fast enough. They left these poor people crying on the side of the road, tugging at these lawyers and then yanking their arms away trying to get into a limousine and get out of town. They came in, they used this city, they ripped the homeless off, they made a fool and mockery of the judicial system and we are paying the price for it."

Autry made up this story about the homeless and their attorneys. I reached out to the former mayor to give him an opportunity to explain his statement, but he had no comment. Michael Risher, a staff attorney from the ACLU, who worked on the homeless lawsuit, did respond.

Risher said, "The ACLU-Limousine comment really shocked me at the time, and it continues to baffle me—I have a hard time explaining it as anything other than his simply saying whatever came into his mind, regardless of whether it was true. My car, then and now, is a '94 Honda Del Sol with faded paint—hard to confuse it with a limo. And for at least part of the time we were litigating the suit the driver's-side door was broken and I'd sometimes have to open it from the passenger side; I remember that because once when I gave one of our clients (Al Williams) a ride from a deposition back to where he was staying, over near the zoo, he laughed at me for having a two-door car where only one door actually worked. I believe I also gave Al a ride after the final settlement approval (by which time I had at least fixed my door), which is why Autry's comments seemed so particularly bizarre. Paul had a nice car, and both Meylissa and Elisa bought new cars (a Mini and a Civic, respectively) while the suit was pending (Elisa because the old one died on the Bay Bridge), but I can say with certainty none of them looked like a limo."

Risher continued, "This certainly affected my view of the other things he had to say about us and our motivations for the suit—*falsus in uno, falsus in omnibus* (false in one thing, false in everything), as the Romans supposedly said. I spent many hours with my clients and many more hours working for them to make sure that the city stopped violating their rights and destroying their already-fragile lives, and I certainly didn't run away from them after the settlement."

I also asked Alexander what he thought about Autry's comments. Alexander said that "Alan Autry's comments about the ACLU descending on Fresno, leaving in a limousine, lawyers leaving homeless crying at the side of the road, and the rest, are pretty much what I came to expect of him: pure crap. This is substance of which he was remarkably full and could create at will in large quantities. I was the lead lawyer for the homeless plaintiffs throughout the entire Kincaid case. I am a private attorney, not an ACLU attorney. I was paid not one penny for the more two years of legal work I did representing the homeless in this case. No one on our legal team ever rode in a limousine, and we never left the homeless in Fresno at the side of the road. In fact, I am still there representing them. We were in Fresno countless times, working with the homeless and representing them in court. Alan Autry wouldn't know about any of this, the facts of the case or what we did for the homeless because he was never there. In fact, he didn't show his face in any of the court proceedings until after the case was settled. He showed up on the very last day, after Fresno had agreed to a settlement, on the day that court was formally approving the settlement that Fresno had agreed to. He strutted around the courtroom a little in the style of Foghorn Leghorn, made some off-the-wall statements that no one could understand, and then left. That was the first and last we saw of him in the case. It is easy to make speeches full of falsehoods and grandiose self-serving statements that you just make up. What's hard is to deal with the real problems and issues presented by vulnerable and sometimes difficult homeless people. Alan Autry was good at the former, but as to the latter, not so much."

It is pretty amazing how the mayor can simply make something up, say it in a public setting and expect there to be no accountability. Credibility? Integrity? One would expect those words to mean something to a person holding public office. Unfortunately, the temptation to use the "Big Lie" must be strong because the tradition continued as Mayor Ashley Swearengin began to confront the homeless issue in Fresno. More about that in a future chapter.

Judge Oliver Wanger and Mayor Alan Autry debated the homeless issue at the Downtown Club in October 2008.

Mayor Alan Autry, in April 2008, said, "We have failed, government has failed on this issue. We are the status quo that has chosen through our wisdom over the last 40 or 50 years to pick the most expensive and ineffective, dis-compassionate way to address the homeless situation."

# Chapter 9

# Poor People Gonna Rise Up!

The lawsuit, Pam Kincaid's death, the legal victory the homeless achieved and the mayor's reaction to the lawsuit were important events, but there were a lot of other moving parts in the struggle to achieve human rights for homeless people in Fresno.

Happening throughout the time of the court hearings were the following:
- An ordinance was passed to stop homeless people from pushing shopping carts.
- The Homelessness Marathon (a national radio broadcast) was held in Fresno, putting Mayor Alan Autry and other elected officials on the hot seat.
- Homeless people near Roeding Park were evicted by the city, with some of their property being stored but later destroyed because of improper protection from the rain.
- The city provided one homeless encampment with portable toilets and trash bins.
- The City of Fresno and Caltrans continued to destroy other homeless encampments.
- A homeless woman was harassed and threatened with arrest for using the bathroom at McDonald's.
- More homeless people moved into tool sheds at the Poverello House.
- One homeless man built his shelter underground.
- Mayor Autry admitted that the city's homeless plan was a failure.
- A 10-Year Plan to End Chronic Homelessness was developed.

The City of Fresno adopted an ordinance in September 2006 that made it a crime to be in possession of a shopping cart. The ordinance criminalized the homeless who use shopping carts as a means of transporting their possessions. The ordinance subjects any person with a shopping cart that has been removed from a business to a $1,000 fine and up to one year in jail.

Several speakers at the City Council meeting to discuss the shopping cart ordinance spoke out and linked it to the city's attack on the homeless. Harley Turner said, "The wheels begin to fall off a city's government when elected officials and city managers begin to harass and attack the poor, hungry and homeless in our city. The City of Oakland attempted to make the homeless disappear. That didn't happen, and a precedent was set in court to give the homeless assistance, not taking their lifelong belongings and kicking them in the teeth."

Barbara Hunt, a regular at Fresno City Council meetings, asked what happened with all of the money coming into the city to address the homeless issue. Hunt said, "We have to protect these homeless, we have to have a place for them to stay, we've got to give them food, we got to get them off the streets." Hunt concluded by saying that the city must address the issue of affordable housing and must provide services for the poor.

Walt Parry, director of Fresno Metro Ministry, said "the shopping cart ordinance is part of a much larger issue." Parry said that some of the homeless own their own carts and that the ordinance does not address the private ownership of shopping carts. The ordinance assumes that all of the shopping carts in town are owned by businesses. Parry said, "We do not have the emergency shelters that we need in this community...and we need to work on that so long- and short-term affordable housing is available. There are also civil liberties issues as to whether a specific vehicle, a shopping cart, can be determined to be illegal and again, some people do own their own shopping carts and there have been some churches that have provided shopping carts to the homeless." Parry said Metro Ministry would like to work with the city to look at the situation of the homeless and work out short- and long-term solutions.

Chris Schneider, director of Central California Legal Services, also focused on the big picture of which the shopping cart ordinance is a part. "Last year, the Brookings Institute published *Katrina's Window*. The study brought to light that Fresno has the highest rate of concentrated poverty of all major U.S. metropolitan areas; in second place was pre-Katrina New Orleans." Schneider said that when the report was released city officials promised to address the issue but that after a year he has seen no results. Challenged at this point in his presentation by City Council President Jerry Duncan to address the issue of the shopping cart ordinance, Schneider replied, "This is about poverty." Schneider argued that the city should be developing a plan to address the homeless issue. He said, "The recent actions of the city through the police department, the sanitation department and now the City Council are directed at eradicating the homeless rather than eradicating the causes of homelessness."

Several City Council members were upset by the public comments and argued that they were not against the homeless. City Council Member Tom Boyajian said that "there are several of us on this board that believe strongly that a lot of the federal money should be diverted to the poor and the homeless." Boyajian said CDBG money should be used for affordable housing and jobs for the poor. "Those monies go to the police department and code enforcement, and I'm sick and tired of having people come up here and saying that some of us don't care. I care a lot; we advocate until we are blue in the face." Boyajian challenged the homeless advocates at the meeting to show up when the budget is discussed and lobby to have CDBG funds used to help the poor and homeless.

Cynthia Sterling, who represented the district where many homeless people live, said she did not see the ordinance as being directed at the homeless. However, in response to the presentations made before the City Council by the homeless advocates, she moved to pull the item from the consent calendar. Sterling said she was concerned about the possibility that some of the shopping carts might be the property of homeless people and that the ordinance would violate their rights.

After the hearing was continued, Sterling said she had checked with the city attorney and was convinced that the ordinance would not be used to target the homeless. Deputy Chief Robert Nevarez, from the FPD, assured the City Council that the ordinance was intended to reduce blight and would not be directed against the homeless. Jim Sanchez, the city attorney, agreed, saying shopping carts that were not identified as belonging to a business would not be taken from the homeless. Sterling said that "this ordinance repeats state law" and that the police would not take a cart that was not identifiable.

Following these assurances that the ordinance would not target the homeless, Boyajian said, "Let's state in the ordinance that it is not targeting the homeless." City Council Member Brian Calhoun, who helped write the ordinance, objected and said that while the point is not to target the homeless, he was against including stating that in the ordinance. City Council Member Larry Westerlund said that he did not think the homeless were in possession of any of their own shopping carts and that the ordinance would apply equally to both millionaires and the homeless. Westerlund said he was offended that people would say that this was a piecemeal attack on the homeless. Earlier, several speakers had complained about the city's lack of a plan to address homeless issues and were concerned that this shopping cart ordinance, a panhandling ordinance and razor-wire-topped fences were an ad hoc approach to the problem. Westerlund was (again) offended at the suggestion.

Sterling moved to approve the ordinance, without changing the wording to say it would not target the homeless, and it passed unanimously.

Within a year, Assistant City Manager Bruce Rudd was back before the City Council with another quality-of-life ordinance, this one to prevent camping (without a permit) in Fresno. That effort would fail, but this would not be the last time City Hall would attempt to harass the homeless by passing quality-of-life ordinances.

Calhoun targeted homeless people with an ordinance, first introduced in March 2008, to stop them from asking for money from median islands. In his introduction to the ordinance, Calhoun wrote that "Fresno Police records will show that the panhandlers are most often alcoholics, drug addicts or have mental health issues." He eventually managed to pass an ordinance that prevents homeless people from asking for money but makes it legal for nonprofit groups to use that space for their fund-raising efforts. This was accomplished by setting up a permit process that included limiting the activity to once or twice a year (per group or individual), the need to have an insurance policy for the event, special clothing, etc.—requirements that a nonprofit could easily accomplish but that no homeless person could reasonably do to panhandle for an hour or two.

Homeless people and their allies came together in Fresno on February 20, 2007, and held elected officials accountable for the recent attacks against unhoused people in this community. The Homelessness Marathon, a broadcast that goes to more than 100 radio stations throughout the country, was the scene for this poor people's assembly in downtown Fresno. The 14-hour program included a panel with Fresno Mayor Autry, two City Council members and Board of Supervisors President Bob Waterston. The event resembled a town hall meeting with an open microphone where anyone could ask questions of city and county elected officials.

There were those in the crowd who described recent city action against the homeless as a scorched-earth policy. They said city policy has included bulldozing homeless encampments, passing draconian ordinances to prevent homeless people from moving their possessions in shopping carts, an outdoor drunk tank for homeless people and the frequent violation of their civil rights by the police. Things got so bad that a federal judge had to order the City of Fresno to uphold the U.S. Constitution. The lawsuit against the City of Fresno was pending at the time of the radio broadcast.

Rebeca Rangel, speaking on the open microphone, demanded to know why the City of Fresno took CDBG money that was intended for the homeless and gave it to the FPD. Rangel said the city has received $8 million to address affordable housing issues and that most of that money has not reached the homeless or the poor in this community. Homeless advocates say that the CDBG money should have gone to help the homeless but was instead given to the FPD's code enforcement division. Speakers on the program pointed out that it was an officer in code enforcement who developed the policy that resulted in the taking and immediate destruction of homeless people's property. The mayor and others on the panel defended their use of the money by saying that CDBG money can be used for many different things.

More than 100 homeless people and their allies attended this event, held on the lawn at the Mexican American Baptist Church in downtown Fresno. As people spoke, a video showing the destruction of homeless encampments by city workers played continuously on a wall directly in front of the elected officials. Angry shouts from the crowd like "time to resign mayor" could be heard as the panel continued.

Jeremy Alderson, the producer of the Homelessness Marathon, asked the mayor if he would put trash bins and portable toilets up at the homeless encampments. Autry did not address the question, so Alderson demanded a yes or no answer. Autry said he did not want to condone illegal behavior and therefore would not support placing these facilities near homeless encampments. City Council Member Sterling said, "I'm willing to look to find a solution, but...people do sleep inside the porta-potties." Sterling went on to say she was willing to consider the possibility of providing homeless people with basic services. Arguably the most conservative member of the City Council, Duncan, unambiguously said that he would support putting trash bins and portable toilets near encampments for the homeless people to use.

On the Friday before the Homelessness Marathon, the City of Fresno did an about face on its policy of trash collection at homeless encampments. At the encampment located just south of Ventura Street on H Street, the City of Fresno came with a garbage truck, a bulldozer and a crew of sanitation workers. Instead of bulldozing the tents in the encampment, city workers carefully cleaned up an area where trash had collected. City of Fresno Public Information Officer Rhonda Jorn said the city was working with the homeless to clean up the area. No homeless person's property was destroyed in the sweep, proving that the city could clean up these areas without massive destruction of homeless people's property.

The Homelessness Marathon was a great opportunity for the community to hold elected officials' feet to the fire on this issue. With the threat of a lawsuit hanging over the City of Fresno, national exposure on the city's treatment of the homeless and a change of policy in the way cleanups are conducted starting to take shape, some homeless advocates were hopeful that homeless people might start to be treated with the dignity and respect they deserve.

The first large-scale removal of a homeless encampment after the preliminary injunction on the city was imposed took place in April 2007 as a group of homeless people living on a sidewalk across from Roeding Park were evicted. Notices went up a week before the "cleanup" took place. Dee, a homeless woman at the encampment, said upon learning about the cleanup, "but where are we supposed to go?"

Dee and other homeless residents in the encampment said the police came by several times and reminded them to get out. Dave, a homeless man at the encampment, said the police came by about every hour on the night before the eviction shining their spotlights into his tent. Dave said he was told by FPD Officer Oliver Baines (who would be elected to the Fresno City Council in 2010) that if homeless people were not gone by 8 a.m., they would be arrested. But, by 8:30 a.m. everything was calm, there was not a police officer in sight and most of the residents were starting to pack up their things.

By 9 a.m., the city started rolling in its equipment. The police in unmarked cars were the first to arrive, followed by squad cars, cleanup crews from the sanitation department, garbage trucks, city trucks with high-pressure water guns and more police. The city crews outnumbered the homeless two to one.

Seeing that the city was serious in its effort to evict the residents and dismantle the encampment, the pace of moving tents, clothing and other property picked up. By a little after 9 a.m., most of the homeless had moved their property to a church a half mile away where they were told they could stay for a few days.

Fresno Police Officer Bruce Hartman told me at about 9:30 a.m. that the police believed the property remaining on the sidewalk was trash. He said a homeless woman told him he could begin the "cleanup." I told him that she does not speak for all homeless people and how does he know that someone, who is not here right now, didn't leave something he or she considers valuable on the sidewalk. The argument left the police and city sanitation department in somewhat of a momentary dilemma. They soon got over it.

Phillip Weathers, a supervisor at the city sanitation department, directed his crew to begin the cleanup operation. The directions given by Weathers seemed some-what vague and ambiguous, leaving a great deal of discretion to the cleanup crew, who were dressed in bright orange jump suits, face masks and breathing filters.

The cleanup crew seemed to do a basically good job of putting anything with ob-vious value in a storage container and the random plastic bags, pallets and old food in the back of the garbage truck. However, I did notice an American flag that was thrown in the garbage truck, as well as some clothes and blankets.

I asked Captain Dave Belluomni, the new commander of the Southwest Police Division where the homeless people dislocated by this action were supposed to go. He pointed in the direction of downtown Fresno and said the homeless should go to the Rescue Mission and Poverello House. The City of Fresno, at that time, was estimating that there were more than 8,000 homeless people in Fresno. The Rescue Mission had more than 100 beds for men only and the Poverello House had beds for about 50 people in tool sheds set up in the Village of Hope. The tool sheds have no heating or cooling. Several homeless people told me they would not keep their dog in one of those tool sheds.

The homeless people at the West and Olive avenues encampment were displaced and no longer visible to those who come to play tennis, right across the street at Roeding Park. The problem with the City of Fresno's policy on the homeless, ac-cording to homeless advocate Bryan Apper with St. Benedict Catholic Worker, is that "it does not provide them with any place to go where they can be safe. They simply chase them from one place to another."

As a follow-up to see how well the new City of Fresno storage policy worked, I went with Dee (one of the homeless women displaced from the Roeding Park en-campment) to find out what the city did with the property it took. It was not easy to find the sanitation building at the city yard on El Dorado and E streets in down-town Fresno. The flyer the city posted said to go to building "E" and that John Rogers, community sanitation division manager, was in charge. After a bit of a runaround, Dee and I were taken to a large container in a parking lot that was full of homeless people's property.

What Dee saw made her upset. "It's all ruined; we can't even use our sleeping bags because they all smell like mildew." Dee was looking in the container where the city had stored the property taken on April 5. In the three weeks since the "cleanup," it had rained and soaked almost everything in the container. There was a tarp, but it only covered about a third of the container. The tarp was partially collapsed with a large pool of water on top.

Speaking of the property she was looking at, Dee said, "They say they are going to put it somewhere that is protected. Does this look like it is protected?" Carlos, a city worker sent with us to reclaim the property, agreed that the container's exposure to the elements could be a problem, saying, "Yeah, and it can cause damage, I will bring it to their attention."

Dee could not find anything worth saving in the pile of property the city had saved from the encampment she lived at. She was angry and frustrated that the city treated her property like rubbish, not taking care to carefully store it.

In May 2007, the City of Fresno gave about 60 homeless people at the H Street encampment (south of Ventura Street) portable toilets and trash bins. But there was a price to pay; Assistant City Manager Rudd announced that it would cost the city $13,000 a month to provide these services. The biggest expense would be the 24-hour a day/7-day a week security subcontracted to CIS Security. The Fresno City Council voted 6-1 to install these services for the homeless at the H Street encampment but saw this as only a temporary measure as they worked toward more permanent solutions.

Mayor Autry announced on April 17, 2007, that the City of Fresno, in a joint project with the county, would set up a homeless center in the downtown area. The center would provide this community's large homeless population with a place to put up a tent, portable toilets, trash bins and a facility (probably a trailer) where homeless people could get information about social services such as job training and employment.

The mayor said this "free zone" where homeless people could live would be operational by June 16, 2007. The mayor's proposed budget for 2008 included $4.9 million for various homeless initiatives, with $3 million being used to purchase property to create more housing for the homeless.

The installation of portable toilets and a trash bin to help the homeless was seen by some homeless advocates as evidence that the city was moving in the right direction. City policy seemed to be moving away from the sanitation department bulldozing homeless encampments. In some cases, the city was actually cleaning up the area around encampments, and then it started providing the homeless with basic public services.

Mayor Autry's idea of a free zone did not get any traction; nobody held his feet to the fire, and the promise began to look like it wasn't going to happen. Instead of a safe place to go, the hammer came down on the homeless encampment on California Avenue, just west of G Street. On June 7, 2007, the California Highway Patrol (CHP) and Caltrans evicted homeless residents from their shelters. As many as 50 homeless people were affected by this action.

Most homeless people had moved by the time the "cleanup" crew arrived. Cynthia Greene, a resident of the homeless encampment, said most of the people had left and whatever remained was junk. She did acknowledge, however, that some homeless residents had been away since before the eviction notice was posted. Their tents remained on the land, which sat under an unused overpass.

The day began with the CHP taking pictures of everything and everyone in the area. They took photos of homeless people, the property that remained on the land and journalists. Next, a crew of Caltrans workers moved in and started to dismantle the remaining tents and other structures in the area. They separated what they considered to be garbage and things of value. The trash was put into a garbage truck and the items of value placed on a truck. From there, I was told, it would be taken to storage for 90 days. It was unclear, at times, how some things were determined to be trash and other items put into storage. Jose Camarena, a spokesperson for Caltrans, explained that Caltrans workers had talked with the residents of this encampment about what to save and what could be thrown out. "We have had a lot of conversations with the people out here. We let them know that we are not going to come through here and shove you out. We want to make sure that we interact with you and you tell us what you want to keep and what you don't want to keep. That allows us to protect their items as much as we can."

Those dislocated from this area moved to other homeless encampments in the downtown area, like on H Street where there were portable toilets and trash bins. The H Street encampment had grown to about 100 residents and was growing rapidly.

The City of Fresno was in the process of purchasing some land, not far from the location of the June 7, 2007, eviction, that it was rumored would serve as the site for the mayor's plan. Autry said the site would include dumpsters, portable toilets and a trailer where the County of Fresno would provide social service information. The mayor and City Council members said this was not a solution to homelessness but a step in the right direction in dealing with the hundreds of homeless people in the downtown area. The expectation was that until more permanent solutions to homelessness could be initiated, at least homeless people would have a place to go to the bathroom and be free from the constant sweeps that force them to move from one place to another.

Nobody that I contacted on the City Council at the time seemed frustrated with the delay in the mayor's plan. City Council Member Duncan said that "nothing surprises me here anymore but at least it is still moving forward. There needs to be a conditional use permit issued to the city for the use of the property for this purpose so there will be a hearing and vote at the Planning Commission in the near future." Duncan said it would be important for interested community members to come out and support the plan because there are several business owners in the area who are less than excited about a large homeless encampment in their neighborhood. Greg Barfield, City Council Member Sterling's aide, did not want to comment. He simply wrote an e-mail saying "the key is getting the services and location."

I asked Camarena, the Caltrans spokesperson, if Caltrans had plans to evict the homeless people living on The Hill. Camarena said Caltrans had no plans to evict them and that Caltrans was in the process of transferring title of the land to the City of Fresno. When asked why Caltrans was evicting homeless people five days before Autry's plan was supposed to be in operation, Camarena said, "This cleanup was coordinated and scheduled independently of any schedule that the City of Fresno has set forth. This is a part of our routine cleanups. We have cleanups like this all over the state and all over our district."

At the end of the day, Caltrans had a clean strip of land but Fresno's homeless still did not have a safe place to sleep.

Assistant City Manager Rudd invited me to a meeting to discuss the possibility of having a safe and legal place where the homeless could live. He and Barfield asked me if I could assure them that homeless people would go to this facility if they built it. I told him that I was not the Pied Piper of the homeless, but that I would ask some of the homeless people I knew what they thought of the idea.

It turns out that most of the homeless people I talked to did not like the idea of being put into a "concentration camp" (their description) located in the old industrial section south of downtown Fresno. Speaking before the Fresno City Council on June 19, Al Williams said, "You are trying to put people into a concentration camp...I'd rather be in jail than a concentration camp." Williams was referring to the city's plan to force all homeless people into a 30,000-square-foot lot that has no shade and is fenced in on all sides.

Williams was not the only homeless person concerned about the specter of being put into a concentration camp. Greene, who lived in a homeless encampment on G and California streets (The Hill), told me that she would not be forced "into that concentration camp. They don't have any shade, it is all fenced in and full of goat head thorns." Williams and Greene spoke as the City Council debated a new city ordinance that would ban camping (without a permit) in the City of Fresno.

The discussion to pass an ordinance banning camping and the proposal to use a vacant lot in the industrial section of downtown as a place where the homeless could live were linked together by the City Council. The homeless and their allies argued against both.

Becky Johnson, a homeless advocate in Santa Cruz, said that local government has passed anti-camping ordinances there and that it has been a dismal failure. Johnson said, "Common sense tells us that if a man doesn't have $40 for a motel room, then he can't afford a $90 camping citation either. Here in Santa Cruz, our city writes nearly 6,000 camping citations a year and we still have a large homeless population. Surprise! Surprise! Surprise!"

Johnson continued, "You can't solve homelessness through fiat. Homelessness is the logical consequence of current economic and political policies over which the individual has little control. When a homeless person gets a citation for the 'crime' of living out of doors because he can't afford to live indoors, this compounds his set of problems. He now is treated as a criminal by law enforcement, is deeper in debt and in the best-case scenario (he serves his sentence/pays his fine) he now has a criminal record which is a further obstacle to obtaining housing and employment. In as many cases as not, these citations go to warrant, and the person ends up spending time in our county jail, which is costly and completely non-productive."

According to Johnson, "The Ninth Circuit Court ruled in 2006 that citing people for sleeping or sheltering themselves at night in a situation in which insufficient shelter exists constitutes 'cruel and inhuman punishment' and is forbidden constitutionally. Those cited under Fresno's new law might turn right around and sue the city for damages."

The ordinance was recommended by a homeless task force headed by Rev. Larry Arce of the Fresno Rescue Mission. The stated goal of the task force is the establishment of a plot of land where the homeless could camp. This was part of Mayor Autry's initiative to set up a "free zone" where homeless people could live.

Instead, what the homeless received were more evictions, harassment and ordinances criminalizing poverty. The 60-day (self-imposed) deadline in which the mayor promised to set up this free zone came and went. With property owners in the area of the proposed encampment up in arms (they organized a protest at a City Council meeting) about the location and the homeless themselves ambivalent if not downright hostile to the proposal, the mayor's plan and the Homeless Task Force seem destined for failure.

Big Sue, a homeless woman in downtown Fresno, told me that she thought the city was trying to push homeless people as far south of Ventura Street as they can. This assessment was confirmed by City Council Member Duncan's call-in to local right-wing talk show host Inga Barks' radio show. Duncan told Barks that the goal was to move the homeless people so they are not so visible in the downtown area and that once they establish this camp it will give them (the city) the ability to clean up illegal encampments elsewhere.

At the June 19, 2007, City Council meeting, Duncan went one step further. He wondered out loud about whether the camping ordinance went far enough. He complained about people who give the homeless food and clothing. Duncan appeared to be seriously considering an ordinance that would ban people from feeding and clothing the homeless.

Could the City of Fresno successfully manage homeless people by forcing them onto a small plot of land and passing increasingly repressive ordinances against them? Greene, speaking before the City Council, said, "If this ordinance is passed, it will be challenged. It was challenged in Los Angeles, and they had to back down because it is not good for the people." The homeless and some advocates in Fresno said they would use whatever tools they have at their disposal to stop this cruel and inhumane treatment, stop the unconstitutional criminalization of poverty and fight against homeless people's forced confinement in the proposed concentration camp.

The meeting about the safe and legal site for the homeless with Rudd and Barfield reached almost mythical proportions in future years. I was told by community and homeless advocates who, after talking with these two City Hall employees, that it was my fault the homeless had no safe and legal place to live. Barfield and Rudd claimed that I was to blame for the horrible conditions in the homeless encampments. If only I had been their Pied Piper, we could have solved the homeless issue in Fresno. This was ironic, I thought, because by 2011 I was the only one supplying the homeless encampments with portable toilets and trash bins. This would not be the last time that those at City Hall would blame me for their failures.

In July 2007, Sherri Williams was issued a citation by the police because she tried to use the restroom at McDonald's on Olive Avenue, just west of Highway 99 in Fresno. Sherri and her husband Al were regular customers at McDonald's; they're homeless and Sherri used a wheelchair. On that morning, Al bought a cup of coffee and Sherri headed to the restroom. That is when McDonald's Manager Michelle Torres saw Sherri and said, "I need you to go; you're not purchasing anything, I need you to go." Al told Torres that Sherri needed to use the restroom and wash her hands and after that she would buy something. Torres went to summon a police officer who was in the restaurant.

Moments later, the officer arrived and said, "They tell me they are asking you to leave but you aren't leaving." Al said, "Why do we have to leave?" The officer replied that "this is a private restaurant and they can refuse service to anybody." Al pointed out that they can only refuse service if they have a reason. The officer responded by saying that if she does not leave "she is going to be arrested."

Sherri was then taken outside and given a citation—PC 602.1 for "Interfering with Business" by Officer D.J. Onruh—that demanded that she show up in criminal court in September. Sherri and Al believed that they were being discriminated against because they are homeless and she is in a wheelchair. In a letter Sherri sent to McDonald's on June 29, 2007, she wrote about an incident that happened three days earlier. In that incident, Sherri wrote, "I was subject to harassment and false accusations by employees of the establishment for use of a public restroom. As a patron at this restaurant, there was no legal cause or justification to be escorted out of McDonald's by a Fresno city police officer."

Sherri said that she might take longer in the restroom than other customers because of her disability. Sherri wrote, "I have been a regular patron of this location for several years and never have had regular customers make complaints about my use of the restroom nor [been] harassed by McDonald's staff as I have in recent months by current management. I am not certain if it's my homelessness or disability, but it seems that my presence annoys these employees regardless of the fact that I have patronized McDonald's for years. I may have left a slight mess when using the restroom, but it is partly because of my health, limited condition and the inadequate dispenser in the women's restroom. I am not clear who sets the policies, practices and procedures at this establishment, but it certainly violates the Americans with Disabilities Act as it relates to accommodating an individual with a disability and the inadequate dispenser in the restroom."

Waiting in the parking lot while the officer wrote up the citation for her crime of needing to use the bathroom, Sherri was getting hot as the temperature climbed above 100 degrees. The officer was sitting in his air-conditioned cruiser as he wrote up the citation. It was at this time when my daughter and filmmaker Simone Cranston-Rhodes arrived on the scene with her video camera. As she filmed the developing scene, McDonald's Manager Torres came out and said, "I'm going to have to ask you to leave; you cannot video on our property." Simone responded that she has a legal right to be there, and Torres said, "You don't have a right to be on my property and video tape, so I'm going to have to ask you to leave." The intrepid journalist stood her ground and refused to leave.

That was when I arrived, hearing Torres say, "Sir, you are not allowed to take pictures...and I'm asking you to leave." I replied that just because Torres didn't want me there does not revoke my rights as a journalist. There was a story unfolding, and I was determined to find out what was happening. She claimed McDonald's had a rule about photography on its property, and I continued to insist on my right as a journalist to cover the story. Torres eventually went inside and the issue was dropped.

The police were now aware that this incident was being documented and decided not to arrest and book Sherri. As one officer stood in the shade and another sat in his air-conditioned car, Sherri continued to bake in the hot sun. Soon, a sergeant and more officers arrived. The sergeant asked for my identification and informed me that I could keep my photos and the video. This generous gesture (allowing me to keep my photos and video) was tempered with a threat that a court order could be issued to use them in a criminal proceeding should this incident end up in court.

Officer Onruh emerged from his cruiser to issue the citation. He told Sherri he was issuing the citation because she was "trespassing and interfering with the business and Michelle is the store manager; she is the one who arrested you." Sherri was fingerprinted and signed the citation.

Earlier in the morning, and the reason why an officer was in McDonald's in the first place, was that there had been a robbery. One officer responded to the robbery call. On the other hand, there were at least three police cruisers on the scene and six or seven officers involved to sort out the alleged crime of a homeless woman needing to use the bathroom.

The incident at McDonald's led to a protest the following week. Protestors said Sherri Williams' rights were violated when she was issued a citation for attempting to use the restroom at McDonald's. Speaking at the protest, Liza Apper, from St. Benedict Catholic Worker, said she was "here today to support Sherri and her husband Al who was discriminated against from getting service at this McDonald's." Apper said that she would "like McDonald's to acknowledge their policy of discrimination toward handicapped people and change. They should give the same level of service to their fully abled customers as they do to their handicapped customers."

Apper had a message for the McDonald's corporation. She said that "McDonald's has roots in helping the homeless. Founder Ray Kroc and his wife were very supportive and contributed millions of dollars to the Saint Vincent center in San Diego and I think that McDonald's, when they are aware of this situation, would feel very upset that their own founders, who had so much sympathy and put their money where their mouth was for the homeless, would have a local McDonald's that exhibits such discrimination against the homeless and the handicapped."

Bryan Apper was also at the protest. Bryan told me that a young man came over to him and asked what the protest was about. "When I told him that McDonald's had issued a citation to this woman in a wheelchair because she took too long in the restroom, he got angry and said, 'You know, I eat here every day and I'm never coming back here again,' and he left. He was very angry."

Sherri and Al were at the protest. Sherri said that she hoped the protest would result in McDonald's allowing homeless and handicapped people to use the restroom. "I hope they don't discriminate against someone else who is in a wheelchair, another handicapped person, there was no reason for them to do that," Sherri said.

Al said, "McDonald's has started discriminating against the homeless and handicapped people. We have approached them and they have become very belligerent about abiding by the laws, so we are going to make this public." Al said that he wanted McDonald's to realize that it is not above the law.

McDonald's Manager Torres was at the scene of the protest. Attempts by several journalists to get a comment from Torres were brushed off. Torres did yell at me for taking pictures of her employees who were serving protestors water. Of course, I continued taking pictures and told her that she had no authority over journalists taking pictures for a news story.

There were no police at the protest. All major television news stations came out to interview Sherri, Al and several of the protestors.

In a 4-3 vote in October 2007, the Fresno City Council agreed to construct 44 10' × 10' tool sheds for the homeless. The tool sheds at the Poverello House would be built with funding coming from the City of Fresno. The funding to build the sheds and improvements at the Poverello House cost about $360,000 for the first year.

The proposal to build 44 tool sheds sparked a significant debate before the vote was taken. About a dozen community members addressed the City Council on this issue. The first speaker, Kyle Schmidt, said he was "concerned about using these prefabricated sheds that are for storage rather than for living. I believe many of them come with a disclaimer that they are not for habitation, and that could be a legal issue." Schmidt also pointed to homeless communities in Atlanta (the Mad Housers) and Portland (Dignity Village) that included homeless people in the planning. Schmidt said, "One thing that sets those apart from this approach is that the homeless have been involved through the process in the planning and in the construction of the dwellings. So they really buy into this as where they're going to stay, not just a concentration camp—where there is security watching their every move."

Al Williams said that "there is lots of money being spent, but it is accomplishing zero. It is making some people rich." Williams said "what we need is for money to be spent to give a person a job, to get a person a house, and we can take care of ourselves." He opposed the proposal to put homeless people into tool sheds.

The next speaker was Jose Luis Barraza from the Center for Independent Living. Barraza said "the fact is that living in a tool shed is not the answer, it is supportive housing." Speaking about disabled homeless people, Barraza said "that they do not need to be on the streets, they need a home, they have a right to live independently, and ladies and gentlemen this (tool sheds) is not the answer."

Speaker after speaker demanded that the city develop a long-term strategy to deal with homeless people in a respectful manner and that the proposed tool sheds were not the answer. But the condemnation of the tool sheds was not unanimous. The Fresno Rescue Mission's Arce agreed that the tool sheds were not a solution to homelessness but he wanted to see them installed anyway. Chamber of Commerce Spokesperson Debbie Hunsaker supported the tool sheds but also urged the city to work toward a long-term solution.

After community input, the issue returned to the dais. City Council Member Sterling, who represented the district where the tool sheds would be located, said "to extend the process without actually taking the opportunity as a city to look at some of the solutions that have been brought before us—I have a drawer full of information on every project throughout the nation concerning the homeless and what people have done for permanent facilities for them and how they went about doing it—but it seems to keep falling on deaf ears." Sterling said that instead of considering the tool sheds the City Council should discuss converting abandoned hotels and motels into affordable housing. She also suggested establishing a "homeless czar" who would oversee developing plans to address the homeless issue. In a couple of years, her staff person, Barfield, would become the city's first homeless czar.

City Council Member Westerlund made the motion to support the tool shed proposal. He said that the proposal "is not the answer (to homelessness). It is a stop gap at best and unfortunately our stop gaps have been our permanent answers." Westerlund said that a forthcoming meeting with the County of Fresno on the homeless would be critical in addressing this issue.

City Council Member Duncan, who represents northeast Fresno, said, "We do have a real complicated problem here, and our problem is complicated by a fundamental fact—that we do not have a community strategy in managing this problem. We have the city which goes one way, the county which goes its way, and some incredible nonprofit groups do the best they can. The reality is that we're not all working together, we don't have our act together, we're not working together. Until we do we're really going to struggle with issues like this not knowing what to do and how to go about doing it." Duncan seconded the proposal to establish the tool sheds.

Duncan asked Assistant City Manager Rudd what the plan was to get the homeless to move into the tool sheds. Rudd said that "the plan is that once this goes into place, we will start looking at the Monterrey Street bridge and G Street encampments. The G Street encampment would be the first location in which we would go out with the county Department of Health and Human Services to encourage people to take advantage of what I refer to as the south campus. At that same time, we will be providing notice that they are on city property and we will go through the same process we have been directed to go through as a result of the court ruling as far as how we deal with encampments. They will be given every opportunity to make that choice, but the first location that will be identified for removal of the encampment will be the G Street location. Those folks who are there will be given every opportunity to take advantage of moving to the south campus."

Duncan asked, "If they choose not to move, what are we going to do?"

Rudd responded, "Then, as that area is cleaned out we will start focusing on the Monterrey Street bridge area." Rudd went on to say that they wanted to see how much "voluntary participation" they get. If homeless people do not move voluntarily into the tool sheds, Rudd said they had ordinances, including a pending "no camping" law, that would be used to force the homeless people to move.

Rudd said the capacity of the "south campus" would be 88 people. Duncan pressed Rudd on this number, saying there are hundreds of homeless people in the downtown area. "What happens when that fills up," Duncan asked.

Rudd, who had a smile on his face, said, "Based on my discussions with both Rev. Arce and Mr. Connell [executive director of the Poverello House], they don't believe and I don't believe that camp is going to fill up completely, voluntarily."

City Manager Andrew Souza said the goal of the meeting with the county "is not to just sit around and all talk about this but to get a firm commitment to implement the 10-Year Plan [to End Chronic Homelessness] and see how that document works, how that plan will work and who are the appropriate community stakeholders involved. We are trying to do a lot of behind-the-scenes work in preparation for that meeting so that on November 7 we walk out of there...with a very firm game plan on how we are going to move beyond just the temporary solutions." Souza said he saw the tool sheds as a temporary fix but that he realized the goal was to look for long-term solutions.

Blong Xiong, the City Council Member who represents the west Fresno district (north of Olive Avenue), asked Souza about the homeless czar. Souza said, "If we are going to engage in the level of solution that we are talking about, including the 10-Year Plan to End [Chronic] Homelessness, we're going to have to have a dedicated staff person whose sole purpose for being here is to address the issue of homelessness."

City Council Member Mike Dages, who represents southeast Fresno, asked if the City Council was still on the 9:30 a.m. item. It was 3 p.m. Dages said the City of Fresno had $4.1 million in the current year's budget to address long-range homeless issues. He asked the city manager what was being done with that money. Souza said he would get Dages a status report. Dages said, "I have a real problem with the idea of creating a tool shed, a shed like I have on the side of my house, for people to live in. I wouldn't ask my relatives to live in it, and I have a real difficult time asking the homeless to live in it. I think the quality of the city really depends on how they treat their poor, their working poor and their homeless. I don't think we are treating them with respect, in my personal opinion. We are struggling with affordable housing, we are struggling with this homeless situation and it just shows to me a lack of respect by the City of Fresno."

City Council Member Henry T. Perea said that he would support the plan if it was part of a bigger program. "If there was a plan to say 'OK, we are going to take this money [the $4.1 million in the city budget for homeless issues] and build transitional housing, provide some real opportunity and some real hope for these people and we had a plan that said this transitional housing will be built in the next year or two and this [the tool sheds] was going to be a stop gap measure until we can get these people into those homes,' I could probably go for it. The problem is—we are not doing that."

The vote was 4-3 with Duncan, Westerlund, Xiong and Calhoun voting yes. Perea, Sterling and Dages voted no. And that is how Fresno's largest collection of beds for the homeless became a reality.

In November 2007, I met Bruce Tracy, who had dug at least 10 feet into the ground to create a multi-room shelter that kept him cool in the summer and warm in the winter. Tracy's home reminded me of the Forestiere Underground Gardens, located on Shaw Avenue in north Fresno. Unlike the Forestiere Gardens, which is a local, state and national historical landmark, the FPD told Tracy it planned to bulldoze his home.

Tracy told me that he has built a lot of these underground homes. "I have been doing this since I was 14," Tracy said. He credited his interest in underground living to a visit to the Forestiere gardens when he was a kid. Sitting in his home on a rainy November day, Tracy said it took him about three months to dig out this home. "I dug it all out with a shovel and an axe."

About a week before I got there, the FPD found Tracy's home, which was on public land (owned by Caltrans) about a mile north of Roeding Park. Tracy said the police came in with guns drawn, searched the place and forced him out in his underwear. He was forced to stand outside in his boxer shorts for two and a half hours while the police interrogated him. "They came back a couple of days later and said I had to leave. They said they were going to bulldoze the place," Tracy said.

The threatened destruction of Tracy's home was consistent with city policy to eliminate homeless encampments and force people into tool sheds, the Fresno Rescue Mission or more isolated places to hide.

John Everett called me at about the same time I met Tracy and told me his story. He said that he owns property near Roeding Park, had set up a couple of trailers on his land and rented them out at reasonable rates to people who were homeless. It gave people a reasonably nice place to stay, at a price they could afford and everyone was happy with the arrangement. Everett said that "code enforcement came in and shut me down. Everyone had to move back onto the streets."

The trailers Everett rented had heating, cooling, electricity, running water and a toilet. The tool sheds at the Poverello House don't have heating or cooling or running water, and everyone shares a portable toilet. Everett said people could come and go as they pleased at his place, but at the tool shed city at the Poverello House everyone is kicked out by 8 a.m. in the morning and can't return until 5 p.m. The tool sheds will cost the city $360,000 for the first year. Everett's operation costs the taxpayers nothing. Tracy's underground home costs the taxpayers nothing. Why was the City of Fresno destroying homeless encampments and forcing homeless people to move into housing that violates building codes, is not as nice as what they had and is costing taxpayers a significant amount of money?

I asked Tracy and his friend Thomas what they thought was behind the City of Fresno's plan to move homeless people into tool sheds. "It's all about control," Thomas said. "I got pulled over 45 times in 30 days," added Tracy. Tracy says homeless people are harassed constantly, "They just want to eliminate the homeless" by making life so hard that they move.

Tracy, who works as a carpenter and a mechanic, said he does not want to spend his money on rent and live the consumer-oriented lifestyle that most people take for granted. He takes no money from the government and would like to be left alone to live in peace. "I'm self-sustaining, self-sufficient and don't get in trouble with the law...as much as I can."

One thing I had learned by this time was that most homeless people live a much more communal life than most Fresno residents who live in suburbs or apartments. They know their neighbors and take time to talk with them every day. While I was visiting Tracy, a friend came by to make sure he was all right. He had seen my car parked nearby. After Tracy assured his friend that everything was OK, he told me that the friend said he would keep an eye on our car to make sure nobody disturbed it. That's what neighbors should do. They should look after each other, not bulldoze their homes.

When the story I wrote about Tracy was published, it went viral and ended up being reported all over the country. The story even showed up as A Ripley's Believe It or Not comic in the *Fresno Bee*. The comic called Tracy the "mole man." When Fox News interviewed Tracy (on national TV), the story reached his long lost brother on the east coast who reconnected with him.

By April 2008, Mayor Alan Autry was ready to proclaim the city's homeless policy a failure. Years later, he spoke about his policy on the homeless as his biggest regret. Autry said, "We have failed, government has failed, on this issue. We are the status quo that has chosen through our wisdom over the last 40 or 50 years to pick the most expensive and ineffective, dis-compassionate way to address the homeless situation." Autry was addressing the joint meeting of the leadership and planning councils of the County/City of Fresno relative to the 10-Year Plan to End Chronic Homelessness.

Autry told the task force, which was meeting for the first time, that he wanted them to develop a blueprint for how to develop a Housing First model that would provide homeless people a place to live without preconditions. The mayor said, "I'm having to change my thinking because we are talking about a home in a neighborhood where a guy comes up and passes out on the front yard. That is part of the process of getting well. There is no requirement on those individuals. I'm ready to go there."

What Autry was encouraging the task force to do was develop a Housing First program in Fresno that would take this community's chronically homeless and provide them with decent/affordable housing. The plan was outlined by Eduardo Cabrera, HUD Region IX Homeless Agency coordinator, who said this meeting would be "the beginning of the end of homelessness." Cabrera gave the same one-hour PowerPoint presentation that Philip Mangano, executive director of the Bush administration's Interagency Council on Homelessness, gave four months earlier.

The presentation makes a powerful argument that government policy on homelessness over the last 20 years has failed to decrease chronic homelessness. The chronically homeless, Cabrera said, are only 10% of the homeless population, but they use 50% of the resources available. Those services include emergency medical services, primary healthcare (e.g., multi-day hospital stays), behavioral healthcare (e.g., psychiatric treatment, detox facilities) and interactions with the justice system (e.g., the police, the courts).

Cabrera said the Boston Health Care for the Homeless Program tracked 119 persons experiencing chronic homelessness for five years and discovered that they had more than 18,000 emergency room visits at an average cost of $1,000 per visit. Research prepared for the Tucson, Arizona, 10-year plan showed that downtown Tucson police officers spent about 200 hours in 1,070 encounters with people who were homeless during April 2007, at an estimated cost to the police department of $64,000. Tucson's Fire Department in 2007 spent an estimated $2 million answering an estimated 3,000 calls—out of a total 76,000 911 calls—from people who were homeless.

In Reno, Nevada, Cabrera said two frustrated police officers tracked the costs of two chronically homeless individuals, who accounted for $100,000 and $120,000, respectively, in hospital expenses in less than a year. The officers determined that one individual, who they named "Million Dollar Murray," had cost more than $1 million in hospitalization, incarceration, detox treatments and ambulance rides. Reno Police Department Officer Patrick O'Bryan said, "We spent $1 million not to do anything about him."

The University of California at San Diego followed 15 chronically homeless people for 18 months, tracking their use of behavioral health acute systems, mental health and substance abuse services, law enforcement interventions on the streets and temporary periods of incarceration. Total cost: $3 million or $200,000 per person.

The solution, Cabrera said, is to provide chronically homeless people with housing so they can stabilize their lives and start getting the help they need. In the Housing First program, people are given housing without any preconditions. They don't have to end their drug or alcohol addictions before they get housing. Housing First gives them housing and offers them assistance.

According to Cabrera, Housing First is working. In Portland, Maine, researchers tracked 99 chronically homeless individuals who moved to permanent supportive housing. They report a 50% reduction in service costs in ambulance and emergency room use, jail nights and police contacts after housing placement, dropping from an average of more than $28,000 per person annually to $14,000. Healthcare costs decreased 59% after housing placement and mental health care costs decreased 41%.

Denver, Colorado, saw a 73% reduction in emergency costs, or nearly $600,000, in the two years after chronically homeless people were placed in housing. More than 80% of the homeless people remained in the housing after six months. Mayor John Hickenlooper of Denver said that city would reinvest $20 million in savings in public systems to create 200 new units of housing for persons who are chronically homeless.

Advocates of the Housing First model say that the old status quo of ad hoc, uncoordinated crisis intervention isn't working; it is more expensive and less effective at helping the homeless than the Housing First model. A Fresno Grand Jury report released in March 2008 came to the same conclusion. The Grand Jury wrote that "the scattered and piecemeal public services provided to the unsheltered homeless add up to a very large public expense. It has been reported that as much as 50%–80% of the total money intended for homelessness is spent on the chronic unsheltered homeless." Writing about the tool sheds at the Poverello House and other efforts by the city to address homelessness, the Grand Jury report says that "these various efforts to provide housing for the homeless have not been effective solutions for chronic unsheltered homeless in Fresno County."

The Grand Jury report said that "Housing First programs provide permanent transitional housing and support services for the unsheltered homeless. Clients receiving shelter are not usually required to be drug and alcohol free in order to be provided housing. Support services, including counseling programs to support a drug-free lifestyle, accompany the housing, rather than being a prerequisite to it. The Housing First model was developed in Boston, Massachusetts, after a study revealed that the community was paying an exorbitant amount to treat homeless individuals at hospital emergency rooms. The study showed that giving the homeless person clean, warm and dry shelter reduced medical costs by as much as 70%. Boston went on to construct permanent buildings to provide temporary or transitional housing for the homeless. Other cities including Chicago and Portland claim to have saved money and improved services by establishing a Housing First program."

Mayor Autry, in his talk to the task force, told them to "think outside of the box" and encouraged them to redirect public policy on homelessness. Cabrera, the HUD Region IX Homeless Agency coordinator, said essentially the same thing. He told the group to "move from managing the crisis to ending the disgrace." The model they are advocating is at odds with the current social service providers such as the Poverello House and the Rescue Mission, which maintain the status quo. Both organizations were represented on the task force but managed to maintain and expand their programs in the years following the shift toward the Housing First model.

Cabrera was clear about the cost of maintaining the status quo. He quoted Albert Einstein, who once said that "the definition of insanity is doing the same thing over and over again and expecting different results." Housing First costs far less than the current public policy, is much more effective at ending chronic homelessness and has gained the support of the mayor and a majority of elected officials.

In September 2008, the City and County of Fresno approved the final draft of the 10-Year Plan to End Chronic Homelessness. The plan was the product of a city/county task force that was mandated with the goal of eliminating homelessness. Attending the September 9, 2008 meeting was Mangano, executive director of the Bush administration's Interagency Council on Homelessness. Mangano said "your goal in this 10-year plan is that your children will have to go to a museum someday to see what homelessness once was." Mangano urged both the City Council and the Board of Supervisors to support the task force plan to end homelessness.

Mayor Autry, speaking before the City Council, said that he made a decision the previous December to move his homelessness policy in a new direction. Autry said, "I have been a miserable failure in terms of the homeless issue in this community. I didn't know it at the time, I felt that we were doing pretty much all that we could...there was a feeling that it would never get better, let's make their (homeless people's) inevitable passing a little more comfortable. That is not only wrong but it's immoral." Autry urged the City Council to pass the 10-year plan.

Mangano explained that by shifting from a policy that maintained/managed homelessness (such as the Rescue Mission and the Poverello House) to a Housing First model, Fresno could not only end chronic homelessness but also save money too. According to Mangano, the current method of addressing homelessness costs $35,000–$150,000 per year per homeless person. The cost is high because of emergency medical services, police intervention and the money that goes to social service providers. In contrast, Mangano says that for $13,000–$25,000, this community could provide the homeless with descent affordable housing and get them on the way to living a more productive life. He encouraged the task force to write a cost-benefit analysis, showing what Fresno could save by switching to a Housing First model.

Mangano said that the federal government was spending record amounts of money on homelessness. He said that "the 2009 budget has $5 billion targeted to homeless people. That has been good for Fresno. More than $25 million has come to Fresno over the last five years. You have received increased resources for the last two years and in three of the last four years Fresno has received record resources from Washington and just very recently, a new award of HUD housing vouchers plus veterans' affairs support services have come to Fresno."

Al Williams, a task force member, a veteran and a homeless man, said he would like to know where that money has gone. Williams, speaking moments after Mangano's presentation, said "too much money has come here that is not accounted for. Mangano said that $25 million has come to Fresno. Well, how many people are still homeless on the street? Where did the money go? It is in somebody's pocket, I guess. I think these social service providers should be held accountable for their spending." Williams has often referred to parasitic social service providers as "poverty pimps" because of their ability to benefit from the suffering of the homeless.

Paul Boden is the executive and organizing director at the Western Regional Advocacy Project (WRAP), a coalition of west coast social justice–based homelessness organizations. According to Boden, the Housing First project and "the administration's current 'Chronic Homeless Initiative' is just the latest in a series of inadequate flavor-of-the-month distractions from the real problem. It does nothing to address the huge cuts to federal affordable housing funding that caused mass homelessness. Housing is a human right, which a democracy should advance, not restrict."

We will explore Boden's analysis in Chapter 15.

Several speakers, including Williams, questioned the 10-year plan's accuracy and the number of homeless people it says are living in Fresno. The task force claimed there are only 4,247 homeless people in Fresno. This was down from an estimated 8,824 homeless people listed in the City of Fresno Consolidated Plan just a few years before. The numbers in the Consolidated Plan were themselves a large reduction in what previous studies had found. A report from the Fresno/Madera Continuum of Care in 2002 put the number at about 16,000.

Because the homeless are extremely hard to count in a street survey, most communities across the country estimate that 1%–2% of the residents are homeless. That is the national average. Communities with more unemployment and a poor economy will be on the high end of that estimate—in the 2% range of homeless people in their city. The 2002 estimate assumed that because of Fresno's chronic double-digit unemployment, poor economy and the highest concentration of poverty in the country, the number of homeless was closer to 2%. The task force instead relied on a point-in-time survey conducted by the Continuum of Care that found the number of homeless in Fresno was well below the national average at 0.05%.

Almost everyone now acknowledges that the point-in-time number was too low and led to a gross underestimation of the help homeless people needed in this community. At the time (2008), there were about 3,000 homeless children in the Fresno Unified School District (FUSD). To give you an indication of how well the 10-year plan is working, by 2013 there were almost 4,000 homeless students in the FUSD. In Fresno County, there were 6,738 homeless students (3.4% of those in public schools) in 2013, according to the California Homeless Youth Project report on "California's Homeless Students: A Growing Population."

If you go with the rather conservative figure of 2% of people in Fresno as being homeless, you would conclude that in 2014 we had a homeless population of about 10,000 in the city of Fresno and 20,000 in the entire county. Given the number of homeless students (3.6%), the number of homeless in Fresno could be much higher. The number of homeless has certainly not gone down, even six years after the start of the 10-year plan.

The task force, claiming that there were only 941 chronically homeless people in Fresno, determined that all that was needed was to provide 100 units of housing a year for 10 years and voila, the homeless problem in Fresno would be gone. It didn't turn out that way.

After six years of the 10-year plan, fewer than 200 new housing units have been built.

There were enormous pressures on the city and county of Fresno to successfully confront the homelessness issue in this community. The financial burden alone motivated local government; if it could spend $20,000 instead of $100,000 per homeless person per year, that would save millions of dollars that could be better spent. Businesspeople, developers and builders in the downtown area were demanding a change. To commercially develop and revitalize downtown, they argued, homelessness must be eliminated or at least dramatically reduced. Those two powerful forces, an alliance of business and government, led to the 10-Year Plan to End Chronic Homelessness.

Homelessness was now on the political radar screen in this community. Both the City Council and the Board of Supervisors said the plan would succeed and both unanimously approved the 10-year plan.

The questions that would become obvious in the next couple of years were: Did local government officials have the political will to end homelessness? Who would be put in charge of bringing the deep and institutional change necessary to change the entrenched (social service) bureaucracy? And, how would the social service providers react to this new paradigm?

Under an ordinance passed in Fresno in 2006, the man in the above photo could be arrested, fined $1,000 and spend up to a year in jail. It does not matter that the police could not prove that he was not returning this abandoned shopping cart to a grocery store. The ordinance says that if you are in possession of a shopping cart, away from the business that owns it, you could be arrested, fined and jailed.
*Photo by Chris Schneider*

The Homelessness Marathon forced Fresno elected officials to listen to the homeless and respond to their concerns. From left to right: Fresno County Supervisor Bob Waterston, Fresno City Council Members Jerry Duncan and Cynthia Sterling, host Jeremy Alderson and Fresno Mayor Alan Autry.

Fresno's homeless were the stars of the show. This homeless woman had the attention of Fresno's elected officials as she asked them a question.

Community activist Rebeca Rangel told Fresno elected officials what she thought about their homeless policies.

Speaking their minds on the Homelessness Marathon were two members of the lawsuit against the City of Fresno (from left to right) Joanna Garcia and Pam Kincaid, along with host Jeremy Alderson.

James Betts, with a tie in the center, shakes hands with Fresno Police Officer Rey Wallace. Betts has defended the City of Fresno in several lawsuits filed by homeless people. Wallace was the architect of the city's policy of taking and destroying homeless people's property, which led to the first lawsuit in 2006.

The City of Fresno forced homeless people to move from this encampment on Olive and West avenues, just west of Roeding Park on April 5, 2007. Instead of taking and immediately destroying homeless people's property, city workers put their things in a large container and hauled them off to a city-owned parking lot in downtown Fresno. The photo above was taken shortly before the cleanup began.

Al Williams and his wife lived about a block from the encampment (above) that was "cleaned up." Fresno Police Officer Bruce Hartman told Williams that he would have to move. Williams was told that all of the nearby businesses signed a letter of complaint against his encampment. Williams claims he has good relations with the business owners and that Hartman forced the business owners to sign the letter.

City of Fresno sanitation workers removed some property and stored some homeless people's property in this "cleanup," which was the first after the federal court order.

Dee and the other residents in the homeless encampment at Olive and West avenues in Fresno were forced to "move on." Dee was not a happy camper and repeatedly complained as the encampment was de-constructed.

The first homeless person to use the new portable toilets is carefully watched by a security guard from CIS Security.

Homeless people in Fresno were evicted from Caltrans land on June 12, 2007. Some homeless advocates considered this a betrayal of Mayor Autry's promise to provide homeless people with a safe place to sleep.

Caltrans workers are seen throwing a mattress into a garbage truck at this homeless encampment near downtown Fresno.

This homeless woman in a wheelchair was harassed, made to stay out in the hot sun and given a citation because she was about to use a bathroom at McDonald's.

There were at least three police cruisers on the scene and six or seven officers involved to sort out the alleged crime of a homeless woman needing to use the bathroom.

This McDonald's manager (far right) claimed the chain had a rule prohibiting photography on their property. I continued to insist on my right as a journalist to cover the story. She eventually went inside and the issue was dropped.

Responding to the harassment of a handicapped homeless woman, who was attempting to use a bathroom at McDonald's, about a dozen protestors held signs and talked to the media in front of the restaurant.

These tool sheds at the Poverello House have a view of the Fresno downtown skyline.

Poverello House staff line up the tool sheds that they use to house the homeless. The tool sheds have no heating, cooling or running water. If you put your mother or father in a tool shed like this, you could be arrested for elder abuse.

Bruce Tracy, a homeless man in Fresno, builds his homes underground. Tracy's homes are cool in the summer and warm in the winter.

These are members of the mayor's task force, which was established to develop a 10-Year Plan to End Chronic Homelessness. On this day, they were on a tour of the Poverello House and some nearby homeless encampments.

The City and County of Fresno voted to adopt a 10-Year Plan to End Chronic Homelessness. At the start of the hearing before the City Council, Mayor Alan Autry apologized for the suffering he has caused the homeless in this community.

# Chapter 10

# Monitoring City Compliance

After the legal settlement with the City of Fresno, homeless advocates monitored the city's actions to make sure it was complying with the new protocols agreed to in federal court. Compliance was, to say the least, uneven. The city's process was random and capricious, leaving it up to the sanitation crew to determine what had value and what did not.

The incident written about in the previous chapter, where Dee had her property taken, put into storage and then destroyed, is a good place to start. It was because of the follow-up to monitor compliance with the court order that homeless advocates knew the city was violating the federal court order.

A couple of months after going to the city yard with Dee, Cynthia Greene and I returned to recover property city workers removed from the area where Pam Kincaid had lived. It was in September 2007, and Kincaid had recently died under suspicious and disturbing circumstances. I was searching for an address on a letter from her husband so I could get his contact information and let him know Kincaid had died. This time, the city seemed prepared for my visit, and I was informed that no cameras were allowed. Perhaps city officials did not like the video that I shot with Dee, which went on a local TV news program, showing the city to be in violation of the court order. I reluctantly left my video camera in the car, as it was more important to find Kincaid's property than to document further violations.

This time, the city had put proper covers over the 8×8×20-foot containers it was using to store homeless people's property. We followed the worker to the storage container; he removed the cover, handed me a pair of gloves and said I was free to look for Kincaid's property. The only problem was that the container was packed solid. There were couches, mattresses and a couple of tons of clothes and other property filling the entire container. How are you going to find something that was on the bottom of the container under a couch and tons of stuff? I started digging. As I did, cockroaches ran down my back, dust swirled around the workspace and the city worker stepped back so he did not get exposed to whatever might be in the dust. Greene flicked cockroaches off my back.

Making someone burrow through a mixture of garbage, other people's clothing, old mattresses and cockroaches was not a respectful or dignified way to return property to the homeless, who had their possessions taken from them in one of the many raids that occurred at that time.

In an amazing stroke of luck, I was able to find some of Kincaid's notebooks but not the letters I had hoped to find. In one of the notebooks was a poem entitled "Homeless Dog," which Dixie Salazar and Teresa Flores made into a short film. That poem is printed in "The Disturbing and Tragic Death of Pam Kincaid" chapter of this book.

There were other interesting adventures as homeless advocates tried to monitor the City of Fresno, which continued to take homeless people's property. In one incident, a Fresno homeless advocate was sent a letter from Homeland Security, informing him that his attempts to help the homeless had been "brought to the attention of the Police Department's Terrorism Liaison Officers." The unwanted attention of the Homeland Security anti-terrorism group followed a "cleanup" of a homeless encampment on the Mariposa Mall (near O Street) in downtown Fresno.

In this incident, several homeless advocates monitored the "cleanup" and removal of homeless people's property on the morning of April 22, 2009, by city sanitation workers. "Cleanups" at the Mariposa Mall site, just west of City Hall, were being conducted at that time about once a month. City sanitation would put up signs announcing the date of the cleanup, and most of the homeless people would move out shortly before the crew arrived and move back later in the day. It was a cruel game of cat-and-mouse that was not intended to help the homeless or make their life better in any way. As a result of this constant harassment, sometimes the homeless would lose their property. This happened if they were gone for a few days visiting a friend or a family member when the city cleaned up the encampment.

The signs announced the start of the "cleanup" as 8 a.m., but on April 22, 2009, they started early. Bill Simon, chairperson of the local chapter of the ACLU, was there that day and said that "Phil Connelly arrived at the cleanup site at 7:20 a.m.

Georgia and I arrived about 7:40 a.m. All three of us had cameras. Phil said the cleanup started just after he got there. One homeless woman was there talking to Phil when I arrived, and no other homeless were in sight. She was all packed up and left as I arrived."

Connelly left the Mariposa Mall "cleanup" and went to the City of Fresno Corporate Yard on G Street in an attempt to see where the confiscated property was taken. Connelly says he spoke with Phillip Weathers at the community sanitation office. "I saw Weathers at the event today and at a previous cleanup on H Street. He supervised both events. He told me the confiscated items were not brought to the City of Fresno Corporate Yard [the large complex at the northwest corner of G and El Dorado streets]," Connelly wrote in an e-mail.

Connelly said Weathers told him "the persons who own the confiscated property are expected to call his office at the number listed on the posted notices [even though his name is not on the notice]. Weathers said that if the owner can provide a description of their confiscated property, Weathers or a staff member will take the property to a location where the owner wants to reclaim it, or the property will be retrieved from its current storage location and the owner can come to the community sanitation office to claim the confiscated property."

A few days after his visit to the City of Fresno Corporate Yard, Connelly was contacted by Sergeant Ronald Grimm, Homeland Security coordinator for the FPD. Here is that correspondence:

> This e-mail is in regards to your visit to the City of Fresno Corporate Yard (2101 G Street) on April 22 of this year. This facility is considered a Key Resource to the City of Fresno, and is critical to the continuity of government for our area. Inasmuch, issues regarding the security (or breeches of security) at this facility fall within the investigative responsibility of the Fresno Police Dept. Your actions during your visit to this facility (primarily the photographing of specific sites on the premises and the contact you had with City personnel) caused concern among several City employees and was brought to the attention of the Police Department's Terrorism Liaison Officers.

> While we assume your visit to the premises was related to an ongoing investigation, I would like to ask for your cooperation for any future visits. If possible, could you please inform City employees

at the facility as to the nature of your visit and the particular public areas you would like to visit. Also, if you could inform these same employees that you will be taking photographs in public-access areas it would probably prevent the issue from becoming a concern of the Terrorism Liaison Officer unit.

Thank you for your anticipated cooperation in this matter. If you have any questions please feel free to contact me directly.

Sgt. Ronald Grimm
Homeland Security Coordinator
Fresno Police Department
(559) 621-2329

\*\*\*

Is being an advocate for homeless rights a legitimate reason for being investigated by Homeland Security and coming under the scrutiny of the FPD's terrorism liaison officers? Were Connelly and other homeless advocates put on a Homeland Security watch list of domestic terrorists?

A month after this incident, I was downtown at the FPD (with a delegation from the ACLU, getting a presentation about the FPD's use of video surveillance cameras) when Sergeant Grimm came over and said "hi." Of course, I asked him why Connelly had been targeted when he was at the City Yard. Grimm explained that the FPD had just conducted a workshop on the importance of City of Fresno employees being "alert" to anything unusual happening in their workplace—or perhaps anywhere in the city. Grimm explained that one "alert" employee saw Connelly at the City Yard, took notes about what he was doing, probably wrote down his car's license number and promptly reported the suspect to the FPD's terrorism liaison officer. Grimm contacted Burke Farah, who is in charge of video surveillance, and his department reviewed the video of Connelly walking around looking for what the city did with the homeless people's property they removed from the Mariposa Mall. The search of the video did not, we can assume, turn up anything too sinister, so the police tracked down Connelly through his car license number or by talking to Weathers at the sanitation department, who Connelly spoke with while at the City Yard.

After talking to Grimm, I drove out to the City Yard and took some photos of my own. The City Yard is wide open, and there are no obvious signs telling people not to step foot on this public property, which we as taxpayers pay for. I, like Connelly, looked around for the property taken from homeless people, but it was not where the property had been stored in the past.

While I was at the City Yard, a reporter from ABC-TV Channel 30 called and asked if he could interview me about the incident. We did the interview on the City Yard property, and I told him that it was outrageous for the police to send Connelly a letter from Homeland Security when all he was doing was helping the homeless. The paranoia that results when people are asked to spy on each other results in a witch hunt. The best-case scenario is that people just waste time chasing their tail. But if homeless advocates get put on a terrorist watch list or if people are frightened away from becoming involved to help the homeless because they don't want the government to suspect them of being a terrorist, then we are all much worse off. If the police are successful in their goal of blanketing the city with video surveillance cameras, Homeland Security has people spying on each other and there is nothing you can do that is not monitored, then we are all going to feel a whole lot safer, right? Either that or we will wake up and realize that we are living in a police state.

More recently, in July 2014, another incident involving the police targeting homeless advocates was revealed. I found out about this when Chris Breedlove, minister of the College Community Congregational Church, contacted me about a PowerPoint presentation being shown around town that listed him as a leader in a resistance movement to stop the demolition of the Grain Silo homeless encampment.

Sergeant Robert Dewey, with the FPD, had produced the PowerPoint presentation that listed Breedlove as the leader and the Brown Berets as the "muscle" behind the struggle to stop the city from destroying the Grain Silo homeless encampment.

Breedlove said he felt concerned by the tone of the presentation. In a slide titled "The Final Line in the Sand!" the FPD claimed that there were "12–15 advocates on hand, intermixed with members of the Brown Berets for 'muscle.'"

The slide goes on to say that the group was "led by Pastor Chris Breedlove of the College Community Congregational Church." Breedlove said he was "outraged, intimidated and concerned that a citizen not charged of any crime, and not under any investigation, could be named and listed in a public document by the Fresno Police Department in what is tantamount to a smear campaign or being proscribed."

The ACLU staff attorney in Fresno, Novella Coleman, would not comment about whether the characterization of Breedlove amounted to defamation but did say that "the city has an unfortunate history of violating the rights of homeless persons by confiscating and destroying their property. So it is troubling that the city may be targeting local advocates who seek to hold the city accountable during these so-called cleanups."

According to Breedlove, it is intimidating to be targeted by the police as the leader of a lawless group. He said, "I worry about how my future efforts, issues and ministries will be adversely impacted by my congregation and myself being negatively branded by the FPD in such a public way.

"I also worry about the well-being of my family. What if we needed an emergency response by the FPD? Is there a bias among the FPD against progressives such as myself? Is there a specific FPD bias toward my ministry?"

Mario Manganiello, who is associated with but not a member of the Brown Berets, was at the Grain Silo encampment during the demolition mentioned in the FPD presentation. Manganiello said that the Brown Berets did not organize a presence there that day and was upset that the FPD was portraying them as some kind of violent gang. "They are saying that we were the 'muscle' and pushing for violence, and that is absolutely not true," Manganiello said.

"My concern is that, with that wording, they are trying to say we are trying to promote violence or encourage other people to be violent towards the FPD," Manganiello said. "But our stance has always been peaceful at rallies and marches, and we are not a violent organization. We are for nonviolent peaceful protests."

Ralphy Avitia, a member of the Brown Berets, said, "I am afraid that the FPD will do as was done in the '60s and '70s with the more left-wing radical groups such as the Black Panther Party and classify us as the 'bad civil rights groups' and thus discredit us. I am hopeful that in this age of the Internet we can fight back against such a characterization. Our youth are better equipped to fight with a smart phone than with a gun as Anonymous has demonstrated. So unless we allow them to manipulate our image, we still have a chance to win the public's trust."

Speaking about the Brown Berets' role in the community, Avitia said it is "to organize, educate and serve communities that are oppressed. Unlike past Beret organizations, we are not nationalistic, homophobic, sexist or conforming to institutions that would oppress others. Also, unlike most groups, we do support the people's right to self-defense and thus will not consider ourselves nonviolent."

Responding to a California Public Records Act request, the FPD provided me with a version of the PowerPoint presentation that did not include the information that offended Breedlove and the Brown Berets. Dewey, who produced the presentation, "An Overview of Our Mission, Accomplishments and Goals," says he changed the references to Breedlove and the Brown Berets, some photos and other minor details.

Dewey said he had reason to believe that Breedlove was the leader of the homeless advocate group because Breedlove had previously held a press conference on the issue and had negotiated with the attorney representing the City of Fresno about the Grain Silo homeless encampment. Dewey added that the information had been removed from the PowerPoint presentation, and if Breedlove was upset he would apologize to him.

"I would apologize to Pastor Breedlove, to say that if that is not what was going on, if that was an assumption I made that was wrong, I apologize. I did take it out. I had been told by one or two other people that maybe it should be a little more generic. That is why I decided to go ahead and change it."

The Brown Berets did not have an organized presence at the Grain Silo homeless encampment on the day of the demolition, but they did catch the attention of Dewey and the FPD. Dewey said, "As far as the muscle, we did recognize people that we had seen in the past that were wearing obvious brown handkerchiefs and brown berets. I have done some dignitary protection in the past, and I know what it looks like when one person is protecting others. That is what it appeared to us as."

Manganiello said the purpose of the group he was with on that day was to give the homeless enough time to move their property. "We were able to stall them (the City of Fresno) for a long enough time so the homeless could put their belongings into storage, so that was the ultimate outcome," Manganiello said.

Dewey saw the situation differently. "As a law enforcement officer, I can't allow that. I can't allow somebody else to control the tempo on a scene that I'm supposed to be in control of. The fact of the matter is that we had a trespassing issue," Dewey said.

About the characterization of the Brown Berets as being the muscle, he said, "If they are upset about this, I apologize. I will apologize to their face if they want me to speak to them. I've got no problem with that."

During the October 23, 2013, demolition of the Grain Silo homeless encampment, Breedlove took video, including a scene where he asked an on-duty police officer for his name and badge number. The officer ignored the request. ACLU attorney Coleman, citing California Penal Code §830.10, says that "any uniformed peace officer shall wear a badge, nameplate or other device which bears clearly on its face the identification number or name of the officer."

Dewey says that Officer Nicholas El-Helou was on duty and should have identified himself but didn't because he was in plain clothes and was told not to "engage" unless there were problems. Dewey is confident that this problem will not be repeated.

Dewey shows the PowerPoint presentation to community groups in an effort to explain the dynamics taking place at the FPD, in the City of Fresno's work to end homelessness. He says that he initially saw the role of the FPD's Homeless Task Force as eliminating the encampments and then to stop them from reemerging. "We can't just ignore the underlying issue of the fact that we still have this huge homeless population that has nowhere to go," Dewey said.

"We very quickly evolved from 'OK, let's move these people along and keep the streets clean.' That was easy! I truly think that was the easy part. That is what we do, we are cops, right? The hard part was, but what do we do now? What do we do after the dust is settled? We quickly transitioned into social work, and that is a very difficult hat for us to wear."

There is a recognition by Dewey and other members of the FPD Homeless Task Force that they will not succeed by traditional police methods alone. They cite statistics about how many shopping carts they have removed and how many new homeless encampments they have cleared, but they get more excited talking about the one-on-one encounters that have led to homeless people getting the help they need to get off the streets.

The FPD Homeless Task Force has no professional training as social workers, their "tough love" approach to ending homelessness has serious limitations and the sometimes awkward encounters with homeless advocates makes them a less-than-ideal group to be on the front line in the City of Fresno's approach to ending homelessness.

Breedlove says, "It is a truly a complex and devastating human rights problem of suffering. Individual citizens need to be engaged. Communities of faith need to be involved. But elected officials cannot abdicate their responsibility on this issue as well.

"There needs to be a multifaceted approach for such a problem of immense complexity. Housing First initiatives are one approach, but that alone will not be a total remedy. Advocates have detailed what an organized safe and secure campsite would involve, but such sincere offers of collaboration have been ignored by all City Council members and county Board of Supervisors' members to date.

"Mayor Ashley Swearengin and City Manager Bruce Rudd only exacerbate the [difficult] lives of [the] homeless by demolishing their communities. Some within the religious fabric of Fresno believe that homeless advocates should collaborate with the city toward solutions. I'm of the mind-set that it's difficult to collaborate with an administration that sends bulldozers and intimidating task forces barreling down on a person that you're trying to help. The City of Fresno first needs to halt harmful and costly policies toward the homeless."

In late 2015, the mayor of Fresno proposed a significant expansion of the FPD Homeless Task Force.

This is the container that the City of Fresno used to save homeless people's property. As Dee found out, all of her clothing was destroyed because the storage container did not protect the property from the rain.

Do Fresno homeless rights activists equal a terrorist threat in the eyes of the Fresno Police Department's terrorism liaison officers? Photo above: The Mariposa Mall in Fresno, where this story begins.

These sanitation workers were being monitored by Kit Williams and Phil Connelly.

## NOTICE OF TRESPASS AND CLEAN-UP

### PLEASE TAKE NOTICE

The City of Fresno has received complaints concerning individuals who are loitering near or residing in temporary shelters that have been constructed in the vicinity of sidewalks on **Mariposa between P and O.** Any individuals loitering or resicing in this area is trespassing, and will need to immediately move off this site and remove any personal property they own.

On **Wednesday, April 22nd 2009, at 8:00 A.M.** the City of Fresno will conduct a clean-up of the area, including the removal of all individuals, personal property, junk and/or garbage from this area. Individuals wishing to reclaim personal property collected by the City as part of the clean-up project may do so by contacting

John W. Rogers  Community Sanitation Division Manager
Community Sanitation Division,
2101 'G' Street Building 'E', Fresno, CA 93706
(559) 621-1447

for a period of ninety (90) days following **April 22nd 2009.** After ninety (90) days, any unclaimed property will be thrown away.

If you have any questions or comments, please contact

John W. Rogers, Community Sanitation Division Manager
Community Sanitation Division,
2101 'G' Street Building 'E', Fresno, CA 93706
(559) 621-1447

The notice posted prior to the "cleanup."

Protestors at the Grain Silo encampment tried to slow the police and the sanitation department so homeless people could safely remove as much of their property as possible. A PowerPoint presentation, produced by a Fresno police officer, would target the homeless advocates as using the Brown Berets as muscle to stop the eviction.

This homeless advocate sat on the claw of a bulldozer, giving homeless people at the Grain Silo encampment more time to save their property from being destroyed.

By the end of the day, the entire Grain Silo encampment was destroyed.

Nancy and Sinomon were residents at the Grain Silo encampment. After the demolition of the encampment, Nancy ended up at the Dakota EcoGarden. Sinomon moved a couple of miles west to an isolated field. Within a couple of months, the police were back to harass Sinomon and tell her to "move on."

# Chapter 11

# Homeless Man Beaten by Fresno Police Officers

A video of a homeless man being beaten by a Fresno police officer went viral in early February 2009. The video, given to Channel 24 (the NBC affiliate in Fresno), was shown internationally. You can watch it at https://www.youtube.com/watch?v=SdoP66bvMGs.

The incident received a great deal of attention. Both city officials and community groups held press conferences. The City of Fresno press conference was held on February 12, 2009, three days after the incident. Newly elected Mayor Ashley Swearengin said she was disturbed by the incident but that she had complete confidence in the police. Swearengin also said that she was committed to establishing an independent police auditor.

Police Chief Jerry Dyer said that the incident would be investigated by the Fresno County District Attorney's office and then reviewed by the State of California Attorney General. He added that "this has been a long two weeks, perhaps the most stressful two weeks I have had in my time as the chief." A couple of weeks earlier it had been revealed that officers in the narcotics division of the FPD were part of a car theft ring. They were arrested, and the narcotics division was shut down. Then a video emerged showing an officer beating a homeless man.

Glen Beaty, the homeless man beaten by the police officer, had been sleeping under a tree near Blackstone and Bullard avenues when he was approached by two officers. Dyer, during the press conference, said that Beaty attacked the officers with a pen and ripped the badge off of one officer. These allegations were denied by Beaty. Anybody watching the interviews with Dyer on the news did not hear Beaty's version, because he was in jail. The information discrediting Beaty spread quickly, and many people started to think that perhaps the police were justified in their response.

Rev. Floyd Harris, who attended the Swearengin/Dyer press conference, was critical of the police department. Harris said the police are "violating our rights, they're violating the homeless people's rights. It seems like the victim is always being blamed for something instead of the people who are supposed to be serving and protecting the people's rights."

Harris added that "our city is in the condition that it is in because of the politicians, not because of us. The $2.3 million settlement in the homeless lawsuit, that was because of our local government. That was because of Mayor Alan Autry, who allowed that to go on. So, I'm tired of always hearing that the victim is being criticized and the victim is always accused of doing wrong. They're [the police] doing wrong. That $2.3 million could have gone towards building a nice shelter for our homeless community. But, no—they violated the rights of poor people in this city and we are sick and tired of it. We're not going to put up with it anymore."

The next day, a press conference responding to the beating of Beaty by a police officer was organized by community groups and held at City Hall. The groups who organized the event were the Central California Criminal Justice Committee, the California Prison Moratorium Project, the National Network in Action, the Mexican American Political Association (MEChA), the *Community Alliance* newspaper, the *Undercurrent* newspaper, the Brown Berets, the Central Valley Progressive PAC, Hmong Justice USA, C.A.F.E. Infoshop, Californians for Justice and the Fresno Area Chapter of ACLU-NC.

Bill Simon, with the ACLU, read the groups' statement. He said that community groups had been concerned for many years about alleged police brutality in Fresno, but this latest incident was outrageous. Simon said local groups were demanding "an immediate Pattern and Practice Investigation of the Fresno Police Department by the Federal Department of Justice Civil Rights Division." Additional demands were that the proposed independent police auditor be established, meetings be set up "so that community members can come and voice their concerns," there be more cultural and sensitivity training for the FPD and the FPD move forward with "the full implementation of a community-based policing program."

While the competing press conferences were taking place, Beaty was in the Fresno County Jail. I visited him several times and attended his hearings in court. Beaty told me he was kept in a small cell with several other men. He was allowed out of his cell one hour a week, but he said he was too depressed to leave. Living like that for several months could not have been good for his mental or physical health.

The City of Fresno and the police department did not push for the District Attorney and the state Attorney General to investigate the incident, as promised by Dyer and Swearengin in their joint press conference. A year later, when I asked Swearengin about her pledge of a thorough investigation, she had absolutely no idea what, if anything, had been done. Her staff got back to me confirming that there had been no investigation other than the internal review by the FPD.

Community activists did succeed in forcing the police to identify the names of the officers involved. The two officers were identified as Jeff Gross, a seven-year veteran, and Scott Payn, who had 10 years with the police department. Their names were released in response to a lawsuit by the ACLU. ACLU attorney Michael Risher said, "We're glad that the city finally, after three months of illegal delay, released the names of the officers involved in the Beaty incident. But it is unfortunate that it took a lawsuit to get the government to follow the law. It's also unfortunate that the city is still refusing to abandon its illegal policy of refusing to obey the clear deadlines of the Public Records Act. As a result, this lawsuit, which should not have been necessary in the first place, is still far from over."

Beaty remained in the Fresno County Jail for eight months on a parole violation charge. No charges were ever brought against Officers Gross and Payn. Beaty was transferred to the Metropolitan State Hospital in Norwalk, California (a mental health facility), where he was confined against his will. He remained there until early 2011 as they returned him to mental competency so he could participate in his legal defense.

Shortly before Beaty returned to Fresno, he was assigned a court-appointed guardian to manage his financial affairs. His guardian quickly resolved the lawsuit that had been filed on Beaty's behalf against the City of Fresno. The $75,000 settlement released the city's exposure to what might have been a substantial liability had the story been heard by a jury. A month later, Beaty arrived in Fresno and soon found himself out of jail and in a halfway house.

I see Beaty around Fresno from time to time. The last time I saw him was at the "We Like Mike" farewell event when I left as editor of the *Community Alliance* newspaper (February 2014). He came up to me afterward and said hi. As always, Beaty was friendly and gentle. Not the kind of guy that chases cops around with a ballpoint pen.

What happened to Beaty has always reminded me of the stories we were told about what happened to dissidents in the Soviet Union. They would be arrested, slandered by government officials, put in jail and then shipped off to a gulag in Siberia. The next time you hear about a Fresno police officer involved in a shooting or excessive force incident, listen closely to what is said by the police chief. Dyer usually tells the public that the suspect is a criminal, violent and often suggests that he has gang affiliations.

Beaty was the victim in this brutal assault but was treated like the criminal. Those who are optimistic and look on the bright side of things will tell you that this incident pushed the city to establish the Office of Independent Review (OIR), which was set up to monitor and report on allegations of excessive force and officer-involved shootings by the police.

The OIR was established and does provide some information about incidents involving the police in Fresno. The most supportive voices in the progressive community say that the OIR is a start and that we need to keep it going and improve it. Others see the OIR as an attempt by local government to give the illusion of police oversight without having any power to hold the police accountable. For better or worse, the Beaty incident is what pushed Mayor Swearengin to set up this department.

Glen Beaty was beaten by two Fresno police officers, put in jail (as if he was the person who attacked them) and then sent to rot in a southern California mental institution.

Mayor Ashley Swearengin and FPD Chief Jerry Dyer held a press conference saying that the incident would be investigated by the Fresno County District Attorney's Office and then reviewed by the State of California Attorney General. That investigation and review never happened.

Bill Simon of the ACLU spoke to the media about the beating of Glen Beaty by two FPD officers. Community groups demanded an immediate Pattern and Practice Investigation of the Fresno Police Department by the Federal Department of Justice Civil Rights Division and for the city to hire an independent police auditor.

# Chapter 12

# A New Mayor, a Homeless Czar and the Weaving of an Illusion

Mayor Ashley Swearengin was now at Fresno City Hall and she had hired Greg Barfield as the new homeless prevention and policy manager. Most people referred to Barfield as the homelessness czar. Homeless advocates at the time were (again) cautiously optimistic that things were going to change for the better.

It didn't take long for Barfield's first challenge to surface. An eviction notice at a homeless encampment went up on Santa Clara Street, between E and F streets, saying that a "cleanup" was going to take place on January 7, 2009, just about the same time Barfield started his new job.

When I called Barfield to ask him about the eviction notice, he didn't seem to know too much about it but asked for some time to sort things out. He said he would look into it and get back to me.

The homeless people living in the area said they had nowhere else to go, and homeless advocates thought the eviction notices were an interesting start to the Swearengin administration's pledge to move in a new direction. Her administration was pushing the Housing First plan and suggesting that these types of attacks were a relic of the past.

Why then was the City of Fresno continuing with the policy of sweeping the homeless off the streets, essentially criminalizing poverty, taking their possessions and forcing them to "move on" when there is no better place to move on to? When asked about this, Barfield wrote in an e-mail that "there is no effort to move anyone except those who might be blocking the sidewalk." He assured me that "there is a new day and attitude" and that efforts were being made to implement the Housing First model.

The City of Fresno blinked, Barfield did his job and the homeless encampment on Santa Clara was not destroyed. The people sleeping on the sidewalk did not receive vouchers to get housing, but they didn't have their property taken away either. Sometimes you take your victories where you can get them.

A couple of months later, a new focal point emerged and that crisis gave insight into the direction city policy was heading. The H Street encampment (south of Ventura Street) had been growing for a while. By March 2009, it was an impressive homeless encampment, probably the largest on the west coast, perhaps the country. There were hundreds of people living on a large vacant lot that extended under an abandoned overpass. There were streets, distinct neighborhoods and some people were starting to build real homes. Some homes had foundations, framed walls and pitched roofs.

It started when Union Pacific Railroad put up a fence topped with barbed wire. The section of fence built along H Street (south of Ventura) completely enclosed the encampment, which was on Union Pacific property. The railroad then decided it wanted the homeless to move and posted no trespassing signs.

When the encampment started, it had the tacit approval of City Hall. This is the encampment where the City of Fresno set up portable toilets and trash bins.

Barfield contacted Union Pacific and said that he had an agreement with them not to evict the homeless. Barfield said the railroad agreed to wait until the City of Fresno's voucher program was up and running before forcing anyone off the property. The voucher program, which had not yet been approved by the City Council, was to provide homeless people with an apartment and social services. It was part of the Housing First program that both the City and County of Fresno agreed to implement.

The voucher program, according to Barfield, was going to be brought before the City Council in February 2009 but was delayed. Barfield said he needed time to evaluate and assess the needs of the homeless at the H Street encampment before taking the proposal to City Council. In a press release from the City of Fresno, it was announced that the voucher program was then expected to be presented in April.

The press release said, "The City of Fresno today again called on the Union Pacific Railroad Company (UPRR) to delay construction of a fence surrounding two large homeless encampments on H Street in downtown Fresno. The City voiced concerns about potential safety risks to those living in the encampments as a result of the fencing."

Barfield said that the railroad is not going to immediately evict the homeless and that he believes the City of Fresno has some time to work out what will happen next. While at the encampment I talked to Guillermo, who is a resident of the H Street encampment. Guillermo, who is from Puerto Vallarta, Mexico, said he was out of work because there were no jobs at local ranches. Guillermo wanted to know what was going on and if he was going to be evicted. He said nobody had told him or any of his friends what was going on and he was concerned that they were being fenced in. Mike Mitchum, another resident of the H Street encampment, said he felt like Union Pacific was treating them like animals in a zoo by fencing them in.

At the time, it was unclear whether the railroad would push the homeless out before or after the city's voucher program was set up and running. Did the city have the authority to stop Union Pacific from conducting the evictions? The railroad has its own police and often behaves independently from local authorities. The railroad company previously had conducted raids on the homeless, destroying their tents and threatening the homeless with detention and arrest. It is interesting that a corporation has the ability to evict, arrest and harass people and that our local government appears unable to do anything to stop them.

The city seemed to be in a race with the railroad company to see if it could implement the first phase of its Housing First project, giving housing vouchers to 200 homeless people, before the evictions began. Union Pacific was cranking up the pressure, which motivated the city to more quickly provide housing vouchers to some of the homeless people living in that encampment.

The housing voucher plan was eventually approved by the City Council. Barfield and his team conducted assessments of the homeless people at the H Street encampment and started issuing vouchers to those they considered most in need. Someone with health issues, a pregnant woman or an elderly person had priority over a young healthy man.

Then, the City of Fresno announced that it needed to immediately remove everyone from the H Street encampment because it was going to construct a water to-wer that would improve water pressure in the downtown area. The homeless, al-ready enclosed with a gate and razor wire, were forced out and a guard was posted. Homeless people were allowed to return for 90 days to reclaim their pro-perty. After that, the remaining structures were bulldozed, the gate was locked and there was nothing but ground squirrels living there for five years. Construction on the water tower started in 2015.

Then, things started to get worse. The city put up eviction notices at the Ventura and F streets encampment saying it intended to destroy that homeless encamp-ment eight days before Christmas in 2009. Homeless advocates talked about buil-ding a manger scene with the baby Jesus and Mary. The city backed off from the eviction, possibly not wanting video coverage of city workers dragging off the baby Jesus and throwing him into a dumpster.

The demolition was rescheduled for January 6, 2010, which was a religious holi-day. The Epiphany is commonly known as Three Kings' Day in the United States. It celebrates the three wise men's visit to baby Jesus and remembers his baptism. Again, the eviction was delayed.

On January 26, 2010, about 50 homeless people from the Ventura and H streets encampment and their supporters were in Fresno County Civil Court. They were there to stop the eviction that the City of Fresno seemed intent on accomplishing.

The city was seeking a temporary restraining order (TRO), which would give it the legal right to evict the residents in the encampment. The city was so confident it would get the TRO that it had already posted eviction notices saying the resi-dents would be forced to move on Thursday (two days from the time of the hea-ring). The judge did not issue the order, however, saying he needed time to think about it.

The homeless marched from the encampment to the courthouse. Several of them were represented by attorneys from the Central California Legal Services (CCLS). Before court started, the room was filled with the homeless and their supporters. One of those supporters had passed out American flags, which several people were holding. The bailiff announced that there would be no waving of flags du-ring the hearing and if there was he would have the person committing the heinous act arrested.

An unexpected development in the hearing was the presence of two men who said they were the owners of the property. One of the city's challenges in evicting the homeless had been that the owner of the property had died and the vacant lot was in probate. Robert and Walt Williams told the court that the city had told them that if they did not "cooperate" with the city and have the homeless evicted that they would have to pay for the cleanup, having a fence built and maintenance expenses. The brothers said they did not want any trouble with the city.

Assistant City Attorney Douglas Sloan said it is typical for the city to ask property owners, "Do you want trespassing laws enforced?" If the property owner agrees to "request" the eviction of the homeless, then they are not charged cleanup and other fees. Sloan told the Williams brothers that they would work out something because they were cooperating. Attorneys for the homeless questioned whether the Williams' brothers actually owned the property where the homeless were living.

One of the owners of a portion of the lot where the homeless were living was said to be Tom Richards. Richards is a developer in Fresno and owner of the Penstar Group. He was also the chairperson of the city's Committee to End Homelessness. This is the group that wrote the 10-Year Plan to End Chronic Homelessness. A City of Fresno official told me that Richards had given the city the "go ahead" to evict the homeless from his property.

Another tactic of the city attorney was to argue that the homeless had no right to due process in this case. They argued that the homeless were simply trespassing and were not entitled to defend themselves in court. The CCLS attorneys strenuously objected.

The next time it appeared in court, the City of Fresno tried a new approach in its ongoing attempt to evict the homeless from the encampment at Ventura and F streets. The city dropped its effort to get a TRO and convinced the judge to dismiss the case.

With the court hearings over, the city announced that it planned to move forward with the evictions, claiming the "owner" of the property had asked the city to clear the homeless people off the land.

Some homeless advocates said the city had misstated the ownership issue of the property and coerced the so-called owner into asking for the homeless to be removed. Robert and Walt Williams were in court and testified that they owned the property. Walt Williams is the executer of the estate and will decide who owns the property.

Bruce Rudd, assistant city manager, told the press that the city would try and force the homeless off the property the next day starting at 8 a.m., without arresting anyone. Alan Simon, one of the homeless living on the vacant lot, told me that he couldn't move. Simon has a cast on his leg and says he is not capable of packing up his tent and moving it. He said that he would stay and see what happens.

The mood in the camp was defiant, with most of the people I talked to saying they would not move. People said there was no place else to go. The City of Fresno had no campgrounds or other facilities where people can go. Rudd claimed that the Rescue Mission had bed space available and that is where the homeless should go. Rudd did not tell the media that the Rescue Mission is for men only, that you have to sit through a Christian religious service before you get a bed or that many homeless people would not go to the Mission because of the way the homeless are treated there.

Rudd also told the media that the homeless should avail themselves of other available services so they can get off the streets. Other city officials attempted to take the moral high ground by saying that they were trying to put an end to the terrible conditions at the encampment. They did not, however, explain why the city had seemingly endless amounts of money to attack the homeless in court and chase them from one vacant lot to another but no money to establish a safe and legal campground where the homeless could live.

The eviction of the homeless at the Ventura and F streets encampment took place on January 28, 2010, but not without some significant resistance. The residents locked arms at one point and refused to leave. Fresno Police Chief Jerry Dyer personally negotiated with them, saying they could move to another vacant lot and the police would not stop them. When asked if they would be evicted from that encampment sometime in the future, Dyer said the police would deal with that on another day.

Most of the residents moved to a vacant lot about one block north and started reconstructing their tents at that location. Within hours, the police were there to tell them to "move on." Cyclone fences were built around the Ventura and F streets encampment and the vacant lot the homeless had moved to.

The homeless organized themselves and headed to a vacant lot that the city had purchased to provide shelter for the homeless but because of political issues abandoned the idea. This vacant lot, about one mile south of Ventura and F streets, had been vacant for years. The homeless thought this would be a perfect solution to their dilemma about where to stay. Unfortunately, the police found them there that night and told them, again, to "move on." The kinder and gentler approach to the homeless by the Swearengin administration officially had come to an end.

In February 2010, I wrote an editorial that appeared in the *Community Alliance* newspaper summing up my thoughts about the developments that were taking place, the impact of those on the homeless and the significance of policy changes at City Hall. I was the editor of the newspaper at that time. My conclusion was that for all of the talk about Housing First, the lives of the homeless were as difficult as ever and what was really happening is that the mayor had simply learned how to spin her version of reality to the media. The problem was that all of the talk about improving homeless people's lives was just an illusion created by a clever and clearly dangerous mayor.

Here is that editorial, in its entirety:

> Like most *Community Alliance* readers, I want to believe that our lives in Fresno are improving as we work through the many serious problems that confront us. In the past year, the City of Fresno has established an Office of Independent Review to improve police accountability and hired a homeless czar to end homelessness. Those two developments should give us hope. Why then do I have this increasing feeling of uneasiness and concern?
>
> My discomfort grew last month when I read about a proposal to change Fresno's name. The argument for changing our city's name is a sincere attempt to break free from the negative stereotypes that surround us. You know, to distance ourselves from the late-night talk show hosts who poke fun at us and the reports that show we have the highest concentration of poverty in the nation, that our air quality is terrible and that our high school dropout rate is off the charts. Changing our name would be similar to what corporations do when they have done something so awful that there is no way out except to start over again with a new name. Blackwater, the war profiteer, comes to mind. After its employees, sometimes referred to as mercenaries, were involved in a series of civilian massacres in Iraq, Blackwater renamed itself Xe. But would changing Fresno to FresYes or any other name change anything?

Shortly after pondering this name change proposal, I drove toward one of this city's sprawling homeless encampments. I passed by the baseball stadium in downtown Fresno, which the City of Fresno has pumped endless dollars into. As I continued on toward the F and Ventura streets homeless encampment, I started thinking about our priorities.

For the wealthy, government bureaucrats and the Visitors Bureau, the stadium was built to attract and encourage people to the downtown area. But to me, the stadium and other recent boondoggles represent the city's attempt to put image above substance. Yes, the stadium looks nice, but it is an illusion that things are getting better in Fresno.

Where this illusion versus reality is really dramatic is with the City of Fresno's policy on homelessness. By any objective measure, there are more homeless on the streets today than there were before the city's 10-Year Plan to End Chronic Homelessness was developed. Greg Barfield, the manager of homeless prevention and policy (aka the homeless czar) for the city, does not have the resources needed to even minimally affect the number of homeless on the street.

What Barfield is able to do is give the illusion that the city has a plan to end homelessness. Unfortunately, instead of helping the homeless, Barfield was reduced last month to joining the police and city sanitation workers as they chased the homeless from one vacant lot to another.

Arriving at the encampment at F and Ventura streets, I thought about how much money the city spent when it built the stadium and more recently gave further concessions to the owners, while at the same time refusing to provide the homeless with drinking water, portable toilets or even trash bins.

How can the city subsidize a baseball stadium while this city's most vulnerable citizens are literally dying from the lack of assistance? What is Barfield doing to help the situation other than providing a fig leaf for the city to stand behind?

I like Barfield, he is a nice guy, but even though he has been at the job for more than a year now, he has not brought us one step closer to ending homelessness. Yes, it looks good that the city has hired someone to focus on the issue of homelessness, but only giving the community the illusion that things are better, without the substance of change, is using smoke and mirrors to confuse and distract people.

As a close observer of this city's policy on homelessness, I can tell you that the situation on the ground is not getting better. Barfield came into his job talking about Housing First, a program that gets the chronically homeless off the streets by providing them with housing. I was encouraged by the talk of this new direction, but Barfield has not delivered on the promise and is now engaged in actions reminiscent of the days when the city bulldozed homeless encampments.

Barfield says, on one hand, that he is so focused on finding housing for the homeless that he has no time to work on providing the homeless with a safe and legal place to stay. He says this knowing full well that it will be years before enough affordable housing can be developed to get a significant number of homeless off the streets. In the meantime, the homeless have no place to live. They are literally being chased around downtown Fresno from one vacant lot to another. How does Barfield have the time to work on chasing them out of one encampment after another, while claiming to have no time to help establish a legal and safe campground with drinking water, trash pickup and portable toilets?

The City of Fresno could make a profound difference if it used resources differently. Instead of spending money to evict the homeless from their meager dwellings, the city could open up abandoned buildings downtown or figure out a way to allow homeless families to be caretakers of vacant, foreclosed, bank-owned homes in Fresno. Studies show that it would actually cost less to house the homeless than to maintain the broken system we have today.

But there are powerful interests (social service providers, the police, business interests and a reactionary/Republican administration at City Hall) that would rather maintain business as usual and spin the illusion that they are doing something to end homelessness than to actually do anything about it.

I'm also concerned about the illusion of police accountability. We had a significant number of officer-involved shootings last year, with many of them ending in death. There was a young man who was shot and killed as he walked out of his house holding a cell phone. He was so sure the police were going to play judge, jury and executioner that he had pre-selected music for his funeral, giving the CD to his girlfriend.

Steven Vargas, 32, of Fresno was involved in a car accident on McKinley Avenue in central Fresno. A Fresno police officer arrived on the scene and ordered Vargas out of his car. When he did not get out fast enough, the officer opened fire killing Vargas. Vargas had no weapon.

Last October, Fresno police officers shot and killed John Cooper in northwest Fresno. According to Fresno Police Chief Jerry Dyer, Cooper called 911 saying he wanted to kill himself. Officers saw Cooper, who had what appeared to be a gun pointed to his head. Dyer said Cooper pointed what turned out to be a toy gun at the officers and they opened fire. Scott Payn, an officer involved in this incident, was also involved in beating Glen Beaty.

The Beaty incident was probably the highest profile case of excessive force in Fresno last year. The video of two officers (one later involved in the Cooper killing and the other promoted) was shown around the world. It showed Beaty on his stomach, being handcuffed, while one of the officers beat him in the face. Beaty, who was never charged with a crime in that incident, was in the Fresno County Jail for seven months. He is still being detained in Los Angeles where he is being involuntarily given drugs.

After years of effort by the Central California Criminal Justice Committee, the Fresno City Council finally agreed to fund an independent police auditor. Late last year, Eddie Aubrey was hired as this community's first director of what is being called the Office of Independent Review (OIR).

Although it is too early to analyze how effective the OIR will be, there are indications that this office also has been set up to give the illusion of addressing an important problem without giving the department the resources it needs to do the job.

Political insiders at City Hall say to watch what happens if Aubrey comes out with a report critical of any police action. The OIR's support on the City Council is weak, the city attorney is concerned that the OIR will be a liability if it finds and reports any information critical of police action and the mayor's support might evaporate if there is a crisis.

The smart money is saying that if Aubrey wants to keep his job he will be a lapdog for the police department. That will keep the City Council, the city attorney, the police chief and the mayor happy. But if there is a controversial case and he does release information that is critical of the police, his job will be on the line.

The reality is that Aubrey probably won't produce a public report critical of the police because his office has no independent investigative authority. Aubrey will be able to review the findings of the Fresno Police Department Internal Affairs department, but he cannot contact witnesses in investigations of police misconduct. Also, Aubrey reports directly to the City Manager's office, which is not a department that will rock the boat even if a controversial report is written. That report would probably never see the light of day.

The job of the OIR, like the homeless czar position, has been set up by the mayor and elected officials at City Hall to give the illusion that we are addressing serious problems, without the substance. Both jobs have been structured with limited resources and authority to guarantee minimal results. If either Aubrey or Barfield were to do what is needed to succeed, they would probably be fired.

A tip of the hat to our mayor for being clever enough to create all of these smoke and mirrors, making these grand illusions a reality. Former Mayor Alan Autry, even though he talked repeatedly about these issues, could never have conceptualized such a scheme. The fact that we have a more skillful mayor is not something for the progressive community to celebrate.

The question that begs an answer is this: What is to be done? How do we process this information without becoming depressed or cynical? Fortunately, the answer is not all that difficult to find. Whether the question is how to create police accountability or how we end homelessness, the answer is that we need to *organize.*

The only way to hold elected officials and government bureaucrats accountable is to build a movement they can't ignore. For example, if the estimated 15,000 homeless in Fresno were to organize a march on City Hall demanding basic campgrounds and public services, the situation would change quickly. Homeless advocates could support the march and help in other ways. Rick Morse, a local businessperson, got tired of government inaction and took it upon himself to clean up an encampment and paid for portable toilets out of his own pocket. Local architect Art Dyson is starting a project to build eco-villages for the homeless.

We need to pressure local government to do "the right thing" and use our creativity to organize a meaningful response to homelessness.

Community activists need to demand that the Office of Independent Review provide honest and useful reports on the recent officer-involved shootings. If the OIR is structurally flawed, as I believe it is, changes need to be made. In addition, public forums can be held to discuss past and future cases of alleged police misconduct. A community Police Review Board can be established where testimony is taken and community leaders question the police and persons involved in these incidents. More people should become involved with Copwatch. The point is, we don't have to wait for local government to act. We need to organize, educate and agitate.

Ultimately, the progressive community will have to build enough unity to elect candidates to local office. Those elected officials will then carry out public policy that meets people's needs, not the wishes and whims of this city's builders, developers and other assorted fat cats. Another world is possible.

It did not take long for the first crisis to hit the Swearengin administration. At about the same time she was taking office, plans were under way to evict homeless people living in this encampment on Santa Clara Street.

Greg Barfield (center), the City of Fresno homeless czar, is talking to Bill Simon (left) about a "cleanup" taking place at The Hill (a homeless encampment on G and California streets).

The H Street homeless encampment in Fresno was fenced in by Union Pacific Railroad.

A view of the H Street encampment at the time when the fence was constructed.

Guillermo, an unemployed worker from Puerto Vallarta, Mexico, wanted to know why homeless people were being fenced in.

The City of Fresno cleared the homeless encampment at Ventura and F streets on January 28, 2010. Fresno Police Chief Jerry Dyer told these homeless people they had to "move on," while they told him there was no place to move on to.

A Fresno Housing Authority worker (left) talks with some of the homeless at the Ventura and F streets encampment. One of the tactics the city used at this time was to sign up people for "possible" housing vouchers during the evictions. The tactic would lead the homeless to believe that if they left the encampment voluntarily, they might get a voucher. Those who resisted the eviction would end up further down the list or not on the list at all—maybe even in jail.

There was a significant amount of resistance to eviction at the Ventura and F streets homeless encampment. Residents here are seen forming a line to stop the police from entering the camp.

# Chapter 13

# Maintaining the Status Quo

It doesn't matter whether you think of them as helpful social service workers, poverty pimps or groups that are responsible for creating a culture of dependency, there are a lot of mainstream groups working on homeless issues in Fresno. As we have already detailed some of the transgressions of the two most prominent homeless social service groups in Fresno, let's see how the Poverello House and Fresno Rescue Mission describe themselves.

This is from the Poverello House Web site:

> Homeless, Hungry, Alone and Sick, with no one to care for them. These are the realities for thousands of people in the San Joaquin Valley. They come from everywhere: transients with no destination; women in need or in fear; children and their families; migrants following the harvests; the elderly, trying to subsist on little or no income; youths with undetermined futures and no hope. Day after day, by car, on foot, or by train, they come to Poverello House seeking food, warmth, and compassion.

> Poverello House is a private, nonprofit, nondenominational organization that has been serving the hungry and homeless of our community since 1973. Mike McGarvin saw a need and addressed it simply: he began handing out sandwiches on the streets. Inspired by his example, others came to lend a hand, and with the help of churches, businesses, and volunteers, the outreach grew. In 1981, through the generous contribution of a supporter, Poverello House was established in its current location on "F" Street. A major ex-

pansion and renovation was completed in 1992, adding office space, a family dining room, a shower and laundry facility, and modernizing the kitchen.

In 2002, Poverello House collaborated with Marjaree Mason Center and Holy Cross Center for Women and established Naomi's House, a homeless overnight shelter for women who are single and do not have children.

In the winter of 2004, after seeing a tremendous need for temporary shelter, Poverello House established the Michael McGarvin Jr. Village of Hope, a shelter for people who are striving to better their lives. In November of 2007, Poverello House and the City of Fresno collaborated to open up a second Village called The Community of Hope. These, too, are temporary shelters established specifically for the homeless.

\*\*\*

And from the Fresno Rescue Mission Web site:

The Fresno Rescue Mission endeavors to glorify God by meeting the spiritual and physical needs of the least, the last and the lost in our community.

Our Vision
Recognizing the teachings of Jesus; that the least, the last and the lost will always be in our midst, we will partner with the Christian community, social service agencies, businesses, families and individuals to meet the spiritual and physical needs of all men, women and children in our community.

Our Values
- Christ-centered by treating the least, the last and the lost with love and compassion.
- Hope shared through God's Word and plan of salvation.
- Relationships established, valued and nurtured.
- Integrity paramount in all that we do and are.
- Service given through stewardship and servanthood.
- Totally committed to loving others as Christ loves us.

\*\*\*

The Continuum of Care is a coalition of groups that coordinates the homeless point-in-time count and is a clearinghouse for writing grants for federal money through HUD. Some of the groups involved, as of late 2014, with the Continuum of Care were as follows:

AspiraNet
Bishop Steinbeck Homeless Advocacy Committee
City of Clovis
City of Fresno
Community Action Partnership of Madera County
County of Fresno/Department of Behavioral Health/Mental Health Services Act
Fresno County Office of Education
Fresno Economic Opportunities Commission
Fresno Housing Authority
Fresno Unified School District
Mental Health Systems, Inc.
Poverello House
Thursday Homelesss Advocates
Turning Point of Central California, Inc.
Valley Teen Ranch, Inc.
WestCare
Fresno Community Development Coalition
Life Skills Training and Educational Programs, Inc.

These are the groups that are likely to apply for and receive the millions of dollars coming to Fresno to address homelessness. In March 2013, Rep. Jim Costa (D–Fresno) announced that the following organizations in his district were going to receive HUD homeless funding:

> Fresno EOC Sanctuary Transitional Living Centers—$1,075,516
> Fresno Housing Authority—$1,399,268
> Marjaree Mason Center—$625,748
> Poverello House—$360,915

And that is just the tip of the iceberg. Currently, the focus is on getting homeless veterans and the chronically homeless off the streets, but a significant amount of money also goes for drug and alcohol rehabilitation programs.

Early in 2010, Mayor Ashley Swearengin established, with great fanfare, Fresno First Steps Home (FFSH) as a nonprofit that she said would work to end homelessness in Fresno. In May, she handed out cards telling the homeless to call 211 and encouraged residents to give those cards to the homeless instead of money. The goal was to raise $1 million a year by getting Fresnans to donate $1 a month. In July 2010, she announced that $221,000 had been donated by three corporate sponsors.

Greg Barfield was the homeless prevention and policy manager at the City of Fresno during this period of transition to privatize the effort to end homelessness. Barfield has since moved on, but he still works at City Hall as City Council Member Oliver Baines' chief of staff.

I asked Barfield in 2011 how much money the FFSH had received and how it has been spent to help the homeless. He refused to provide me with that information, saying he was not required to do so because the FFSH is not an official government project. At the time, I wondered why there was no transparency or a willingness to share information about all of the wonderful things this group was doing.

Three years later, I returned to the question of what the FFSH had done with the money it was given. I found out that the nonprofit gave no money to help the homeless in its first two years of existence (2010 and 2011). Yet, in October 2011 City Hall sent out a press release announcing a $250,000 FFSH grant to the Fresno Housing Authority, but evidence of that contribution is not included in the IRS reports the FFSH filed for that year. While homeless people in downtown Fresno were dying on the streets, the FFSH sat on more than $500,000 while publicly claiming to give assistance to the homeless.

As late as 2013 (the latest information available when this book was written), the FFSH Web site shows that it still had more than $500,000 in the bank. Its income is down from previous years and the amount given to help the homeless, primarily through the Fresno Housing Authority, was a little more than $100,000 in 2013. That amount is nowhere near the $1 million a year goal the mayor had when the organization was set up, but nobody is talking about that. The FFSH was a success in that it gave City Hall a justification for removing a line item in the budget for the homeless and thus privatizing an essential public service. In addition, the Housing First project, which the FFSH supports, is what Swearengin uses to claim success in her effort to end homelessness. Many people, but not all, are impressed by her sleight of hand and ability to create the illusion that there are fewer homeless people in Fresno now than when she became mayor.

The mayor sets up a nonprofit, uses it as a shield to show that the city cares about the homeless and gets public relations mileage out if it by saying that it is contributing money to the homeless when the nonprofit's IRS reports (three years later) prove that to be a lie. Drug and alcohol rehab groups rake in federal dollars, developers get wealthy building affordable housing and the homeless living on the street don't see a dime.

This is business as usual in Fresno and might be what social service providers and the government do everywhere. But I can understand why some of my homeless friends refer to these people as poverty pimps and corrupt politicians.

# Chapter 14

# Alternatives to the Dominant Paradigm

The reality for the homeless in Fresno is pretty harsh. There are few shelter beds in the city, their property is constantly being taken from them and the homeless are forced from one vacant lot to another. The City of Fresno passes an endless number of quality-of-life ordinances to stop the homeless from pushing a shopping cart, asking for money or sleeping in the park.

In addition to fighting against these ordinances as they get introduced, some homeless people and their allies are creating alternative institutions and proposing changes to the public policies that are harming the homeless.

Food Not Bombs (FNB) has provided free meals to the homeless in Fresno since 1996. It serves meals once a week at Courthouse Park in downtown and at Roeding Park. The FNB serves everyone who comes, doesn't force any religious dogma on those who come, doesn't conspire with the city to bulldoze homeless encampments and doesn't ask permission to operate from government entities.

The St. Benedict Catholic Workers group also serves food downtown and assists the homeless in other ways, such as bringing homeless people into their home. Liza Apper from the Catholic Workers recently told me that they "are serving on the porch of Fresno County Jail on Tuesday nights from 7 p.m. to 9 p.m. and will be adding one Saturday and one Sunday a month soon. We hope to increase our presence at the jail incrementally. In 2012, we did hospice for a former sheriff's lieutenant and suspended our line for that year. We are also facilitating a 12-week grief support and education group twice a year; a Friday night Bible study, an emergency food pantry [and] giving workshops at Holy Cross Center for Women (HCCW) to both staff and those women who come to HCCW. We also are still helping one client from the Kincaid lawsuit. We do hospitality for those who need a place to stay who are visiting at the jail from out of town, released inmates who need a day or two for a PO appointment and homeless women. We also are open to hospice care for those with no place to turn." Liza and her husband Bryan do all of this on a shoestring budget. For more information about this project, visit http://www.sbcw.org/home/.

Writing about the FNB group, Kelly Borkert says, "What Food Not Bombs offers is a little food and a lot of love. That there is a place for anyone to find food and friendship every Saturday and Sunday from Food Not Bombs surely means a lot. Decent food and excellent clothing, free to all. Bicycle repairs and sleeping bags for those in need. Priceless services available to those able to be at Roeding Park on Saturday afternoons starting at 1 p.m., on the north side of Storyland children's park." Sunday Food Not Bombs serves free food at Courthouse Park to anyone who is hungry. Cooking starts at 1 p.m., and the food is served at 3 p.m. The best way to get involved with either of these FNB groups is to just show up at one of their food servings and ask them what you can do to help.

Art Dyson is a Fresno architect who has a passion for building creative and innovative housing. Dyson was on the city's commission to develop the 10-Year Plan to End Chronic Homelessness and continued working on the homeless issue even after the group finished its work. I spoke with him about his vision for eco-villages on the *Community Alliance* "Street Heat" radio show on KFCF-FM 88.1. Here is some of what he had to say about the Eco-Village project:

Dyson: You would take a group of homeless people that have already learned how to live together; they have already developed a charter about how to run an encampment. You take those folks and put them in a holistic setting that would address many issues. It would be self-sustaining, it would be using recycled materials, it would be in as beautiful of an environment as is possible, so that when people drove by, it would look like a park. It would be off the grid; we would use rainwater harvesting, photovoltaic cells for electricity and geothermal heating and cooling.

They would grow their own food, they would have a common restroom, laundry room, and then a huge part of this in each one of these villages would be the economic driver. That would be a building that would possibly be built out of straw bales or used tires, and that component would be a venue for the folks that live in that community. So, if you have a series of artists you might have pottery wheels where people do pottery work. They might teach pottery classes. And they would have a venue to sell their pottery. If they had woodworking skills, they might take discarded furniture and recycle or refinish it and put it back on the market and sell it there. They might teach other people how to refinish wood.

This is not intended as a permanent home; it is intended as a way to get people back into the job market. They would have the legal right to live there. They would have a safe environment to live in, and they would have the opportunity to develop skills and develop a job/employment resume.

Rhodes: I have heard you talk about eco-villages before and compare them to what currently exists, that is, the harsh reality and the loud sounds that homeless people endure as a part of their lives right now. Talk a little about how a person's environment affects them as human beings.

Dyson: There is a study of neuroscience that has come to the forefront in the last few years. It substantiated information that we have known anecdotally over the years. We know that when you are in a natural environment the human condition improves. Studies have verified that; it has shown us that in a hospital setting, for example, if one has a window and looks out on a natural landscape, they use less medication, they recover faster, their spirits are higher. Everything is elevated from that situation.

We know from studies that when you have the look of a natural environment, as opposed to what most homeless folks have right now—next to a railroad track or a paved hard-scape area—without any of the sounds of nature that have soothed human beings for eons, aggression and violence increase. But with a natural environment and with the wind and birds singing, aggression and violence decrease.

Everything we do is affected by the environment we are in. So, it is either a draining environment or an uplifting environment. That is what excites me: Putting people into an uplifting environment. As an architect, where my heart is—is in trying to uplift the human spirit. I'm trying to do more than just provide shelter from the elements, but to embrace the elements and provide a shelter for the human spirit, something that will uplift the soul of a human being.

To hear the complete interview Art Dyson, visit www.indybay.org/newsitems/2010/05/29/18649168.php.

The Eco-Village Project of Fresno has built a model unit at the Dakota EcoGarden. Here is how they describe the project:

In July 2012, Nancy Waidtlow purchased a 0.6-acre lot in west Fresno, where she founded the Dakota EcoGarden in late 2013. It is the original site of the Eco-Village Project of Fresno and the first of its kind in the city. There are many resources for the homeless in Fresno, but none offer the same uplifting environment and democratic approach.

The Dakota EcoGarden is open to people of all walks of life, regardless of gender, race or creed. The mission of the Dakota EcoGarden, as part of the Eco-Village Project of Fresno, is to empower formerly homeless individuals with the skills needed for self-sufficient lifestyles that enable happiness, health and success.

The Dakota EcoGarden represents Waidtlow's version of architect Dyson's original vision for an eco-village. Although the Dakota EcoGarden does not include a standard community building, the home on the property provides the same basic elements of a shared kitchen, living space and bathrooms. The Dakota EcoGarden will encompass up to five single living units (eco shelters), whereas the original model called for up to 18.

Lastly, Dyson's concept incorporates a commercial building that includes an art studio and an art gallery (pottery, sculpture and other art), a furniture repair shop and a showroom and a bakery. Although the Dakota EcoGarden does not incorporate this framework, it does provide residents with counseling, mentoring and employment opportunities.

For more information about this project, visit https://ecovillagefresno.wordpress.com/dakotaecogarden/.

At the beginning of 2011, many of the homeless advocates I work with got tired of waiting for the City of Fresno to start providing basic public services for the homeless. That led to my setting up portable toilets and trash bins at several homeless encampments in the downtown area.

I set this up because the homeless people living on the streets had no place to go to the bathroom and allowing trash to build up in piles on the street is a health hazard, not only for the homeless but also for the entire community. Initially, these services, which cost about $600 a month, were paid for by the Reality Tours I conducted at the homeless encampments. I would take a group of 5–15 people on a two-hour walk through the encampments of downtown Fresno, exposing many people for the first time to the realities of homelessness in Fresno. Participants' donations paid for the project for the first six months or so.

On the Reality Tour, we would often stop and talk to the homeless about their lives and wonder out loud how millions of dollars could be coming into Fresno to end homelessness, yet none of that money reached the people who needed it most. Providing portable toilets and trash bins seemed like the least we could do to address the immediate needs of the homeless.

I realized that it was not sustainable to continue begging money from my friends month after month to keep this project going, so I started reaching out to faith-based groups for help. I tried to convince them that for a relatively small amount of money we could provide portable toilets and trash bins for all of the homeless who live in the downtown encampments. There were four or five major homeless encampments downtown at the time.

Although the faith community was unable to fund this project, one generous donor approached the Fresno Regional Foundation and provided the funding to keep the services going for another year. By the time we were running out of money, the next round of demolitions was taking place and the homeless encampments disappeared.

For all of the years I have been in contact with homeless people in Fresno, there have been individuals, faith groups and independent projects that take food and other supplies to the homeless. These groups are greatly appreciated by the homeless and sometimes are the difference between life and death.

Being a homeless advocate, I sometimes hear people say that we are not realistic about how to end homelessness. Or that we don't offer any holistic and concrete proposals for how to address this crisis. Some people even say that by encouraging people to give a homeless person food or money, you are actually hurting them—the "you have to be cruel to be kind" approach. But homeless advocates have time and again offered workable solutions and new approaches to government officials and anyone who would listen.

For example, shortly after the demolitions of the homeless encampments in late 2011, an unusually large coalition of the homeless and advocates came together to encourage the City of Fresno to move in a more enlightened and humane direction. One of the outcomes was the following proposal, which put in writing the need for a coherent plan that had short-, medium- and long-term goals that would result in ending homelessness.

This proposal started with the following:

## The Need

The City of Fresno allowed homeless encampments to exist and grow for several years but in the past couple of months has cleared out all the major encampments in the city. This dislocation has resulted in thousands of homeless people in Fresno having no safe and legal place to live.

Existing shelters cannot house all of the homeless who are now sleeping on sidewalks and other locations not intended for human habitation. As temperatures dipped below freezing in late December, one woman died as she slept on the sidewalk outside of the Poverello House. Many others are sick with pneumonia and other illnesses related to their exposure to the cold weather.

The cost to city and county government, if we allow the situation to continue as it currently exists, will be enormous. The price of providing emergency medical care and hospitalization would be dramatically reduced if we redirected those dollars to provide the homeless with a safe and legal place to live.

Although the city's goal of decent, affordable and permanent housing for everyone is a good goal, we all know that it cannot be achieved anytime soon. Therefore, there will be homeless people who do not make it into a shelter and have no place to sleep. It is those people, and there are currently thousands of them in the City of Fresno, that this proposal is intended to assist.

## Safe and Legal Campsites

The fastest and easiest way to dramatically improve life for the homeless would be to allow them to construct shelters and provide them with basic public services. With shelters like tents, the homeless can get out of the rain and stay considerably warmer than if they have no protection from the rain, wind and cold.

These encampments will exist on public and private land. The City of Fresno could determine which property it owns that will be used for these encampments. The city will allow encampments to be developed, through a conditional use permit, for any owner of property who wanted to use his/her land for that purpose. The city will work with other state, federal or county governmental entities to facilitate the use of the land for encampments.

Initially, Phase I of this proposal seeks to allow the establishment of encampments at existing sites, with limited development of infrastructure. A longer-term project will see some infrastructure put into place to better serve the needs of the homeless residents.

These campsites will be self-governing and not overseen by any social service agency or government entity. The residents will be like any other group of people living in a small neighborhood. They will be provided with drinking water, portable toilets and trash pickup. Those services could be paid for by the city, the county, community groups, churches and/or individuals.

The individuals living in these safe and legal homeless encampments will be responsible for maintaining the campsite. No illegal activity will be permitted in the camp. If there are legal problems, they will be handled in the same way as they are in any other neighborhood in Fresno.

These campsites will be distributed throughout the city and consist of no more than 100 residents per encampment. The purpose of the multiple locations is an acknowledgment that homeless people live throughout the community, and the intention is to equitably distribute the encampments throughout the city as much as possible. The purpose of limiting each camp to 100 people or less is to avoid concentrating the homeless in one location and affecting any single area with a high density of homeless people.

Possible campsites include vacant lots, churches, parks and unused government property.

Phase I of this proposal will start immediately and utilize the areas where the homeless are already living. Phase I will allow the homeless to construct simple structures (tents and tarps) and live in them until something better is available. This will take away the stigma of living illegally and being told to "move on," when there is nowhere better to move on to. This decriminalization of poverty is an important first step in allowing people to live with dignity and respect.

Phase I will provide every group of 10 or more homeless people living together with basic public services (drinking water, toilets and trash service). Providing the homeless with these services will not only dramatically improve their lives but also clean up our city. Having access to drinking water should be a service provided to every citizen of this community, whether rich or poor.

Phase II, which will take a couple of months to start, will seek new locations for the homeless encampments. These new locations will have improved infrastructure and might be associated with a church or a community group, or they could be independent and located on property owned by someone who allows the encampment on his/her property.

The range of shelters in Phase II might include tents, wooden buildings, modified tool sheds and other structures deemed appropriate by the residents. Although residents in the Phase II development might stay for a while, none of these encampments are intended to be permanent. The goal is to work with the residents, address any issues they have that are holding them back and get them into decent and affordable housing as soon as possible.

The primary goal of Phase I and II of this project is to improve the lives of the homeless while saving taxpayers money and improving public safety. By stabilizing and improving their lives, it will improve their chances of getting a job and/ or getting the help they need from social service agencies. That assistance includes health services, mental health services, alcohol or drug addiction treatment, job training and getting a better education. Being in a stable location will help the homeless get the assistance they need.

A cost-benefit analysis of this proposal would show that it will save the taxpayers money. Our streets, businesses and residential neighborhoods will benefit by providing homeless people with basic public services. Homeless people will benefit by improved living conditions, better contact with social service agencies and ultimately getting into a house.

In Phase III, we recognize that there is both an independent and resourceful spirit among homeless people. A portion of the population will never be served by traditional housing. In addition, many homeless individuals possess underutilized construction skills or the capacity to learn those skills.

In Phase III, we would like to identify a location(s) suitable for the development of permanent self-sustaining communities that are being designed by architect Dyson and the nonprofit organization Eco-Village. At a location agreeable to the residents and the jurisdictions, an Eco-Village will be planned for phased development. Residents who will work on the site will establish a temporary camp onsite. Through sweat equity and volunteer labor, the shared facilities (e.g., bathrooms, kitchen, community space) and individual dwellings will be built and occupied by the residents.

The work will be guided by tradespeople and trained professionals.

Alternatively, the city or county could determine an existing unused public facility that it desires to convert for use as shelter. As with the Eco-Village, a temporary camp will be located onsite and homeless individuals will work on the adaptation of the facility for shelter. In turn, they will gain skills and earn equity in the final product.

Additional suggestions are to establish a true 24/7 emergency shelter for up to 30 days, following acquiring federal funding for emergency shelter and services, and the development of transitional housing for up to two years. We also support a permanent housing development utilizing existing and foreclosed homes in Fresno and new affordable housing being developed as part of Housing First.

The proposal was presented to City Council Member Oliver Baines. Baines represents the district in the downtown area where many homeless people live. After initially being optimistic about reaching an agreement, Baines cut off all contact with the group after several homeless people filed new lawsuits against the City of Fresno in early 2012.

It is frustrating to be ignored and undermined by those making public policy on homeless issues, but we understand that Fresno City Hall is run by a right-wing Republican administration that is not interested in our point of view. Sometimes the best that homeless advocates here can do is to create alternative institutions that make the lives of homeless better and point in a new direction. Independent groups will continue these creative projects that are alternatives to the dominant paradigm, treating the homeless with the dignity and respect they deserve.

Those efforts deserve our support.

Volunteers with Food Not Bombs feed the homeless and anyone else who shows up a couple of times a week.

A group of volunteers, mostly from the Unitarian Universalist Church in Fresno, delivered everything from water to firewood to the homeless encampments in downtown Fresno.

An artist's conception of the Eco-Village Project.

# Chapter 15

# The Big Picture

Homelessness is the result of the economic and political system in which we live. If we had the political will and changed our priorities, homelessness could be ended within a year. I have been telling this to everyone who would listen for years. But it wasn't until I ran into Paul Boden, executive and organizing director of the Western Regional Advocacy Project (WRAP), that I understood the details of how government policy directly led to the situation we are in today. Boden's book, *Without Housing: Decades of Federal Housing Cutbacks, Massive Homelessness and Policy Failures,* is a real eye-opener.

I met Boden during a series of encounters around the time of the homeless lawsuit against the City of Fresno. Homeless people and their allies from Fresno, Sacramento, Merced, San Francisco, San Jose and other communities started to get together and share strategies, tactics and solidarity as we faced similar problems in cities throughout California.

One thing Boden said during this time caught my attention. He said that because of the mainstream media focus on daily events "it is hard to cut through the never-ending news cycles that bombard us daily to deliver a message." Furthermore, "if your organization lacks resources and political clout, it becomes even harder. If the message has anything to do with human rights and homelessness, forget about it."

The primary reason for the increase in homelessness, Boden says, is that "in 1979, the Department of Housing and Urban Development spent $77.3 billion in today's money developing and maintaining housing to ensure all people could afford a place to live. Yet since 1995, the federal government has done nothing while more than 500,000 of these units have been lost" with hundreds of thousands of more units threatened.

Figure 1 illustrates the decline in funding for affordable housing and the increase in the money that now funds HUD priorities. These new priorities include veterans, the chronically homeless and families, but the result is that these temporary campaigns are not capable of ending homelessness because the resources are not available. The budget priorities have shifted from the building and maintenance of affordable housing to something else.

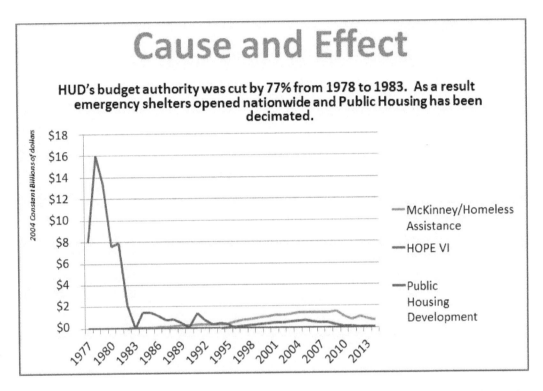

A similar de-funding for rural housing has occurred affecting places such as the Central Valley more than urban areas. Nationally, the U.S. Department of Agriculture built 38,650 affordable housing units in 1979 and only 763 in 2011; in 2012 and 2013, the number was zero (see Figure 2).

# Rural Housing Cuts

**USDA built 38,650 affordable housing units in 1979 & only 763 in 2011 — in 2012 & 2013 the number is 0.**

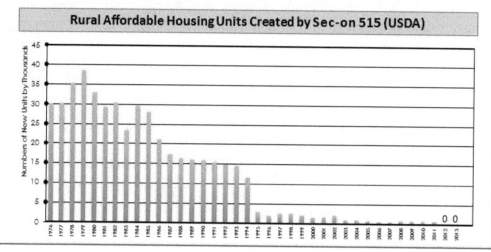

WRAP shows both the cutbacks in federal spending on affordable housing and where the money is being spent. Although low and moderate-income housing assistance has gone down over the years, the amount of money going into tax breaks for homeownership has remained high (see Figure 3). People earning enough money to buy a house, a second home or a vacation home are getting significantly more resources from the federal government. This decision to prioritize resources for middle- and upper-income earners and not for affordable housing is one of the reasons why homelessness has increased.

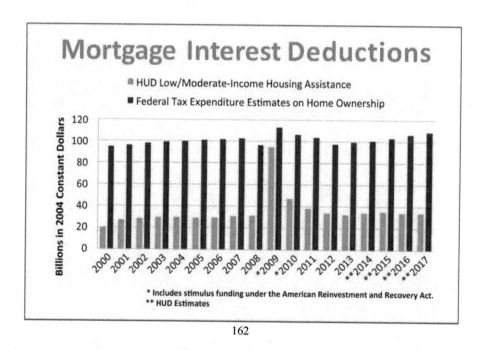

When you look at where else tax dollars are being spent, it becomes even more obvious that ending homelessness is not a priority at the national level (see Figure 4). The amount of money spent on military adventures in the Middle East, on military hardware and to maintain the largest military force on the planet dwarfs the resources given to address ending homelessness.

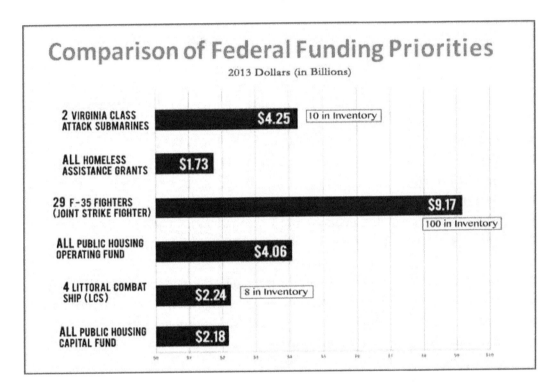

I interviewed Boden in late 2014 at WRAP headquarters in the Mission District of San Francisco about this critically important topic. How did we get to where we are, and how can we end homelessness? The interview was heard on KFCF 88.1 FM in Fresno and posted on the Central Valley page of Indymedia.

The interview with Boden was long and took some interesting twists and turns that go back to what he sees as the beginning of the massive homelessness problem we have today. He was homeless himself, so he understands firsthand what it is like to live on the streets and speaks in a colorful language that leaves no doubt about his authenticity. He is no pointy-headed intellectual, but he knows how to get his narrative across to anyone listening.

Boden said that if you "go back and look at it from a cause-and-effect systemic perspective instead of looking at what drugs are available or de-institutionalization, something clearly happened shortly before October 1982. New York City started opening shelters in 1981, and police stations, empty police stations, were the first shelters in New York City. Here in San Francisco, it was empty Muni buses that they put out in front of St. Anthony's [an organization providing essential support to San Franciscans living in poverty] and in front of the old welfare department, and everything was temporary short-term crisis, but yet no one really seemed to stop and say what's creating it."

Working at the National Low Income Housing Coalition and looking at reports put out by Cushing Dolbeare, a pattern started to emerge about what was happening to funding for public housing. "[We] looked at those funding trends, looked at those charts and then started digging deep into exactly when the cuts came, who was the president at the time [and] what was appropriated versus what was allocated, and it showed so clearly that from 1979 to 1983 in 2004 constant dollars [that] $54 billion a year in affordable housing funding was cut by the federal government. So, when you have this cumulative series of cuts that equals $54 billion a year that then expands…out at $54 billion a year over the next 25–30 years, you ain't going to do nothing but create homelessness for people that are poor." There was a similar pattern in rural housing, which you can see in the chart above.

"The de-funding of low-income public housing was accompanied by creating smaller and less expensive versions of the programs that existed before. Maintenance and upkeep is reduced, rents are increased and older units destroyed. Boden said that "as they started implementing those decisions, there's always a strong necessity to pretend like you're still doing something about the lives of the people that you're screwing over."

Drawing a parallel to mental health cuts and homelessness, Boden said that "residential treatment, which was the solution to institutionalization—it wasn't putting people on the street and in jail that was the recommended solution to that. As that got dismantled, all of these little quasi semi-innocuous programs started popping up all over the place and all funded by the state because the state was making the deepest cuts. In housing, they're now funding homeless programs. They know goddamn well since they passed McKinney [in] 1987 that homeless programs are being created because we're cutting affordable housing. That was in all of the testimony [that justified] Reagan, of all presidents, sign[ing] the McKinney Act. Everybody at the table knew that this was a response to the cuts to affordable housing, and now it's the answer to homelessness.

"What?

"It wasn't a lack of homeless programs that created homelessness; it was a deci-mation and the demolition and the selling off of and the de-funding of our housing programs that created homelessness, and now homeless programs are talking about Housing First with no freaking housing money or redefining when a person is homeless versus when they are poorly housed."

Housing First is the primary program that City of Fresno officials point to when they talk about ending homelessness. Everyone from the mayor and City Council to Preston Prince at the Fresno Housing Authority talk about Housing First. The irony of it is that I was the first person to introduce the idea of Housing First to the Fresno City Council. You can ask former City Council Member Cynthia Ster-ling about this. I supported the concept at the time because it seemed a whole lot better than bulldozing encampments and it was providing homeless people with housing.

Not everyone is a fan of Housing First and even I have become much more criti-cal, in part from what I learned from Boden. In the interview, I asked Boden to expand on his comments about current government programs aimed at the home-less. He said that "the most obvious target these days is Housing First, which is the one that everybody's hearing about…When you actually go to look at HUD and look at the federal government's budget and look for the funding stream and the line item—in the Blue Book of the federal government is a line item for every single dollar they spend or allocate—there's no line item for Housing First. Hou-sing First was created in the public relations office. It wasn't created in the fun-ding office.

"If we really were serious about Housing First, we would obviously, of course, restore the funding for housing. How the hell can you do Housing First without any housing? It just begs itself to the ridiculousness and the lack of depth connec-ted to social policy and public policy issues in the mainstream media…and even from the left mainstream media."

Why does Housing First focus on the chronically homeless? Because they are the most visible, and if you can reduce the number of the visibly homeless, you can declare you are dramatically reducing homelessness, which is exactly what the mayor of Fresno has done. A June 2, 2015, headline in the *Fresno Bee* said that "Fresno's Homeless Decline by Half," supporting the mayor who gives credit to the Housing First effort. But as Boden explains, in a country where "we have 1.2 million kids that go to school every day that don't have a home to go to that night

—our No. 1 priority is the visible single adult. And then we wonder why the numbers of families keep growing and the numbers of teenage suicide and abuse and beatings of homeless people, you know, continues to just get worse and worse and worse because people are being told one thing, but the reality is something completely different.

"The days of women and children first are long freaking gone. If HUD had been driving the Titanic, the life raft would've only been filled with single adults so you could say you saved more people. It's a recipe for disaster, and it's blown up in their face."

The point-in-time headcounts used to quantify the number of homeless are inaccurate, expensive and misleading. "If you really gave a shit about how many people are homeless in America at any given time or over the course of the year, local communities spend millions and millions of dollars to hire consultants and trainers and staff investing in flashlights, writ[ing] reports and do[ing] all this crap—because they love to study poverty. They love to study racism, and they love to study homelessness because they don't have any intention of addressing any of those issues," Boden said.

The methodology of going out once every two years on January 25 to get an accurate count is absurd. "January 25 in Bozeman, Montana; in Detroit, Michigan; in Chicago; in New York; and in Portland, Oregon. January 25 tends to be pretty freaking cold, so to think that going out and counting the numbers of heads of people that you see sleeping in the streets on that night will result in an accurate count is foolish...And the most amazing part is those numbers that come out from that process are now the official numbers," Boden said. In Fresno, they have bulldozed all of the encampments, scattering the homeless who now hide in remote areas, the police have relentlessly harassed them forcing them to act like they are invisible and you expect to get an accurate count? And...on what might be the coldest day of the year? Good luck with that!

Where do these bad policy decisions emerge from? Is it poor judgment, an ideological bias or something else? It matters because some homeless advocates think that if we just used logic and explained things to government officials, things would change. Or, as Boden so eloquently said, "Why wouldn't the U.S. government want a socially just governance structure? Why wouldn't the government want people to be educated, to be healthy, to be housed and if they really wanted to support a capitalist system to have some freaking money in their pockets? Why is that considered bad? It's been considered bad because it's been beaten into the heads of all of us for the last 35 years that government [is] bad, business [is] good. So, now our downtowns are public-private partnerships, our parks are public-private partnerships, our public housing is now going to be a public-private partnership, our military, and it just goes on and on and on. There is no legitimate role that government plays in the lives of the people that we govern because the only ones that can do that are private industry."

Instead of providing enough affordable housing, government (including Fresno City Hall) passes quality-of-life laws to stop homeless people from sleeping or sitting in public, asking for money, pushing shopping carts, etc. Boden said that they found a poster from 1936 put out by the mayor of New York. There were images of poverty and homelessness in the center, and at the top it said, "Must we always have this?" At the bottom, it said, "Why not housing?"

Boden said, "Why are local mayors and state elected officials and state departments allowing the federal government to just pull out and get the hell out of the social issues of people's lives—the healthcare, the education, the housing issues of people's lives? Why are they allowing that to happen, and why are we electing people that allow that to happen?" Why does Fresno City Hall give huge tax breaks to corporations, builders and developers while thousands of people are sleeping on the streets?

Boden answers the question like this: "Well, how are you going to deal with that? You're going to use your jails. You are going to use your courts. You're going to create laws that say it's illegal to sit down in public spaces. Everybody's going to sit down in public spaces…everybody knows that. Everybody's going to stand still. Everybody's going to lay down. Everybody at some point in time whether they like it or not is going to go to sleep. Everybody's going to have to eat at some point in time. So we're passing all these laws that make sitting, standing, sitting, sleeping [and] laying down [illegal]; closing our public parks; making it illegal to eat; making it illegal to serve food.

"And everybody in the game knows—just like with Jim Crow laws, just like with sundown towns, just like with anti-Okie laws—this is about certain people. These are laws that are universal…but the application of these laws is about certain people. It has been about Japanese-Americans, it has been about African-Americans, it's been [about] mentally ill people, it's been about homeless people and again it's about homeless people. But this has been done against other people, *braceros*, people from Mexico, so everybody in the process knows."

The Western Regional Advocacy Center and its allies have conducted close to 1,700 interviews with people on the street, and the top three criminal offenses reported are sleeping, standing and sitting. Those are illegal acts if you're perceived to be in a certain class. According to Boden, WRAP is "pushing legislation in Oregon and California, working with a lot of groups in Colorado, working with groups now on a campaign in Washington, that says local governments cannot criminalize the act of sleeping, sleeping in a vehicle so long as it's legally parked, sitting, standing, laying down, eating or sharing food. Those are protected acts and cannot be criminalized anymore in the future. Because those are acts that get criminalized but you know everyone's going to violate [them].

"So the fact that we have historically allowed local governments to pass laws to make it illegal to sleep or to sit or to stand still, you know everyone's going to do that, so our bill says you can't make those activities illegal anymore. Basically, under the assumption that if we build power, if we keep working on this—because I don't think these bills are going to be easy, but nothing worthwhile is—[then] they lose the ability to get rid of us and make us disappear. Our right to exist gives us power. If you can't say 'go away, disappear, I'm closing my eyes I don't want to see you anymore'; if you can no longer do that to us, then maybe as human beings you're going to have to start talking to us. You're going to have to start dealing with us as human beings and as people with rights…I live here, I have a right to be here, and we need to figure out how we're going to work together because you no longer have the legal authority to make me disappear."

As this book goes to press, WRAP's Homeless Bill of Rights legislation is in Sacramento. Regardless of whether it passes, there is still much to be done. We need to elect city, state and federal officials who have the political will to end homelessness by prioritizing affordable housing and providing the social services to help each person live the best life they are capable of living. If that means reducing tax breaks to billionaires, fewer concessions to big corporations and an end to the endless war against terrorism, then that is what needs to be done.

Paul Boden

# Chapter 16

# The War Against the Poor Goes into Hyperdrive

The time after the settlement in federal court until the fall of 2011 was full of contradictions with the City of Fresno's policy on the homeless. The city would tolerate some homeless encampments if they were out of sight and neighbors didn't complain too loudly. There were even stories (which turned out to be true) about parole officers dropping off people recently released from prison at the Santa Fe Avenue homeless encampment. Many of the residents at that encampment were sexual offenders with ankle bracelets. They were told by their parole officers to stay there.

Forcing recently released sexual offenders into homelessness is unconscionable. It is bad for the community and bad for the men involved. Being a sexual offender, just released from prison and being homeless are the single biggest factors in recidivism. Maintaining a homeless encampment for sexual offenders was tolerated by the City of Fresno for years and encouraged by the local state parole office.

Some of the homeless encampments were unambiguous drug bazaars that got a nod and a wink from the police department. City government didn't do anything to shut these drug operations down or do a damn thing to help most of the people living there.

The vast majority of the homeless are neither drug dealers nor sexual offenders, but other than issuing housing vouchers to a lucky few, city policy during this time was one of benign neglect. The millions of dollars coming into Fresno to help the homeless was going to social service organizations and a couple of construction projects that would house a handful of homeless people. If you were actually homeless and sleeping on the sidewalk, the city did not provide drinking water, portable toilets (after the H Street encampment was shut down) or trash containers.

That phase ended in October 2011 when notices went up that a "cleanup" was going to take place at the major homeless encampments in the downtown area. Homeless advocates rallied, held a press conference and denounced the demolitions during an October 26 press conference in front of City Hall. That event was held on the day before the bulldozers were scheduled to destroy the Santa Fe Avenue encampment. Video of the speakers at that press conference can be seen at www.indybay.org/newsitems/2011/10/26/18695320.php.

The City of Fresno and Caltrans did what they said they were going to do—they attacked and destroyed the homeless encampment on Santa Fe Avenue, just south of Ventura Street. But they could not do this without being confronted with significant resistance by community members and the homeless who protested the eviction.

Although there were more than 100 community supporters to protest the destruction of the homeless encampment on Santa Fe Avenue, that was not enough to stop Caltrans and the City of Fresno. The encampment, which was spread across a long block in the old industrial section of downtown, proved to be strategically impossible to defend, with so few people. If there had been 1,000 advocates and homeless people, the city and Caltrans would have had an extremely difficult time carrying out their assault.

The north end of the Santa Fe Avenue encampment was on Caltrans land, and the south half of the encampment was on City of Fresno property. Caltrans was involved because the north portion of the camp is under the Highway 41 overpass. When homeless supporters were defending shelters on the far south end, Caltrans and the California Highway Patrol (CHP) started to work on the north end. Ultimately, it was impossible for the advocates, whose numbers diminished over the course of the day, to stop the destruction. On the other hand, this was the strongest and most militant show of public support for the Fresno homeless—ever!

The City of Fresno claimed that the destruction of this encampment was necessary because of work that needed to be done in the area around the Highway 41 overpass. Four years later, no construction work in that area had been done.

Supporters of the homeless expressed concerns about the destruction of homeless people's property as the evictions on Santa Fe Avenue took place. In the settlement with the City of Fresno and Caltrans, the court ordered that any property of value found during "cleanups" at homeless encampments would be put into storage for 90 days. There were clearly tents, beds and other property destroyed on Santa Fe Avenue, in apparent violation of the federal court order.

Homeless advocates took photos and video of the destruction of property on Santa Fe Avenue in the hope that it would be useful to defend homeless people's civil rights should legal action be taken. They also visited the other encampments, taking photos of people with their property, helping them make signs to ID items such as tents, and getting contact information from them about how they could be found after the evictions.

A couple of days later, the "cleanup" continued on H Street, south of Ventura Street.

Laynette Johnson put her name on the shelter where she lived on H Street under the Monterey Street bridge. She knew there were signs posted warning of an eviction on November 1, 2011, but she had to attend classes at Cesar Chavez Continuation School that day. Bill Simon, then chair of the Bishop John Steinbock Homeless Advocacy Committee, was there and told Caltrans workers that Laynette was at school and that they should not destroy her property. It was not abandoned.

Simon described what happened next: "The bulldozer would use its bucket to smash the tent and other structures with their contents, then ran over it and finally dump everything in a dump truck. Everything she had except four plastic trash bags of small items were bulldozed. Every tent/structure with belongings that I could see north of her on H Street was similarly bulldozed." Simon said that video of the destruction, which appears to be a clear violation of the federal court order, is available should legal action be taken.

A large number of homeless people's tents and shelters were destroyed that day in and around H and San Benito streets. Property was picked up with bulldozers and put into the back of waiting garbage trucks.

The demolition of homeless encampments continued the next day (November 2) on G Street as City of Fresno sanitation crews, backed up by the FPD, bulldozed most of the structures in that area. It was a little confusing because the area of destruction was under Highway 41, which is usually in Caltrans' sphere of influence. Caltrans, in fact, had just posted signs giving the homeless a couple of extra days to move out. Without regard to those newly posted signs, the City of Fresno crews rolled in and started destroying the encampment.

At one point, the city crews were led by a self-appointed homeless man who was telling them which structures they could destroy and which ones they should leave. I was told later, by residents of the encampment, that the homeless man directing the city crews was mentally ill and that he was simply pointing to the shelters of people he did not like and having them destroyed. He would tell the workers that "the person in that tent has left, so you can destroy it." This is not the first time I had seen this happen; I had heard supervisors on city crews ask homeless people if it was OK to destroy a shelter. The homeless person would say, "OK, I don't care," and that is all of the authority the supervisor thought was needed to declare the shelter abandoned. Never mind the fact that the homeless person being asked was not the shelter's owner and didn't live there.

When the city sanitation crew was a little further down G Street, they were confronted with an angry group of homeless people defending their shelters. One of the participants held a large stick over his head, and others stood with fists clinched. The crew made a hasty retreat and called in the nearby police. After things calmed down, the sanitation crew continued to destroy the encampment.

November 3, 2011, found the city crews destroying shelters on Golden State Boulevard and doing mop-up operations in the other areas. I had a couple of interesting conversations with city workers that day. My overall impression was that none of the workers wanted to be doing this, and nobody thought that it would result in anything other than displacing the homeless. One Fresno police officer told me that he felt bad because these people had nowhere to go. He explained that he was just following orders and that this was not a solution to the problem. A city sanitation worker told me that he was trying to comply with the mandate of the federal court order. He said the sanitation crew was only destroying the shelters if the owner said they could or if it was abandoned. The crew did seem to pack up more property and put it into storage than on the previous days, but there was still obvious destruction of property taking place.

I watched as a homeless woman riding her bike back to her shelter was almost hit by the claw of a bulldozer.

The destruction of The Hill began on November 7, 2011, with Caltrans destroying tents and other structures at the north end. This was part of the coordinated two-week effort by Caltrans and the City of Fresno to destroy all of the homeless encampments in the downtown area.

The first person I talked to as I was walking toward The Hill on G Street was an older man who was crying and saying that his home had just been destroyed. He said he had nowhere to go. Other homeless people were trying to save as many of their possessions as they could before the bulldozer got to their shelter. The City of Fresno gives lip service to helping people find housing, but none of the people I talked to that day had a place to go.

The City of Fresno set up a tent at Santa Clara and G streets and was helping homeless people fill out applications for housing, although nobody, as far as I could tell, was being offered immediate housing. The city said it had 140 slots available (if you qualified) and that more might be available the following year. Those vague promises seemed to mean little to the homeless, whose lives were made more difficult by losing the only shelter they had.

The Hill, where city sanitation crews were working on this day, was probably the largest encampment in the downtown area, with some shelters now two stories tall. The combination of a Caltrans crew on one end and city workers on the other destroyed the encampment in one day. The following morning, there was just a mop-up crew removing the few odds and ends that remained.

It was now Day 13 of the City of Fresno and Caltrans attack against downtown homeless encampments. Witnesses saw continued assaults on G Street, The Hill and Golden State Boulevard. On November 8, new attacks against the homeless were initiated on Santa Clara Street between G and F streets and on F Street between Ventura and Santa Clara streets. The City of Fresno estimated that 200 homeless people were dislocated. Homeless advocates estimate the number at closer to 500.

On Santa Clara Street, bulldozers plowed through the shelters, leaving more homeless people with nowhere to live. Nobody seemed to know where they were going to spend the night. There was some talk of joining Occupy Fresno at Courthouse Park, but for the last three nights, Occupy Fresno activists had been arrested for exercising their right to assemble.

City workers visited each of the shelters on Santa Clara and F streets telling the residents that they had to remove their property and leave. They told them that what they did not take with them would be destroyed and taken to the dump. There were some conflicting reports about whether they were being told that the city would store their property for 90 days, but some homeless people were given trash bags and those bags were being loaded onto trucks destined for the storage facility. It is probable that if the person who owned the tent or shelter being targeted was not in or near their shelter, he/she did not get the warning.

Right after the demolition of these shelters, you could see homeless people pushing their shopping carts, with all of their possessions, throughout downtown Fresno—they were looking for a place to sleep. Many homeless people, particularly single women, became more vulnerable because they no longer had neighbors who could help protect them from predators.

In a statement sent to the media, the City of Fresno quoted (now reduced to part-time) homeless czar Greg Barfield as saying that "the City and its partners are devoting a tremendous amount of resources to finding long-term solutions to our homelessness issue. We're in the midst of a methodical process that involves collecting many documents and matching the needs of individuals with the resources available in the community, but the reality is that we're all working together and making progress in getting these homeless individuals the help they need."

Most progressive homeless advocates didn't agree with the city's approach and complained that the destruction of the homeless encampments in the downtown area would make people's lives more difficult. A better approach, they argued, would be to provide the homeless with basic public services—drinking water, a place to go to the bathroom and trash service. Phase II would be to establish safe and legal places for the homeless to stay, until the City and County of Fresno could provide them with the housing they claim to be working on. Forcing the homeless to live on the streets, with no access to shelter, is cruel and heartless.

Many of the people pushed out of their modest shelters ended up on Santa Clara Street, near the Poverello House, where they would try to sleep at night. I heard from homeless people that the police came through almost every night, would wake them up and tell them to move on. While I was there one night, interviewing homeless people about this situation, a patrol car pulled up and announced over the loudspeaker that camping was not permitted. The announcement went on to say that "violators will be subject to arrest."

During this time, homeless people on Santa Clara Street had no choice but to sleep on the sidewalk usually without a tent and sometimes without a sleeping bag because those had been taken by city workers. In a video taken on December 15,

2011, given to me by a homeless man using his cell phone, city sanitation workers can again be seen taking and immediately destroying homeless people's property. On the same day and at about the same time, Fresno City Council members were discussing an ordinance that would make it illegal for the homeless to camp on city property (e.g., City Hall, an alleyway, sidewalks).

The video shows that when police, garbage trucks and a flatbed truck arrived on Santa Clara and F streets, there were no signs posted and no warning of this cleanup. Shopping carts were collected, homeless people's clothes and other items were thrown on the ground, and the carts were put on a flatbed truck and taken away.

Judy Hess, a homeless advocate who went down to talk to the homeless people after this incident, said the city not only took blankets and sleeping bags but also took homeless people's firewood too. Because the city destroyed all of the shelters that the homeless people had built, they were keeping warm at night by building fires. Hess also said that one person lost an urn that held his grandfather's ashes.

Bobby Gray, who first alerted me to this situation, said the city had taken all of her clothes and bedding materials; she had not been on the street at the time because she was inside the Poverello House making Christmas decorations. Gray also said that one man had been injured when he was pushed off a couch by a city worker.

While the "cleanup" on Santa Clara and F streets was going on, the City Council was discussing the adoption of an ordinance that would make it a criminal offense for anyone to camp on city property. The item, which originally appeared on the Consent Calendar, was pulled, and a three-hour-plus discussion ensued. About 20 homeless advocates and a couple of homeless people spoke out against the proposed ordinance. Several Occupy Fresno activists spoke out against the ordinance, saying that it appeared that the city was trying to stop them from "occupying" city property.

Some of the reasons given for opposing the camping ordinance were as follows:
- City Council Member Oliver Baines had asked homeless advocates to propose a plan that would establish safe and legal homeless encampments. If this ordinance passes, it would be illegal to use City of Fresno property for that purpose.
- It is wrong to criminalize the poor.

- Criminalizing the homeless for sleeping does not help them. It makes their situation worse by giving them a criminal record and fining them.
- The City of Fresno can't put violators in the Fresno County Jail—it is already full.
- The Jones decision in Los Angeles ruled that you can't arrest homeless people for sleeping if there are not enough shelter beds to accommodate the homeless population. There are not enough shelter beds in Fresno for the homeless.
- This ordinance is an admission of failure and runs contrary to the city's 10-Year Plan to End Chronic Homelessness.

Although claims were made that the ordinance would be revenue neutral, homeless people would probably not be able to pay fines and cleanup costs if they can't even afford a place to live. The ordinance says there are campsites in Fresno where the homeless can stay, but it does not say where they are at. Homeless advocates were aware of no such campsites.

After the public presentations, in which everyone who spoke called on the city not to pass the proposed ordinance, City Council members spoke. City Council Member Sal Quintero said he was undecided until he received a letter from Larry Arce at the Rescue Mission, which he read aloud, talking about how the homeless needed to have their shelters destroyed—that the tough love would bring them into the programs they needed to get off the streets.

Baines insisted that the camping ordinance was not directed at the homeless. He speculated that the ordinance was directed at the Occupy Fresno movement. That sentiment was repeated by other City Council members and staff.

The City Council voted not to back the anti-camping ordinance but intends to bring it back up for discussion at a future date.

The City of Fresno spent more than $200,000 to destroy the shelters and property of people living in downtown homeless encampments in the fall and winter of 2011–2012. This was done as freezing weather arrived and city representatives told homeless advocates that they did not have enough money to open warming centers, which previously had been set up at community centers around town. Somehow the city found money to destroy homeless people's shelters but could not find any money to help keep the homeless warm.

Not only did the city fail to open the warming centers, but police officers also extinguished the small fires on Santa Clara Street that the homeless built to keep themselves warm. This was after earlier "cleanups" in which the police stood guard as city sanitation workers took down tarps, tents and anything else the homeless used to protect themselves from the cold and rain. Homeless people told me that city workers also took their sleeping bags, blankets and clothing.

The result has been massive illness, with many homeless people coming down with pneumonia and other illnesses. The emergency room at Community Hospital was overwhelmed on some days because so many people were seeking medical assistance. It was in this context that Sharen "Big Sue" Bobbitt died on December 28, 2011. Big Sue died on the sidewalk outside of the Poverello House.

Dr. Jean Kennedy, speaking at Big Sue's funeral, said, "Her death is not going to be in vain." Kennedy vowed to bring the situation of Big Sue's dying on the sidewalk in front of a homeless center to the attention of the community. Kennedy said she will do everything she can "to make sure that we look at policy so that we won't have this sort of a situation—so that people have a room, so they have a roof over their heads if they so desire."

Big Sue's funeral went from the spot where she died on Santa Clara Street to Ray Polk's homeless ministry at Broadway and San Benito streets. A memorial plaque was placed there alongside dozens of other plaques of homeless people who have died on the mean streets of Fresno.

Two days after Big Sue's funeral, homeless advocates took their concerns about how the city is treating the homeless to the annual Dr. Martin Luther King, Jr., march. There were signs and banners demanding safe and legal campsites for the homeless, a large photo of Big Sue and criticism of the "cruel and heartless" city policy on homelessness.

Many of the displaced homeless, caught in the raids that took place from October to December of 2011, reestablished a camp just west of Palm Avenue and H Street on a canal bank behind the large grain silos. Police told those residents to "move on" by February 1, 2012, although there was no place for them to move on to. Polk, who runs a homeless ministry, was told to clear out in March. Polk, who is homeless himself, was spared in the 2011 round of "cleanups" but was again being threatened with eviction.

Bill Simon continued speaking out against the injustice of homeless people having nowhere to go. He asked, "Where are they supposed to go?" Without a safe and legal place for the homeless to live, the city is essentially criminalizing poverty. The unsurprising result of that policy is the death of Big Sue and the hundreds of others who die and end up at the county morgue. Many of the homeless who die on the street end up cremated and dumped into a mass grave at a county cemetery.

One of the problems with moving forward with the eviction of Polk and his ministry was that he had been featured in numerous radio and newspaper stories, and his Homeless Memorial was a well-known landmark in the area. The city thought long and hard before removing Polk and the memorial.

But once the decision to move on Polk and the Monterey Street bridge encampment was made, city workers smashed apart the shelters of a dozen homeless people. Enoris Williams (also known as Mother Nature) was one of the people who watched in horror as the city destroyed the shelter that kept her warm at night. "That's my home, that is my home," she wailed as a group of sanitation workers kicked her home down.

The City of Fresno claimed it was destroying the encampments because of construction projects in the area that required their removal. Barfield said that the city was finding housing for those affected by the destruction of the encampments. Yet, at an impromptu meeting I held at the encampment on the day of the demolition, not one person said he/she had been offered housing.

On a live TV show the night of the eviction, Barfield was asked why the homeless were being evicted now, just as the weather is getting cold. He responded that "no time is a good time" to evict the homeless but argued that it was the right thing to do. The city also defended its policy of providing no safe and legal places for the homeless to live. Preston Prince, executive director and CEO of the Fresno Housing Authority, said that he does not support the concept of safe and legal campgrounds. Both Prince and Barfield said they wanted to provide housing for the homeless and not encourage temporary encampments.

Other panelists on the show, hosted by the Catholic TV station KNXT, argued passionately about the need for a short-term solution for the homeless because nobody is saying that the City of Fresno or the Housing Authority is going to find all homeless people housing any time soon. Chris Schneider, executive director of the CCLS, challenged Barfield to support the safe ground concept. Barfield refused to express support for safe and legal places for the homeless to live.

Kevin Hamilton, deputy chief of programs at Clinica Sierra Vista, said there are more than 3,000 homeless people on the streets of Fresno and that while it is nice that city efforts have found housing for some of them, the reality is that people need a safe place to sleep at night. That point was repeated throughout the 90-minute program by other panel members, the in-studio audience and callers.

Simon asked why the City of Fresno destroyed homeless people's property even though it was clearly marked with their names on it. He showed a video of a shelter being destroyed, even after he had told workers who it belonged to, that the owner was at school at the time and that she wanted her property saved. Simon argued that the destruction of homeless people's property appears to be in violation of a federal court order, prohibiting the city from taking and immediately destroying their property.

Later in 2012, the City of Fresno destroyed a long-established growth of oleander bushes to remove a couple of dozen homeless people from their encampment on Weber Avenue, between Olive and Belmont avenues. The oleanders provided some beauty for drivers and a haven for the homeless from the scorching temperatures that went significantly above 100 degrees for much of August. Without shade, homeless residents were forced to move to other locations, where they stayed until they were forced to "move on" again.

Several homeless advocates were on Weber Avenue to witness the demolition and had signs that asked the question, "If not here, where?" Advocates had been demanding safe and legal campsites for the homeless but had not been successful in reaching a sympathetic ear at City Hall.

California Public Records Act requests revealed that the City of Fresno had spent about $1 million to remove the homeless and destroy the Monterey Street bridge. What was left at that location was a now weed-infested vacant lot that is fenced in so the homeless can't live there.

The oleanders are gone, and city crews return regularly to Weber Avenue to spray herbicide on the ground so no new life emerges. Every time I drive down that stretch of road I think about how the bare lifeless ground that is constantly under attack reflects city policy on the homeless. The oleanders try to survive, they sprout new twigs, but every time they do the city sends a crew to kill them. They put up fences around vacant land, poison the ground and bulldoze encampments because they don't want the homeless to have any place to live. The policy of the City of Fresno can best be described as being developed and directed by a culture of death and destruction.

The Santa Fe Avenue homeless encampment (south end) before the destruction began.

Homeless people, joined by community supporters, tried to stop the city from destroying the Santa Fe Avenue encampment.

City of Fresno workers, with rakes, garbage trucks and bulldozers, cleared out the homeless living at the Santa Fe encampment on October 27, 2011.

Homeless people's property, like this camping tent, were destroyed as city workers plowed through the encampments.

Sometimes the confrontations between the homeless and city workers got up close and personal.

These two homeless men on H Street (south of Ventura Street) held out for as long as they could. Eventually, the city crews were ordered to move in and take everything these guys decided to "leave behind."

As Caltrans moved in on the upper portion of The Hill (a homeless encampment on G Street near California Avenue), people took what property they could carry and escaped before the bulldozers knocked down their shelters.

This homeless man held a sign to express his feelings about the destruction of the downtown homeless encampments.

Sometimes the City of Fresno crews could not get into a homeless encampment with their bulldozers. When that happened, they got creative about how they destroyed homeless people's shelters.

As city workers kicked down her home, this homeless person known to everyone as Mother Nature cried. Mother Nature died after her shelter was destroyed.

Most homeless people in the downtown area knew Big Sue. She died sleeping on the sidewalk in front of the Poverello House shortly after her shelter was destroyed by city work crews. Big Sue died on December 28, 2011. *Photo by Dixie Salazar.*

Many supporters of human rights for homeless people carried signs about Big Sue in the annual Dr. Martin Luther King, Jr., Day march in January 2012.

Yolanda, a homeless woman living under the overpass near H and San Benito streets, was unable to stop the city from destroying her shelter.

The City of Fresno destroyed all of the oleanders on Weber Avenue (between Olive and Belmont avenues) to get rid of a few homeless people camping behind them. For the past several years, the city workers have killed every reemerging oleander that has appeared at this site—a fitting and symbolic action illustrating their policy of death and destruction.

# Chapter 17

# More Lawsuits Filed Against the City of Fresno

Following the homeless encampment demolitions of October and November 2011, 36 individual lawsuits against the City of Fresno were filed in federal court. The lawsuits alleged that the city again took and immediately destroyed homeless people's property. This was not a class action lawsuit, like the previous one filed in 2006, so it was possible that each case would involve a separate trial.

The decision to file individual lawsuits rather than a class action lawsuit was made by the attorneys involved and was based on their belief that this was the most likely path to victory. The two law firms representing the homeless in the litigation were Arnold & Porter LLC and the Central California Legal Services. Because the CCLS is prohibited from engaging in class action lawsuits, that made the decision to go with individual lawsuits an obvious choice.

Arnold & Porter hired me as a consultant to help keep in touch with the clients, get them to meetings and update clients on the status of the case. Therefore, you might conclude that I'm not exactly an unbiased casual observer. Of course, as Howard Zinn has been quoted as saying, "You can't be neutral on a moving train."

Instead of fast action in federal court, as in 2006, these lawsuits moved much more slowly through the judicial process. By the late summer of 2014, several of the homeless plaintiffs had dropped out of the case, one moved to Mexico, two of them had died and several others were in poor health.

Three years of litigation included dozens of depositions, including all of the homeless clients, City of Fresno workers involved in the demolition of the encampments, the city manager and the mayor. There were motions for dismissal, mountains of paperwork and mediation efforts. With the number of homeless clients continuing to decline and no trial in sight, it was starting to look like justice delayed was going to result in justice denied.

Although the attorneys representing the city challenged every client's claim, the homeless people were confident that they would prevail. Their stories were compelling, like this one submitted to the court by Steven Ward, describing the factual allegations in the case:

> Beginning in or about September 2011, defendants created, planned and began implementation of a continuing custom, policy and practice of destroying the shelter and other personal property of plaintiff and other homeless residents in the City of Fresno, of seizing and immediately destroying their personal property even though that property was valuable and not abandoned by plaintiff, and of continuing to destroy plaintiff's attempts to shelter himself from the cold and to remain safe, including but not limited to destruction of limited shelter at times when that shelter is most needed, exposing plaintiff to conditions that impair his health and safety, and threatening plaintiff with arrest and incarceration when he seeks shelter against the cold and elements in the City of Fresno. Defendants have destroyed vital shelter, clothing, sleeping bags and other property essential to the continued survival of plaintiff. None of these actions were authorized by a warrant. This custom, practice and policy is continuing.
>
> On or about November 7, 2011, acting pursuant to the custom, practice and policy alleged above, defendants seized and immediately destroyed substantially all of the personal property belonging to Steven Ward, including but not limited to his tent and its entire contents, which included all of his clothing, his furniture, his personal papers, photographs, letters, books and other property necessary for life, and property of a personal nature of significant value to plaintiff.
>
> In addition, certain of the property seized and destroyed by defendants had personal significance to plaintiff: pictures of his grand-

mother, work boots and blankets. Plaintiff had not abandoned any of the personal property destroyed by defendants but at all times sought to maintain possession of their property upon which they depended for their ability to live. Defendants had provided no adequate notice of their intent to seize and destroy plaintiff's property. On December 12, 2011, Ward tried to put up another tent; defendants tore it down within a day.

Following the demolition of his shelter and destruction of his property by defendants on or about in November 7, 2011, Ward has been forced to move to different locations in an attempt to protect themselves and survive. Acting pursuant to their ongoing custom, practice and policy, defendants have forced Ward to move, forced them to take down his limited shelter, seized and destroyed his property on subsequent occasions, and continue to threaten him with arrest and/or destruction of their property with no or inadequate notice. During this period, temperatures have fallen below 36 degrees Fahrenheit on several occasions and Ward has been exposed to cold and rainy weather with little or no shelter. Despite the extreme conditions, and despite the fact that they have destroyed Ward's shelter, defendants have failed and refuse to provide any means of protection from the cold and wet weather.

Defendants have not stored any of Ward's property and have failed and refused to provide for the return of their property or for any adequate means for plaintiff to identify and recover their property.

Despite the extreme conditions, and despite the fact that they have destroyed plaintiff's shelter and property essential to protection from the elements, defendants have continued their custom, practice and policy as alleged herein. Defendants know or should reasonably know that their conduct presents a threat to the ability of Ward to continue to survive, but nonetheless continue their conduct in a manner that creates substantial risk to their ability to continue to survive and is shocking to the conscience. Plaintiff has suffered injury to his health and physical well-being as a result of the conduct of defendants. Ward has suffered and continues to suffer not only property loss, but physical harm and extreme emotional damage proximately caused by the conduct of defendants.

Defendants knew, or reasonably should have known, that their conduct would also cause extreme emotional trauma and damage to plaintiff and, in addition, threaten Plaintiff's ability to continue to survive. The nature and timing of defendants' conduct and the cumulative effect of that continuing contact have combined to worsen the emotional trauma and damage caused by that conduct. Defendants timed the demolitions and destruction of property to occur at the onset of the winter months that would bring cold and freezing temperatures, rain, and other difficult physical conditions. Defendants knew or should reasonably have known that their conduct would have a substantial harmful effect on homeless residents because they engaged in this conduct at a time when they were particularly vulnerable and when that conduct would cause substantial physical and emotional damage to plaintiff and create a substantial and ongoing threat to plaintiff's right to life and liberty.

As a further direct and proximate result of defendants' conduct, plaintiff has been left without any shelter or adequate clothing or other protection from the elements, and has suffered adverse physical and mental health effects as a result of that conduct. Plaintiff's right to life and liberty is substantially threatened and jeopardized by defendants' conduct.

Defendants, who timed the destruction to occur at the onset of the winter months that would bring cold and at times freezing temperatures, rain, and other difficult physical conditions, knew or should reasonably have known that their conduct would cause substantial physical and emotional damage to plaintiff and create a substantial and ongoing threat to plaintiff's right to life and liberty. Plaintiff lacks the financial or other means to avoid defendants' conduct. As a further direct and proximate result of defendants' conduct, plaintiff has been left without any shelter or adequate clothing or other protection from the elements, and have suffered adverse health effects as a result of that conduct and plaintiff's continued right to liberty and life is substantially threatened and jeopardized by defendants' conduct.

Defendants' policies, actions and conduct have proximately caused and continue to cause enormous damage to plaintiff, including loss of property, physical and emotional damage and further loss and injury for which there is no adequate remedy at law, constituting irreparable injury, including but not limited to the loss of their fundamental rights under the U.S. Constitution and the California Constitution to be free from unreasonable seizure and destruction of their property and to the right to life and liberty, among others. Plaintiff has no plain, adequate or complete remedy at law to address the wrongs described herein. Defendants have made it plain by their actions, the ongoing nature of their activities, and their public statements that they intend to continue the unlawful conduct described above. Defendants intend to continue the unlawful policies and practices as alleged above and will in fact continue that conduct unless and until restrained by an injunctive decree of this Court.

The acts of defendants as alleged above constituted violations of established constitutional rights of plaintiff, and defendants could not reasonably have thought that their conduct in intentionally seizing and immediately destroying all of plaintiff's personal property and threatening the life and liberty of plaintiff as alleged herein was consistent with plaintiff's constitutional rights. Defendants have engaged in this conduct either with the intent to cause the destruction of plaintiff's property and both physical and emotional damage, or with reckless indifference to the foreseeable consequences of their conduct. Further, the acts of defendants as alleged above were arbitrary and conscience-shocking in their manner and timing, including but not limited to the destruction of vital property and shelter at the onset of winter, maximizing the injury and harm that their conduct would proximately cause to plaintiff.

Effective as of May 28, 2008, defendants City of Fresno, Caltrans and certain other defendants entered into Settlement Agreements (the "Agreements") with representatives of a class that the Court in Kincaid, et al. v. City of Fresno, et al., Civil Action No. 06-CV-1445-OWW, had certified. The commitments by the City of Fresno, Caltrans and certain other defendants in the Agreements represented binding commitments by those defendants for the benefit of plaintiff, among others. The conduct of those defendants, as alleged above, violates their contractual obligations to plaintiff under the Agreements and the Order of the Court, which incorporated those Agreements.

An actual controversy exists between plaintiff and defendants in that defendants have engaged in the unlawful and unconstitutional conduct as alleged herein and intend to continue this unlawful conduct as an ongoing practice and policy, whereas plaintiff claims that these practices are unlawful and unconstitutional and therefore seeks a declaration of rights with respect to this controversy.

As a direct and proximate result of the unconstitutional and unlawful policies, practices and conduct of defendants, plaintiff has suffered, and will continue to suffer, damages, including but not limited to deprivation and destruction of property, including clothing, bedding, medication, personal documents and other personal possessions, severe and continuing physical and emotional damage, including loss of health, emotional damage, loss of personal dignity, and, if defendants are not restrained, the likely loss of life.

Plaintiff is informed and believes and based thereon allege that the acts of defendants were willful, malicious and oppressive and done with intentional and conscious and deliberate disregard for plaintiff and their rights as alleged herein. The acts of defendants as alleged herein have been and are of such a continuing and cumulative nature that they shock the conscience and go beyond basic standards of human decency.

Plaintiff has filed and/or will timely file administrative claims with the City of Fresno pursuant to California Government Code § 910 et seq.

The above motion, filed in federal court on behalf of Ward, is representative of the 36 lawsuits filed against the City of Fresno. Evidence of an agreement to settle the lawsuit started to emerge in September 2014. Finally, after years of work and weeks of negotiations the City of Fresno and homeless plaintiffs in these lawsuits came to an agreement.

The smile on the faces of homeless people as they cashed their checks left no doubt about who was victorious in the lawsuit. Angelita Soto was one of the homeless people who filed a lawsuit and received a check in October 2014. Soto had lived in an encampment near E and Santa Clara streets. On the morning of November 7, 2011, city crews arrived at Soto's shelter. After forcing her out, they searched inside her shelter, removed her chest of drawers, a chair, a bookshelf and other household furnishings. Those items were put on the curb next to the road. Soto watched as a bulldozer drove by, grabbed her furniture and put it into a garbage truck. Next, the bulldozer returned and destroyed her shelter.

As a result of being without shelter and sleeping on the street in November and December, Soto contracted pneumonia. During this time, several homeless women died in the area.

Chris Schneider, executive director of the CCLS, said, "My hope is that the settlement represents the city recognizing that the *Kincaid v. City of Fresno* case made clear that all residents of Fresno, including the homeless, have constitutional rights, and that if those rights are violated, there will be consequences.

"The city clearly hoped to wear down the plaintiffs and their attorneys through tens of thousands of pages of documents, discovery demands, hundreds of hours of depositions and the passage of time. The city wanted to send a message that it is futile for homeless residents to insist on their rights and to demand dignity. They were unsuccessful in that."

Homeless people harmed by the city's bulldozing of the encampments that I talked to said they would use the money to get an apartment, a couple of them will use the money to continue their education and several of them will buy used cars so they can get back and forth to work.

By mutual agreement, both the homeless plaintiffs and the City of Fresno decided not to disclose the amount of the settlement. Most likely they had different motives for their decision. Maybe City Hall did not want taxpayers to know how much of their money was spent to resolve this lawsuit alleging that the City of Fresno took and immediately destroyed homeless people's property. On the other hand, because these were individual lawsuits, it is a reasonable assumption to make that homeless individuals did not want everyone to know how much money they received. Being homeless and having just received a financial settlement in a lawsuit might make you a target.

The city's defense of its actions largely consisted of claims that everything destroyed was trash. Attorney James Betts, who represented the city in this case, attended the 2011 demolitions and inspected many of the shelters before they were destroyed. In video of these "cleanups," city workers can often be heard saying that homeless people's property was trash and smelled of urine or feces. City video also documented the destruction of Soto's property.

The definition of what property is of value and what is trash was a critical factor in the recently settled lawsuit. The Kincaid decision mandated that the city save any property found during these "cleanups" and store it for 90 days. Was the city's uncertainty about its ability to convince a jury that Soto's furniture was trash a factor in its willingness to settle? To prevail, the city would have had to convince juries in 30-plus trials that no property of any value was destroyed. That is a pretty high bar to clear.

I asked Schneider if there were any surprises in this lawsuit. He said, "I was shocked to find that a number of the city officials believe that the Poverello House, is 'part of the problem' of homelessness in Fresno. They basically view the Pov as a magnate for the homeless and think that if the Pov was closed the homeless would magically disappear.

"I was also surprised to find out how adamantly opposed they are to even consider any idea about addressing homelessness other than Mayor [Ashley] Swearengin's First Steps Home program. It seems that city and Housing Authority officials both have an inability to recognize that the Housing First approach at its present pace can only help a few dozen individuals per year or they know its limitations and just don't care about the thousands of people who will continue to be on the streets for decades."

Paul Alexander is senior counsel with Arnold & Porter and the lead attorney representing the homeless. I asked him the same question. He said, "There were two surprises for most of us on the legal team. The first of these centered on the Renaissance at Santa Clara. This is a project developed by Penstar Corporation and its executives basically using federal money. It houses only 69 homeless residents, but the total cost of this project exceeded $11,000,000. What's more, of this enormous amount, the Penstar Corporation took $1,000,000 off the top in a 'consulting fee.'

"It isn't hard to imagine how much good could really be done for this enormous expenditure of federal money and how little was actually done. Maybe we shouldn't have been surprised. The rich do get richer.

"Second, some of us were surprised that the City of Fresno's executives testified that making some provision, however small, for the homeless is 'not our job.' The city leaves this to others, such as the Penstar executives, while turning its back on far less expensive and more meaningful alternatives such as the Eco-Village concept.

"What this means is that, for the most part, the city provides no sanitation facilities, no garbage pickup, no fresh water, not even a porta-potty, much less any shelter, for any of its homeless residents. All this does is make the problem worse. Then the City spends large sums, including sanitation department overtime, police supervision, extra heavy machinery and the like, to destroy homeless encampments.

"Fresno can do better, spend less and over time have a positive impact in reducing homelessness and its impact on the community. This should be the job of city government."

It is probably not a coincidence that Penstar CEO Tom Richard was a big contributor to Swearengin's campaign for state controller, giving $6,800 in 2014. Other Penstar executives made significant contributions to Swearengin's run for mayor in 2012.

The mayor's Housing First program, which is intended to benefit the homeless, ends up enriching wealthy developers and, not surprisingly, some of that money ends up back in Swearengin's campaign accounts. It is a small world after all.

Alexander says the legal team has "learned what we always knew—that litigation is long, difficult and expensive for all concerned. The city was well represented and fought hard. In the end, the city was wise to settle. We would all be better off if this process did not repeat itself. We don't get paid for bringing this litigation. We do it only when we feel it is absolutely necessary. Who knows—maybe everyone involved can learn some lessons for the future. Hope springs eternal."

Schneider said, "I would hope that city officials have this time actually learned a lesson and will pursue a proactive approach to addressing homelessness. Such an approach would cost the city a lot less both financially and morally. The city needs to realize that there are plenty of people and organizations in the community ready to work together to find collaborative solutions. We would much prefer that over further lawsuits."

The three years of litigation in the homeless lawsuit cost the city more than $865,000. That does not include the money paid to homeless people to settle the case. The cost for taking and storing homeless people's property from October 2011 to November of 2014 was $525,000. The amount spent on the FPD Homeless Task Force for fiscal 2015 is projected to be $192,000.

When City of Fresno officials tell you that they don't have any money to address homeless issues, that is not exactly true. They have money to spend on the things they are interested in—like bulldozing encampments, issuing citations and hauling homeless people's property off. It is the things that would actually improve homeless people's lives—like drinking water, portable toilets and trash bins—that they don't have money for.

Homeless people cried out in anguish as their property was being destroyed by city crews during the destruction of a downtown homeless encampment. Lawsuits were filed alleging that the City of Fresno took and immediately destroyed homeless people's property during the October–November 2011 action.

# Chapter 18

# What Is Motivating the City of Fresno?

To understand the forces that are at work in determining public policy on homeless issues, you have to both "follow the money" and look at the philosophical beliefs of the right-wing ruling elite in this community.

You start with the premise that the pathetic stream of money made available from the federal government is not enough to end homelessness. Most of the resources available come through HUD, but there are just enough grants available to put a Band-Aid on the problem and create the illusion that something is being done to address the issue.

The limited resources made available through the federal government push local governments to support one approach after another. Sometimes they focus on veterans. Sometimes the focus is on youth or families. As of late 2015, most resources were going into Housing First projects, which seek to find a place for the chronically (most visible) homeless to live. Therefore, what little money there is to address homelessness comes to Fresno through HUD, which distributes the money into projects that are consistent with the Housing First approach.

Cities seeking federal dollars are encouraged to develop a 10-Year Plan to End Chronic Homelessness, count the homeless every two years and establish a Continuum of Care organization to coordinate the work. The City of Fresno does not get money from the federal government to provide temporary shelter, portable toilets, trash bins or drinking water, so that does not happen.

Representatives of the federal government sometimes encourage local entities, such as the City of Fresno, to destroy homeless encampments. They do this by making it clear that federal dollars will be available for Housing First and similar projects but not for providing public services to the homeless encampments. Barbara Poppe, executive director of the U.S. Interagency Council on Homelessness, said during the 2011 demolition of homeless encampments that "I applaud the City and its partners for focusing on the Housing First approach to addressing this issue and getting the public, private and nonprofit sectors aligned to provide services and housing to the men and women living in the encampments." In a press release sent out by the City of Fresno, Poppe went on to say that "the City and its partners have shown true leadership in energizing the community to respond in a way that is compassionate to individual needs and also makes sense for the greater community."

The City of Fresno and the Fresno Housing Authority, which works with HUD on distributing federal money to address homelessness, can de-code what Poppe is saying and have positioned themselves to receive as many federal dollars as possible. Our local government officials know that there are not enough federal, state or county resources to end homelessness, but they are willing to do whatever is necessary, even if it means bulldozing and destroying homeless people's property, to get that HUD funding.

There is also a philosophical and, in some cases, religious motivation that drives homeless policy in the City of Fresno. I'm convinced that since becoming mayor in January 2009 Ashley Swearengin is the driving force behind this right-wing/conservative culture of death and destruction. I think her own words as she gazed upon the bare ground of her scorched-earth policy that destroyed homeless encampments in November 2011 says it best. According to an e-mail from her deputy chief of staff, Kelli Furtado (to Assistant City Manager Bruce Rudd and Homeless Czar Greg Barfield), she said, "It looks amazing, Wow, Wow, Wowzers."

Swearengin worked through the city manager, the chief of police and other department managers to destroy the encampments. The demolitions would not and could not have happened without her enthusiastic leadership.

After the demolition of homeless encampments in downtown Fresno in October–November of 2011, city crews returned to take not only what little the homeless had left but also stacks of firewood—the only thing the homeless had left to keep themselves warm. That happened 10 days before Christmas! If Mayor Swearengin isn't the grinch who stole Christmas, she sure is giving the grinch a run for his bragging rights.

I was intrigued when I heard City Council Member Sal Quintero (on the same day and about at the same time when the attack described above took place) say that he was going to vote for an ordinance banning the homeless from sleeping on sidewalks because he agreed with the tough love message it sends to those who are down and out. City Council Member Oliver Baines yelled at homeless advocates at that meeting because he said the ordinance was actually targeting Occupy Fresno, but that is another story.

Some friends and I started dissecting the "tough love" approach the city has implemented on the homeless, and we came to the conclusion that it explains a lot. One of my friends put it this way: "I think the right-wing logic goes something like this: To help the poor, the best thing to do is punish them until they are not poor because punishment builds the character they need to be not poor, or in this case homeless. In addition, to give the poor assistance compromises their motivation to change their situation because it creates dependence on other people rather than promoting independence. So if I'm following this logic correctly, destroying the property of the homeless, over and over again, and chasing them all over the streets is the right's way of trying to help them."

I think my friend nailed it. The policy makers at the City of Fresno, whether they are articulating it this way or not, believe they are being cruel to be kind. Another friend added: "It's known as 'prosperity theology,' a relatively recent phenomenon in American Christianity. In short, riches are the result of piety; lack of riches stems from lack of faith; so to offer assistance to the poor is to 'reward' their lack of faith. Helping them equates to opposing God's will. While the civil servants in question might not be adherents, they work in an institution led by those who are. Those at the top set the tone or culture of our city government."

How else can you explain the heartless and cruel policy of taking poor people's shelters, waking them up in the middle of the night and chasing them off of public sidewalks, and then stealing the last stick of wood they have to keep themselves warm?

The other explanation, of course, is that this is all about the money. City elected officials carry out these attacks against the homeless so they can maximize the federal dollars they are entitled to receive. That money allows them to get rid of some of the most visible manifestations of homelessness, like the encampments, but does nothing to end homelessness. Swearengin has even figured out a way to spin Housing First to the media to make the public believe there are fewer homeless in Fresno, enrich her developer friends and have some of that money end up as campaign contributions in support of her political ambitions.

This is what Swearengin and her political allies were able to accomplish with the opening of their premier Housing First project, the Renaissance at Santa Clara.

I went to the grand opening of the Renaissance at Santa Clara in November 2012. The $11 million project was built to provide 69 units (340 square feet each) to help end homelessness in Fresno. If you do the math, that is more than $159,000 per unit. Although the units are a little bigger than the tool sheds for the homeless located at the Poverello House, they are a lot more expensive.

Opening the Renaissance created the illusion that progress is being made to end homelessness, while leaving the overwhelming majority of homeless people still on the streets. I was struck by this realization at the grand opening. Hundreds of homeless people were outside on Santa Clara Street, in the cold, while the "dignitaries" and "city leaders" were patting themselves on the back and congratulating each other for a job well done. While awards were handed out under a heated canopy, the homeless simply stood on the other side of the barbed wire uninvited to the celebration.

I was also unfavorably impressed with the massive video surveillance presence. I counted 40 cameras that monitor the outside, every entrance and the hallway in the complex. The Renaissance looks more like a minimum-security prison than a home for traumatized individuals who are trying to overcome their difficult circumstances. These cameras raise significant civil liberties and privacy issues for the residents of this complex.

As the "love fest" among the politicians, developers and the well-connected Fresno elite was taking place, I kept thinking to myself, "Why did they spend $11 million to get a mere 69 people off the streets." I asked Barfield, the city's homeless czar, what was next. Because Barfield and other city representatives say that projects like this are their solution to ending homelessness, I expected more of an answer than I got. Both Barfield and a representative from the Fresno Housing Authority told me that they had no future plans to construct housing to help the homeless. Nothing. Zip. Nada.

Preston Prince, director at the Fresno Housing Authority, met with me after the grand opening, telling me about his credentials as a leading advocate for the poor and affordable housing. He sincerely believes that he is taking the moral high ground on the homeless issue.

One revelation that caught my eye in the financial information he gave me was that the Penstar Group was awarded the contract to build the Renaissance at Santa Clara project. Tom Richards is chairperson and CEO of the Penstar Group, a Fresno-based development company. Richards was also the chairperson of the committee to develop the 10-Year Plan to End Chronic Homelessness and is the chairperson of Fresno First Steps Home. The Penstar Group was awarded $1 million as the consultant on the Renaissance at Santa Clara project.

I'm impressed that the ruling elite in Fresno has figured out how to create the illusion that it is ending homelessness, while at the same time enriching political allies who use the same money to further the career of Republican Mayor Swearengin as she aspires to higher political office. The hutzpah, if not downright corruption, is breathtaking.

For years, city officials have been relentlessly demonizing the homeless as being criminals, dangerous, dirty and something that we need to eliminate. The homeless, as a result, are probably the most vilified minority in this community. They are a scapegoat that many people fear, some hate and others are confused about (even though they might be one or two paychecks from homelessness themselves). City spokespersons and other right-wing demagogues blame the homeless for causing their own misery. We are told they are all drug addicts, mentally ill and not to give them any money (because it only encourages their deviant behavior).

When the ruling elite, corporate media and dominant ideology converge to present a group of people like the homeless as being the enemy, then watching the bulldozing of their shelters becomes acceptable. Can you think of another time in history when other groups of people were singled out for us to fear and hate?

When the power elite can manipulate our minds with its propaganda, history has shown that people will allow the police and military to do what is necessary to get rid of the problem. Somehow it made sense that Jews, homosexuals and Gypsies were vilified, their property confiscated and that they disappeared into concentration camps.

Ask yourself—what would you do if the government was bulldozing Fresno's African-American community because it said those neighborhoods were unsafe and crime was taking place? What if the government did that to a Jewish neighborhood? Is it somehow OK to do this because the people under attack and being persecuted in Fresno today are poor, destitute, powerless and homeless? I believe that the homeless are our version of the canary in the coal mine. In other words, watch closely what happens to the homeless because our future is tied to their fate.

One might ask how the "good Germans" in the 1930s and 1940s could have allowed or encouraged the Nazis to carry out their horrendous crimes against humanity? All it takes is for good people to do nothing and allow the culture of death to roll over the weak and powerless. After all, City Hall is not coming after you (yet). And, certainly, someone would speak out if you became City Hall's next target because you are Muslim, a union member or gay. Right? I'm reminded of the famous quote by German pastor and theologian Martin Niemöller, which is as follows:

> First they came for the communists, and I didn't speak out because I wasn't a communist.
> Then they came for the socialists, and I didn't speak out because I wasn't a socialist.
> Then they came for the trade unionists, and I didn't speak out because I wasn't a trade unionist.
> Then they came for me, and there was no one left to speak for me.

There is an alternative. What the City of Fresno should be doing is not really that complicated. First, the city should not be bulldozing homeless encampments and destroying homeless people's property. First rule—do no harm. Within a week, the homeless should be provided with basic public services, which would improve their lives—drinking water, portable toilets and trash bins should be set up. Within a month, unused vacant lots (owned by the city, county or individuals) could be established as safe and legal homeless encampments. That would remove the homeless people from living on the street, sometimes in front of homes in a residential neighborhood. Phase III, which is a longer-term project, is to get every homeless person in the city into affordable and decent housing. Housing should be a human right.

With these short-, medium- and long-term goals, our community can help improve the lives of the homeless rather than making their already difficult lives even harder. Of course, some of the homeless need job training, mental health assistance or help to end addictions to drugs and alcohol. Everyone who is living on the streets of Fresno can live a better life than they are now if we come together as a community and help them, just like they were our brothers and sisters, which they are.

Of course, Mayor Swearengin sees it differently. In sworn testimony for a deposition on the lawsuit against the City of Fresno, which alleged that city workers took and immediately destroyed homeless people's property in October and November of 2011, Swearengin gave her narrative about what drives homeless policy.

According to Swearengin, there were several factors that motivated the city to clear out the encampments in 2011 and to stop any new encampments from emerging. The biggest factor driving city policy, according to her testimony, was the belief that the homeless encampments were not good for the people living in them, for the residents living nearby or for the surrounding businesses.

Swearengin said that the city believed it could help most of the homeless people living in those encampments into transitional housing using new streams of revenue coming from private, state and federal sources. Other motivating factors to destroy the encampments, again according to the mayor's testimony in this deposition:

- They were being encouraged by the federal government to put a stop to homeless encampments.
- This was part of the 10-Year Plan to End Chronic Homelessness.
- She believed that most of the homeless would get vouchers and be put into housing.
- Construction projects are planned for the area.

Commenting in the deposition about the influence of the federal government on city policy, Mayor Swearengin said that "Philip Mangano served in that capacity (former national homeless policy czar) under President Bush and directed the development of the 10-year plan to address chronic homelessness with the input from the City of Fresno and the County Board. His advice at that time, and I'm relaying what I've heard from city staff, I wasn't directly involved, was that encampments are not good for the people who live in the encampments, and that as a community, we should aim higher."

She continued, saying that "Barbara Poppe (who is with the U.S. Interagency Council on Homelessness) has provided that same input to the City of Fresno, to me directly, and has on several different occasions encouraged us to keep pushing for housing instead of allowing camping to be the approach for addressing homelessness."

She cited the Renaissance housing project, with 120 new units for the homeless, as evidence that more housing for the homeless was available. She also said that the city was starting to shift money from low-income housing to housing for the homeless.

Swearengin said that the city would save money in the long run by getting the homeless into transitional and then permanent housing. This is a foundational assumption of those supporting the Housing First model.

The attorney representing the homeless asked the mayor, "Now, was the construction, destruction [and] demolition of the Monterey Street bridge, was that a reason at all for the removal of the homeless shelters in 2011?"

Swearengin replied, "It was a concern raised by staff and certainly factored in. So my experience beginning in 2009 that I have already relayed that led to my overall belief that we need to seek housing instead of encampments, as I was pursuing that and directing that policy approach, city staff raised the issue about there is a public works project that is in this area that is also going to require that the encampment area be cleared. So that factored into my overall assessment of the situation. I knew that at some point the bridge would come down."

She was convinced that homeless people were not having their rights violated when the "cleanups" occurred in 2011 because she had confidence in her staff. When homeless advocate Bill Simon sent the mayor an e-mail telling her about the violations taking place, she did not investigate. When the ACLU sent a letter expressing concern, she claimed to have never received it.

The mayor stated Simon's e-mail did not raise any concerns "because of the reports I had received about the care and the diligence that was being taken by city crews and overseen by our legal counsel and videotaped by people onsite that things were in fact being handled properly and that personal property was being stored." In other words, because her staff said everything was OK, she believed that no human rights violations were taking place.

I include Mayor Swearengin's narrative not because I agree with it but because it is important to understand how other people view things.

Fresno Mayor Ashley Swearengin and Fresno County Supervisor Henry R. Perea cut the ribbon at the grand opening of the Renaissance at Santa Clara.

Fresno Mayor Ashley Swearengin and developer Tom Richards sat together at the grand opening of the Renaissance at Santa Clara. Richards' company, Penstar, made $1 million in consulting fees to build this facility. Richards and several other top executives at Penstar have given generously to Swearengin's electoral campaigns (for mayor and state controller).

On the day the Renaissance at Santa Clara had its grand opening, there was a barbed-wire fence outside to keep the homeless from entering the facility. The grand opening was for invited guests, dignitaries and the media.

National Homeless Policy Czar Philip Mangano joined newly elected Fresno Mayor Ashley Swearengin at a press conference in January 2009 to talk about the Housing First project.

# Chapter 19

# A New Homeless Policy Emerges in Fresno

A new City of Fresno policy on the homeless started to emerge in the summer of 2013 when new notices went up notifying the homeless that "cleanups" would take place. Although the endless game of "whack a mole" had gone on for a decade, things were different this time. The FPD formed the special Homeless Task Force to focus on keeping the homeless from developing any new encampments.

There was a zero tolerance policy following the next round of evictions that the police enforced. The new policy would allow the homeless to set up a sleeping bag or a tent as it got dark, but the police made sure they were gone by the early morning.

The FPD's Homeless Task Force started writing citations for homeless people for having their property in what they considered to be a disorganized fashion. The citations claimed homeless people were littering or had left rubbish on the street. Homeless people said they were being given citations for sitting on a curb next to their property.

Another phenomenon that started to happen after the "cleanups" in mid-2013 was that when the FPD's Homeless Task Force found a shopping cart (or other container) with a homeless person's property, it called the city sanitation department. The sanitation workers would drive a flatbed truck to the site, load up the property and haul it away. The property would be stored for 90 days. A written notice would be posted on a wall near where the property was taken, informing homeless people where they could call to make an appointment to reclaim their property.

Many shopping carts were taken when homeless people were in the Poverello

House getting something to eat or taking a shower. Because they had no permanent encampment where they could leave their property and the Poverello House would not allow them to bring shopping carts into the facility, they were left outside the gate. It did not take long for most homeless people to lose their property. Yes, they could go through the process to reclaim it, but not everyone had a phone to make the call, wait for the call back and set up an appointment. Besides, even if you did get your property back, where could you put it so that it would not get taken again? There was no safe place for homeless people to put their property.

The new policy forced many homeless people to move away from the Poverello House. Some moved onto the Fulton Mall and other downtown locations. Many more moved north and east into other parts of town, increasing the visibility of the homeless as they wandered the streets of Fresno. For those who stayed near the Poverello House, it was a challenge to always be on the move and to never take your eyes off your property.

In addition to preventing any new encampments from emerging, the FPD's Homeless Task Force was expanding its zone of influence and destroying any remaining homeless encampments that were outside of the downtown area. In a PowerPoint presentation produced by the FPD's Homeless Task Force in early 2014, it boasted of having removed 1,640 shopping carts, issuing 265 citations and clearing 333 new homeless encampments.

This new policy resulted in many homeless people moving to north Fresno. William Lewis and his friend Lori Bryson, who are homeless, found themselves living in the Herndon Avenue and Blackstone Avenue area during this time. Lewis called me to complain of police harassment, saying they had been arrested and taken downtown for allegedly "blocking a sidewalk and trespassing." Lewis told me that the officer who threatened him with arrest issued a citation and took him and Lori to the downtown police department for processing.

"Officer Lee threatened to take our two dogs from us if he sees us anywhere north of the Poverello House," Lewis said. He claims Officer Lee told him "that if I'm north of the Poverello House and see him coming for Lori and I to empty our pockets, put our hands behind our backs and to consider ourselves under arrest." Lewis said he was having a hard time sleeping from all the stress.

Another example of the problems encountered when homeless people are forced out of downtown and end up in other parts of the city is what happened in July 2013 when an encampment emerged on a ditch bank near Ashlan and West avenues in northwest Fresno. When I arrived, the Fresno Irrigation District (FID) was in the middle of destroying the encampment and everybody's property.

Most of the structures had already been pulled out of the protective shrubbery on the southwest side of the canal bank. A bulldozer was busy picking up homeless people's property and putting it in a dump truck.

I asked Murray, who said he was a supervisor for the FID, if they were saving any of the property. He said they had not found anything of value yet, but my question got him thinking about the implications of their actions. Murray said that notices had been put up informing the homeless people that there was going to be a "cleanup." I asked for a copy of the notice, and he said he didn't have one.

I walked away for a moment to take some photos, and when I came back the driver of the machine with the large claw said, "We don't have time for this shit. Call the police."

Someone (probably Murray) must have convinced the crew that they better make a show for the press because then they started going through the shopping carts and putting things aside, which they said they were going to save.

Another example of how the new City of Fresno policy on the homeless is playing out for the homeless people it affects is illustrated by Kate's story. I met Kate (not her real name) in early 2014. Kate is a retirement age homeless woman with breast cancer who until recently lived in a tool shed at the Poverello House. She was evicted from her tool shed in the Village of Hope, she says, because she came back late from the hospital, where she was receiving treatment for her medical condition.

"I'm going through Stage 3 breast cancer treatment, and with that I get nose bleeds, so I decided on Saturday I would take care of my chores before I left for the hospital. I was worried because I could not get the bleeding to stop. I walked to Community Hospital, but because of flu season there were 100 people there and it was a 12-hour wait to be checked," Kate said.

When Kate returned, she was told that she was being evicted from her tool shed for not following the rules. She ended up on the streets outside the Poverello House and Rescue Mission with her clothes and little else.

Kate was given a tent by a friend and set it up on Santa Clara Street, in front of the Poverello House. Since the demolition of the homeless encampments in 2013, the police do not allow anyone to keep their tent up during the day. Kate put her tent up at night and in the morning went into the Poverello House to use the restroom. When she returned, an FPD officer was in the process of having her property removed.

She told the officer it was her property and that she wanted it back. "He told me I could have it if I asked him nicely. I told him that I'm not going to beg you for my stuff. If you are going to take it, just give me the address and I will be fine." Kate said the officer asked if she was just going to let him take it away and "I said, but what else can I do? I'm not going to beg you. It is embarrassing enough (to be living on the streets). I think he was getting some kind of enjoyment out of the whole thing."

Kate eventually got her property back, but this incident illustrates what is happening all over downtown, as the City of Fresno continues to crack down on the homeless. Bob (not his real name), a homeless man sitting on the curb on Santa Clara Street in mid-March of 2014, told me that the police come by several times a day taking people's property and handing out citations.

"The other day a friend of mine was sitting over there, and the police wrote him a citation for having his property with him. They said his property was trash and it was littering the street," Bob said. Bob told me that people were being given citations for crossing the street and throwing a cigarette butt on the road. "Some of my friends have 10–15 citations. Nobody is paying them. It is just a waste of time and resources!"

Kate said, "I'm wondering how long the judges are going to take up all of this time, because these people are homeless. They don't have any money. These tickets range from $100 to $500. The officers don't care; they just keep writing them. To me, it is like harassment. It is a waste of taxpayer money."

On March 6, 2014, the Fresno City Council passed an ordinance that makes it easier for the police to remove shopping carts from the homeless. This follows ordinances to stop the homeless from using median islands to ask for money and another one that prevents the homeless from aggressive panhandling.

These "quality-of-life" ordinances are having an impact as the homeless experience more pressure to be constantly on the move and never have a place to stay that is safe and legal. As we were saying goodbye, following the interview, Kate broke down and cried, saying that the stress of living on the street, the insecurity of having to always be on the move and worry about whether her tent and sleeping bag would be taken away have led her to stop the cancer treatments at the hospital. The level of stress was too high for her to continue. Without treatment, Kate will probably not survive for long.

The mayor and City Council members say they want an end to homelessness, they want to revitalize downtown and they are willing to put the resources necessary into making this happen. Kate's experience makes the argument that there is a human cost to eliminating the homeless and gentrifying downtown so builders, developers and businesspeople can make money. That cup of coffee the urban hipster drinks as he or she watches cars drive down the newly redesigned Fulton Street will be built on the foundation of Kate and other homeless people's lives.

In an above-the-fold front-page story in the *Fresno Bee* on November 16, 2014, city officials were congratulated for a significant drop in homelessness in Fresno. The article claimed that the number of homeless people in Fresno and Madera counties "fell nearly 40% in the past four years." There was a similar story in the November 29, 2015, *Fresno Bee*.

The propaganda and lies never stop.

What are *Fresno Bee* readers to think when on September 11, 2014, it was reported that there were 6,738 homeless students in Fresno County and then on November 16, 2014, reporter George Hostetter claimed that the homeless population in all of Fresno and Madera counties is only 2,592?

The Hostetter front-page story went on to praise efforts by local government officials to end homelessness and quoted them about what a good job they were doing. As soon as the self-congratulation is over, I hope our elected officials will ask staff if the recent HUD count, citing the 2,592 number, was accurate.

Everyone involved in the HUD count of the homeless knows that it is inaccurate. The reason it is not accurate is that homeless people are really hard to find, especially now that the homeless encampments in downtown Fresno all have been destroyed. They obviously did not count the homeless students. The methodology of the count guarantees that it is, year after year, inaccurate.

The only way to end homelessness is to have the political will and resources to get the job done. The *Fresno Bee*'s reporting of inaccurate homeless counts that make local government officials look good is not helping.

My experience has been that the *Fresno Bee* and most of the mainstream media will give Mayor Swearengin a free ride on the homeless issue. That is why it is essential to support alternative/independent media such as the *Community Alliance* newspaper and KFCF 88.1 FM, which offer a more accurate and critical perspective about what is going on with homeless people in this area.

Homeless people in downtown Fresno are kept on the move, and if they leave their property (even briefly) it will probably be taken and put into storage. After 90 days, if it is not reclaimed, it is destroyed.

This is where hope goes to die. Homeless people's property is brought to this lot on H Street in downtown Fresno. Most property is destroyed after 90 days because nobody can keep all of their property with them 24 hours a day, seven days a week. If a homeless person in downtown Fresno takes his/her eyes off of his/her property for a couple of minutes, it is taken away.

When the police see any "abandoned" homeless property in downtown Fresno, they call the sanitation department, which brings out a flatbed truck, loads up the property and hauls it off.

When the homeless move to north Fresno, they continue to be harassed by the police. Lori Bryson and William Lewis were living at Blackstone and Herndon avenues when they were taken downtown by a police officer. Lewis said he was told "that if I'm north of the Poverello House and see him coming for Lori and I to empty our pockets, put our hands behind our backs and to consider ourselves under arrest."

Chris Breedlove spoke at this press conference to denounce the City of Fresno's ongoing attacks against the homeless.

Amid the destruction on Santa Clara Street (August 21, 2013), as the city bulldozed another homeless encampment, this woman emerged out of the dust.

This group of workers from the Fresno Irrigation District destroyed a small homeless encampment on a canal bank near West and Ashlan avenues in north central Fresno.

City workers are telling this homeless woman to leave, shortly before her shelter was destroyed.

# Chapter 20

# What Have We Learned and Where Are We Headed?

The best answer to what we have learned about homelessness in Fresno and where we are headed is best discovered by listening to the collective voices of those involved. I will attempt to answer this question from my perspective and then turn to homeless advocates and homeless people for their insights.

It seems painfully obvious to me that the current approach to ending homelessness in Fresno and around the country is not working. The core problem is that there are deep political and economic forces in motion that are the cause of homelessness. There are policy decisions that have been made at the highest level of government that have prioritized funding for the military and reduced resources for public and affordable housing to the point that homelessness is the inevitable result.

There is no political will at any level of government (local to federal) to do anything other than create a system that responds to homelessness with shelters and programs that focus on one subgroup of homeless people and then another. This constant activity provides cover for the social service providers and government officials involved by creating the illusion that the problem is being addressed and things will get better if we just follow the course set by the experts.

Social service providers in Fresno get millions of dollars in funding and local elected officials always have something to point to that illustrates they are addressing the problem, but the homeless always find themselves with the short end of the stick. Make no mistake—the social service providers and City Hall can dazzle you with their 10-year plans, big buildings and stories about individuals who have risen from homelessness, but at the end of the day homelessness in Fresno has not ended. Why? Because the political will and resources to end homelessness simply are not being used to solve the problem.

In my opinion, the City of Fresno could do a lot more, but it cannot end homelessness on its own. Although the City of Fresno certainly could do a better job of handling the situation, without more resources, there is only so much that can be done.

On the other hand, if you follow the Housing First logic, you do have to wonder why the city doesn't do more. Even if all you cared about was the money (and not the lives of the people involved), you might appreciate the argument that local government would save money by housing the homeless. On the Fresno First Steps Home Web site (Mayor Swearengin is on its Board of Directors and basically created this organization), the content goes on about how much money could be saved on emergency medical services, police and social services if homeless people were given housing. Why would they put that information out in public and then not follow through?

There has to be something more going on here. If City Hall really could house all of the homeless and save millions of dollars a year doing it, why wouldn't they do that? Why spend limited General Fund dollars issuing homeless people citations, storing their property, bulldozing encampments, passing ordinances criminalizing poverty and suffering through endless lawsuits if you really could end homelessness? It really doesn't make any sense.

There are multiple explanations for the disconnect between City Hall's rhetoric about Housing First and the reality of its public policy. Starting with the obvious—the resources coming from the federal government are not enough to build the public and affordable housing units needed to end homelessness. City Hall does not have the money to build thousands of units of low-income housing on its own, and it has not figured out a way to utilize the potential savings in housing the homeless and put that money into Housing First. In the meantime, the city is able to get money for the police and the county pays for indigent medical care.

Another reason for this disconnect between rhetoric and public policy is that most homeless people don't vote or make major political contributions to elected officials. Therefore, they have little political power or leverage to encourage City Hall to come up with a plan to house the homeless.

Builders and developers have figured out a way to make money building low-income housing like the Renaissance at Santa Clara so they are not anxious to change business as usual. Social service organizations get grants and other funding because of the current system so they have a financial incentive to maintain the status quo. Many of these organizations would go out of business if all of the homeless had housing. These people vote and contribute to political campaigns.

All of these economic and political factors are intertwined with the dominant ideology that views homeless people as somehow being responsible for their situation. Never mind the fact that the system has created the conditions that makes homelessness inevitable, the people at City Hall like to blame the victim. Homeless people have become a scapegoat for society's problems, and they are told that they need to get into a drug, alcohol or mental health program and save their soul, preferably in a Christian church. As long as homelessness is looked at as a personal problem, we are not going to end homelessness.

If we continue down the path that we are currently on, we will see more of the same. We will be told that things are getting better when we know that they are not. The police will be used to issue more citations to the homeless, new ordinances attacking the homeless will be passed by the City Council, homeless people will die on the streets from both the heat and cold and the level of homelessness will remain more or less the same.

But another world is possible. Every religious and faith-based group in Fresno could have an epiphany that homeless people are their sisters and brothers. Churches, mosques and synagogues could open their doors and house the homeless. There are more than enough religious institutions to take in all of the homeless if they had the will and vision to do so.

Individuals and groups could set up more housing for the homeless like what has been done at the Dakota EcoGarden. Faith-based groups, individuals and groups could come together and make a huge difference. But that would not be enough. We need to involve city, state and federal governments in the solution.

Within a week, a march of the homeless, the dispossessed and their allies should head toward Fresno City Hall. The 100,000-plus marchers would illustrate to the nation and the world that people really do care and want to end homelessness. This would inspire millions to join in the biggest movement for human rights this country has ever seen.

This movement will demand the federal government provide the resources to rebuild the public and low-income housing needed to end homelessness. They will also demand job training, educational opportunities, resources for mental health departments to provide the services needed and drug and alcohol programs for everyone who needs them so that everyone in this country has the tools needed to improve their lives.

The productivity of the people, when given the resources they need to succeed, will bring this nation back to the greatness that it can achieve. And that is how we are going to end homelessness.

An alternative, less ambitious approach, was detailed in Chapter 14, "Alternatives to the Dominant Paradigm." This approach would greatly improve the quality of life for many of the homeless in Fresno who are sleeping outside every day by establishing safe and legal places to live that include public services such as drinking water, trash bins and portable toilets. If City Hall did that, rescinded "quality-of-life" ordinances targeting the homeless and ramped up access to affordable housing, we would at least be moving in the right direction.

There are other ways to get from where we are today to where you would have to visit a museum to see what homelessness was about, so let's see what some of the other activists and homeless people in this community think of the current City of Fresno policy and what we should do to end homelessness. All of these interviews were conducted in December 2014 in person, by e-mail or by phone.

**Larry Collins**
Larry Collins was homeless but is now living in the Renaissance at Santa Clara, which is the $11 million transitional housing complex across the street from the Poverello House.

Rhodes: What have we learned over the last decade about what it is like to be homeless in Fresno?

Collins: I know I have learned that there are more homeless people. I think it has like tripled compared to 10 years ago, and the age group is a lot younger. There are a lot of young kids out here 18 or 19 years old. In my experience, being homeless was not that nice. You have to live out in all the elements and try to get to sleep, keep heathy and eat right. It's not good from that point, but you have to do it to survive. It's all about survival. It's like living in the jungle, you just have to survive and take it one day at a time. Can't make no promises, can't make no plans. If you don't have a phone or an address, you're really lost. If you don't have a phone, you can't get in touch with anybody, and nobody can get in touch with you. You never know when the city is going to move you around. You might be at one place, and you tell your family you're in one place, and then you get moved and they can't find you.

Rhodes: What is the City of Fresno's current policy on the homeless?

Collins: Nothing, to be honest with you. The city's not doing a thing except waking them up in the morning and harassing them. You know they give homeless people citations? How are they going to pay it, and how are you going to get a letter in the mail with the court date? It's awful. It's crazy. I was talking to one guy who said he has about five citations and said he ain't paying them. Homeless people can't pay them. The city is just wasting their tax dollars.

Rhodes: Have the policies of the City of Fresno helped or hurt the homeless?

Collins: I can't see any helping. It is not the city helping the homeless, it's the County of Fresno that has offered the apartments and stuff. The city's only thing is controlling the homeless. Out there, cleaning up and harassing, the city is not benefitting the homeless. If the homeless want to get some help, it has to be from the county. The city is hurting the homeless by making them move, scattering them out.

I will have to give this to the city because they have started to come out here every day to clean the streets. They don't clean the sidewalks, so I push things onto the street and they have a crew that comes out and cleans up the streets on Santa Clara [Street] every day. This just started about two weeks ago. They have also started sending a street sweeper out here once a week.

Rhodes: If you were in charge of homeless policy in the City of Fresno, what would you do to improve homeless people's lives?

Collins: I would find some property or a building. I'm quite sure the city or the county, if they can come together maybe with some investors, can get some of these great big buildings and renovate and get some staff and security and give people a place to sleep rent free. Rent free. Get them off the streets. They could use the old Fresno Hotel. Fix that up. Look how big that thing is. That is a big building that could fit all of the homeless and have room for some newcomers. It's not far from the Poverello House. They could eat and go back home. I would also create some kind of jobs, clean up or something for each person. Then I would have a staff to help them get their ID and Social Security cards. If you promised them that you would get them a job, you can get an ID and a Social Security card, that would motivate people to do something. Keep homeless people busy, and from there they'll feel good about themselves. It would be like a plane taking off and lifting up.

Rhodes: What would it take to end homelessness in Fresno?

Collins: Jobs. First housing and then jobs. But they've also got to get their ID. I think jobs and housing would be the key to get most people off the street.

\*\*\*

## Chris Breedlove

Pastor Chris Breedlove is with the Community United Church of Christ, Fresno. Pastor Breedlove is the chair of the Faith in Community Board in Fresno County and a community activist focused on human rights, racism, systemic homelessness, income inequality and environmental justice concerns.

Rhodes: What have we learned over the last decade about what it is like to be homeless in Fresno?

Breedlove: Being homeless in Fresno is only one small step from death itself, a cruel death at that. There is a vehement hatred directed at homeless communities and individuals by the city and county Fresno governments. Being homeless in Fresno is akin to being left for dead.

Rhodes: What is the City of Fresno's current policy on the homeless?

Breedlove: Currently, the city is considering ordinances and practices toward homeless communities and individuals that are tantamount to criminalizing homelessness. Fresno has made it illegal to sleep in one spot on consecutive evenings; homeless individuals are forced to constantly and tirelessly be on the move. Fresno has essentially outlawed homeless individuals from forming communities for better protection. Fresno has cracked down on individuals using shopping carts for their belongings. Fresno has looked at over-regulating recycle centers, and such regulation appears to target the homeless specifically.

Rhodes: Have the policies of the City of Fresno helped or hurt the homeless?

Breedlove: Fresno government policies and practices toward the homeless have further endangered the lives of the homeless. As a minister of a church, it's increasingly difficult to minister to and keep up with homeless individuals because of the harsh and senseless policing of homeless that results in the scattering of homeless individuals throughout the city.

Rhodes: If you were in charge of homeless policy in the City of Fresno, what would you do to improve homeless people's lives?

Breedlove: Optional (voluntary) organized camp sites with ample and safe restrooms and showers. There is a severe lack of housing available for the homeless and those on the brink of homelessness. In conversation with an unnamed staff person with the Housing Authority back in September 2013 I learned the following: "We looked into Ms. _____'s application. Her application was received, and she is currently on the preliminary list. As all applicants were informed, the preliminary list (applicant pool) does not mean they have a position on the wait list. As vouchers become available, the system will randomly draw names (lottery) from the preliminary list to establish the actual wait list. This allows for people to apply at any time and have [an] equal chance of getting placed on the wait list as others, regardless of [the] time and date they applied. It also allows us to keep the application process open rather than only for 45 days and closing it for several years as we've done in the past. Since the list was established in July, we have had two system draws totaling 500 applications. It is important that Ms. _____ provides any changes to her contact information should it change from what was provided on the application. I believe we currently have close to 50,000 applicants on the preliminary list. I hope this helps with knowing her status although I know it does not help with her current housing needs."
- I would end ordinances that in effect serve to criminalize homelessness.
- I'd call for a multi-approach with multiple partners to help the homeless instead of an overly simplified and singular approach of "housing first."
- I'd add considerably more mental health and drug treatment subsidized programs.
- I'd increase emergency shelters with more generous condition parameters, for example, current weather temperatures that trigger emergency shelters. Plus, emergency shelters should allow for personal property allowances.

Rhodes: What would it take to end homelessness in Fresno?

Breedlove: To end homelessness in Fresno, Fresno needs to first stop oversimplifying the problem, and Fresno needs to stop generalizing what causes homelessness. Mayor Ashley Swearengin often touts that she has kept the City of Fresno out of bankruptcy, however, Fresno continues to rank second in the United States in rates of poverty. The systems of inequality and structural racism embedded in Fresno need to be dismantled.

I've been struck that many homeless individuals work or attend school. Underemployment and lack of fair wages saddle many homeless individuals with persisting burdens and continuing cycles of homelessness. Many of the homeless are also hurt by lack of healthcare and health services; there are many homeless with severe or terminal illnesses and chronic diseases of addiction.

Individual citizens need to be engaged. Communities of faith need to be involved. But elected officials cannot abdicate their elected responsibility on this issue as well. There needs to be a multifaceted approach for such a problem of immense complexity. Housing First initiatives are one approach, but that alone will not be a total remedy. Advocates have detailed what an organized safe and secure campsite would involve, but such sincere offers of collaboration have been ignored by all City Council members and county Board of Supervisors members to date. The mayor will not attend Catholic summits on homelessness.

The City of Fresno spins a PR narrative that encampments have to be destroyed because fires and crimes are pervasive within their ranks. The city narrative of encampments plays in to the unfair generalization that all homeless persons are criminals and drug addicts, or simply individuals not taking responsibility. The real story is that there are a number of complex reasons for the societal existence of homelessness.

Mayor Swearengin and City Manager Bruce Rudd only exacerbate the lives of homeless by demolishing their communities. Some within the religious fabric of Fresno believe that homeless advocates should collaborate with the city toward solutions. I'm of the mind-set that it's difficult to collaborate with an administration that sends bulldozers and intimidating task forces barreling down on a person that you're trying to help. The City of Fresno first needs to halt harmful and costly policies toward the homeless.

Homelessness for Swearengin is an unsavory obstacle that thwarts her ambitions for a revitalized downtown that caters to corporate commerce and venture capitalists. Swearengin's real homeless policy is to keep the homeless out of sight and out of mind. Otherwise, why would she make hard lives harder?

The city often invokes the promise of housing vouchers. The truth of the matter is much more complicated. In fact, most recently, both the Housing Authority and certain City Council members were unaware of the city's slated destruction of the Grain Silo encampment. Encampment residents also explain how impossibly hard it is to actually receive housing.

The Housing Authority has two lists of persons seeking housing, a waiting list and a preliminary waiting list. The preliminary waiting lists, as of this summer (2014), included over 50,000 names. The actual waiting list is compiled of names pulled out of the preliminary list by a lottery system. It's easily conceivable how individuals lose hope while lost within such a system.

Fresno is spending tens of thousands of dollars destroying the last efforts of vulnerable people trying to survive harsh realities of an overly impoverished region. Fresno is a place where a quarter of its population exists below the national poverty line. The City of Fresno has previously destroyed encampments in both 2005 and 2011. One would think that even fiscal hawks would readily see the foolish management of taxpayers' dollars, nearly a quarter of a million dollars, to destroy encampments. Rather, Fresno needs to work with the homeless and advocates toward safe and legal campgrounds. As the city deploys bulldozers and dump trucks aimed at homeless communities tucked away in the shadows, one is left to ask Swearengin and Rudd, "If not here, where?

\*\*\*

**Melissa Ohler**
Melissa Ohler is currently homeless, and this interview was conducted on F Street near Ventura Street.

Rhodes: What have we learned over the last decade about what it is like to be homeless in Fresno?

Ohler: I've only been homeless for about three years. Before that, recycling was something I did in my kitchen's 10-gallon trash can so my son could buy a treat at the end of the week. I have a very different view of what homelessness is now. I thought the Poverello House was a place people went on Christmas to help people. I never knew people lived like this, and I worked in the hospital for a long time, but I had no clue. Life for homeless people in Fresno is very hard. We have some of our most educated and intelligent people out here. Veterans. It is mind-boggling why people are out here. It can be especially hard when the winter comes and there is rain. The city keeps taking our things and getting them back is hard. You have to work for every little thing, and it makes you realize how much in your life before you took for granted. I will never see a shopping cart in the same way again.

Rhodes: What is the City of Fresno's current policy on the homeless?

Ohler: Their plans are to eradicate the homeless, but just because they want to see an end to homelessness doesn't make us any less homeless. So they set up these policies and procedures that they think will help us. But in reality you can be on all the housing waiting lists that you want. It doesn't put you any place any sooner. I was on the Renaissance waiting list for a year and a half and still never got a call. I could never understand why they didn't help me. Was it because I'm not a veteran, I'm too healthy or I'm not disabled? Over time, you just get discouraged. You just get stuck in the same hamster wheel every day. You do what you need to do to survive that day, but you don't have time to do what is needed for the bigger picture. Those little things, like getting your ID. Because if you did that, you didn't do the work you needed to do to survive and so you can't eat.

Rhodes: Have the policies of the City of Fresno helped or hurt the homeless?

Ohler: The mayor and all of them—I don't know what they're doing up there in their office but we don't see any of them out here. But the police come every morning and every day, and they make life very difficult. They wake you up. Depending on the cops that day, if they're in a bad mood, they will come earlier around 5:30 or 6 a.m. Making us move our things the way they do, we can't go to breakfast. Therefore, we are freaking hungry all day because were trying to move our stuff.

We can't get into the Poverello on time to get the clothing because you have to get in at a certain time to stand in a certain line at a certain time. Same thing for a shower and laundry, but we are out here messing with our stuff and messing with them (the police) so we don't lose our stuff. Because they take our stuff, we have to get more stuff and it just means we get more stuff that they end up taking anyway. We get it all back out, but then they take the shopping carts, which is most people's means of transportation. They (homeless people) get them from stores that are closed down. Shopping carts that are no longer being used by the stores.

It is a vicious cycle that happens every day, and if they are in a really fun mood they make examples out of us and take people to jail because we don't have certain things done at certain times. There will be a bunch of people on the sidewalk with their stuff still hanging on the fence and people that are almost done and have their stuff packed up they just have to move it. The police will take that person to jail.

They just took me to jail because my stuff wasn't moved fast enough. I was at the Fresno County Jail for 15 or 20 minutes while they gave me a citation. It is a waste of taxpayers' dollars, it is a waste of time and it was just to make a point. For them to take me to jail when I'm struggling to do the best I can, it is very discouraging and I think it is a mental physical and emotional tactic against the homeless.

Rhodes: If you were in charge of homeless policy in the City of Fresno, what would you do to improve homeless people's lives?

Ohler: For one thing, I would get, like you guys talked about a long time ago, a huge piece of property from the city. If the city wants they could somewhat regulate it, but for the people that have been out here for a decade or more, they're not going to change by trying to make them. I don't know how to explain it. I would probably get a big piece of land that is within access of the Poverello House and that would be the welfare system. I would give each person a little square piece of the land. I would make it easier for them to get Social Security. I would make jobs more accessible for people who can work. Most people want to work. If full-time jobs were available, people wouldn't even need Social Security so much, if they could work. Because most of these people don't want to live like this. If people had a job, they could probably provide their housing.

Rhodes: What would it take to end homelessness in Fresno?

Ohler: I would say work. Work that might be more individualized to meet a person's needs. If they found people and put them in jobs they could handle, they could take care of themselves and their lives and families. They could provide the rent. Vacant houses could be given to the homeless to watch so they don't get vandalized. There are a lot of vacant houses in Fresno that could be used like this.

\*\*\*

**Edie Jessup**
Edie Jessup, when she lived in Fresno, organized the Coalition with the Homeless in 2012. The coalition formed following a well-attended community forum held at

the Unitarian Universalist Church. Jessup now lives in northern California.

Rhodes: What have we learned over the last decade about what it is like to be homeless in Fresno?

Jessup: Fresno is a hard place to be homeless. There are models throughout the country of successfully reducing the incidence of homelessness. The dilemma is that the attempt in Fresno is to privatize homelessness, criminalize homelessness and people in power buying into myths of who homeless people are. Because of these issues, and the likely misappropriation of public funding from HUD and CDBG funding intended to create a Continuum of Care for the homeless for years, Fresno has failed to address the thousands of homeless individuals, refused to see to their needs and ignored the fact that there really is not a lack of housing. Ignoring the de-funding of mental health, health services, addiction treatment and not creating a stable 24/7 shelter where folks can begin to get well and move on is ceding to neglect of the neediest and blaming the victims of public policy.

Rhodes: Have the policies of the City of Fresno helped or hurt the homeless?

Jessup: The policies of the City of Fresno have hurt the homeless. Witness several successful lawsuits over treatment of the homeless. Witness the ruse of instituting a mistaken vision of Housing First, spending federal funding building too expensive and too few housing units with funding from HUD and the state, while there are empty homes and empty abandoned businesses. There is no scarcity of housing in Fresno, just lack of will to allow it to be accessible by the very poor. Witness the ruse of the mayor's idea of privately funding responses. The result has been that this charity model leaves the houseless with the seven deadly "ins": insufficiency, inappropriateness, inadequacy, instability, inaccessibility, inefficiency and indignity.

Rhodes: If you were in charge of homeless policy in the City of Fresno, what would you do to improve homeless people's lives?

Jessup: I believe that there are some basic things we can all agree on. We all want justice and fairness, strong and vibrant communities, healthy people, sustainable public systems and thriving economies. The policies on homelessness need to be developed with the idea that, bottom line, the issues of fairness, justice, economic and ecological sustainability, and healthy people need to be the results of the policies for the betterment of our community. And there is "enough." There is no scarcity of housing, food or healthcare; there is enough if distributed fairly and intentionally.

There is a need to address the dilemma of solely charitable or religious solutions to homelessness and poverty. It will never be enough to address the systemic issues of deep poverty. Our country has created poverty and homelessness and can un-create it more economically than criminalizing homelessness or leaving people in ill health on the streets, or insisting that they pray to access human services.

The fear of the homeless perpetuated by the city and county, and the constant battle between the city and county over "who is responsible for Fresno homelessness?" has to be understood. Each has a role, and wrangling with each other, blaming each other, is not what we elect leaders to do. The policy should be to create safe and legal campgrounds/communities with water, sanitation and garbage services, so people are no longer "illegal" and so they can rest, and recover, and work on moving forward. I would immediately declare a shelter emergency, which would trigger state mandates for responses by the city and county. I would set up and utilize the four "mash" units the county has for emergencies.

Long term, a 24/7 emergency shelter must be created as the place of entry to transitional and permanent housing. That is what is meant by "housing first": a stable roof over one's head, food and medical care. Then appropriate housing. A medical detox should be developed. Health services should be available at the shelter and any camps established. The tools of recovery need to be available to folks especially utilizing best practices. Most homeless cannot begin to be employed or return to school until they have recovered from the trauma of houselessness and have a stable situation 24/7. One size does not fit all. Individual recovery needs to be based on achieving the highest independence possible. There needs to be a possibility of second chances. Persistently creating respect for people's potential, sustainability and an array of supported possibilities is the answer.

Mostly, there is nothing wrong with what currently exists in the Fresno Continuum of Care, except it is not a continuum. It remains a fragmented non-system, fighting over too little funding, and without addressing the gaps in services. There is funding to do all of this. There is not currently political will.

Rhodes: What would it take to end homelessness in Fresno?

Jessup: Addressing the conundrum of solely charitable answers to homelessness and poverty by persistently creating respect for people's potential, sustainability and an array of supported possibilities. The homeless have to be participants in developing the solutions.

There are ways to achieve the elimination of homelessness in our area. Shelter, 24/7, from day one. Time to recover, and engagement with case management on-site, substance abuse and mental health programs onsite, work that benefits the community and the ability to stabilize lives with permanent, truly affordable housing. There are solid examples of successful shelter programs that have accomplished a very small recidivism rate and ongoing support as long as needed. We could learn to do that here in Fresno. There are scientifically proven ways and programs to end homelessness, and they use resources wisely.

The "overnight to life" model of addressing the issues underlying homelessness, and providing 24/7 responses that ensure stability for the houseless, very poor, addicted and mentally untreated individuals on the streets.

\*\*\*

**Kelly Borkert**
Kelly Borkert was introduced to issues affecting Food Not Bombs participants and the Sleeping Bag Project by Jean Chipp in 2003, around the time the City of Fresno began bulldozing homeless camps in downtown Fresno.

Rhodes: What have we learned over the last decade about what it is like to be homeless in Fresno?

Borkert: The homeless in Fresno seem to serve many different functions. A source of funding revenue. Scarecrows of economic inequity and misfortune. Scapegoats for their own plight. Trash can rattling neighborhood nuisances. Sidewalk landscaping and cause célèbre for local peace and justice advocates—all this from a much longer list. The burgeoning size and impact of the homeless population over the years in Fresno nearly defines the town.

The last decade was a rollercoaster for those without shelter in Fresno County. With swiftly changing services and attitudes toward those facing freezing winter temperatures, tents and sleeping bags disappeared much faster than they could be found when City of Fresno anti-homeless operations were in full swing. When it becomes cooler and moist, things become very difficult. At their coldest, winters in Fresno kill people.

There has been a particularly mean spirit and malicious inconsistency in warming center operations over the last 10 years by the City of Fresno, an indifference that few communities would care to match. Obviously, oversight is lacking, and even the most minimal safety measures are not guaranteed. An inevitable lesson in the first reality of homelessness—extreme vulnerability.

Rhodes: What is the City of Fresno's current policy on the homeless?

Borkert: Not particularly clear. More incursions into personal property seizure with less regard for prior agreements, it appears. Fewer recent attempts at nuisance ordinances, with little evidence of follow-up with the measures previously "implemented" other than camping restrictions, which probably sums up their current policies. They are presumably following a prescribed time and way which people can sleep on the sidewalks in tents.

Over the years, a good bit of radio discussion by elected officials encouraging people not to donate to sidewalk solicitors, demonizing the meridian menace homeless people present, shopping cart theft rings, lobbying for passing ordinances against these things while leaving the doors shut on warming centers seems to shed light on the spirit of [City] Council members toward their poorest constituents. Whether any part of that attitude has changed over the last few years, it seems doubtful that it has improved.

As far as stated policies or expressions of intent, they contradict themselves (if you can corner them for a response to a question), refuse serious dialogue for absurd reasons and ignore clearly expressed concerns and overwhelming public sentiment. Whatever their actual policies are, they leave a lot to be desired and should be subject to public input.

Rhodes: Have the policies of the City of Fresno helped or hurt the homeless?

Borkert: They did not help the community, judging by responses to camp dispersals, which suggests they have not helped the homeless. I see a few particular investors, contributors and developers may have benefitted from blight-induced property devaluation, government programs and government-assisted demographic or infrastructure changes. Their investments stand to do very well. So one out of three. Is that bad?

A series of 10-year plans and two-minute promises turned into an $11 million project that benefits a few. That is a lot of money per occupancy (enough to buy three houses outright in a foreclosure crisis for each occupant) for a 69-tenant project which opened while larger, less exclusive low-income mainstays on Motel Drive were closed down at the same time. What was gained?

In terms of disrespect—summarily removing and destroying possessions is a world-class hurt for anyone. As if indifference, hostility, nuisance ordinances and evictions during cold wet weather isn't enough, they go the extra mile of seizing and destroying what little property homeless people have, year round, even from the Poverello sidewalks. Tents, sleeping bags, blankets, personal items of great sentiment, medicines and IDs necessary to survive—taken from people not always mentally capable of being 100% responsible, or wary of unforeseen risks.

Closing down the warming center and/or hours of operation while much smaller communities throughout the Valley took care of their own? No words are nasty enough to describe this abrogation from vindictive local officials. Completely unacceptable and inexcusable in this country, utterly anti-Christian behavior from people who hide behind pulpits and podiums. The shameless self-congratulating flourish of reopening the warming center after outdoor deaths?

I suppose that is the only policy I am clear upon.

They cannot support or abide small, clean campsites with porta-potties and trash service. They can close the doors on warming centers, and no one even knows it until it is far too late. The number of homeless people who have died of exposure in plain sight on sidewalks in downtown Fresno the last 10 years stands as the clearest description of the city policies on homelessness. Grievous and reprehensible.

Rhodes: If you were in charge of homeless policy in the City of Fresno, what would you do to improve homeless people's lives?

Borkert: We should maximize Census efficiency and demographic accuracy to focus resources and attention where it should be, beyond the already over-serviced fully funded sectors like veterans and women with children. Knowing exactly how many people are homeless in Fresno County should not be a bad thing. Knowing who is homeless at a given time could inform a more effective response. Elderly residents should not face the ever-present dangers of living on the street alone. While veterans are sought-after recipients of aid, the elderly can face lethal challenges we can scarcely begin to comprehend, but we should face that problem immediately.

I would want to ensure some warming and cooling shelters when appropriate, while hoping very few ever needed them but had easy access.

Those are areas of service I would prioritize, while other aspects need to be cultivated downtown. Community relations, mitigation and mediation rather than shrugged shoulders, which forced the downtown business community to drag the police and city into their self-organized discussion in the aftermath of the last major cleanup at the Pov. While city policies, formal and informal, have moved homeless people in and out of the areas around G [Street] and south of Ventura [Street], the reality and repercussions of those decisions were always borne by neighboring residents and businesses. All three parties that are effected by city policy and practice should have a functioning dialogue with the local government, working toward an effective solution in everyone's interest. It is a matter of public health, safety and life quality. The policy architects simply fail to incorporate wider interests into their patchwork approach of conga line rhetoric, bunny-hop policy decisions and cakewalk plans for downtown Fresno's wealthier interests.

There are so many untapped possibilities involving the wider community. It is a matter of stubborn will, selfish interests and faulty preconceptions to overcome. Not nearly so much a budget problem as a moral logjam.

Rhodes: What would it take to end homelessness in Fresno?

Borkert: Homes. Whether a tent in a safe place, or a makeshift dwelling of some sort on private property, or better yet, four walls, decent insulation and a working roof. Whatever the abode, if someone is secure in their location and has good contact opportunities like an address, phone or e-mail, they will very likely make the most of their means.

The amount of money it would take to better accommodate those who do not find their way into subsidized housing opportunities is minimal, especially compared to the money that can be had (and might be lost) for "ending" or "solving" homelessness in the "next 10 years," again.

That appears to be a real problem.

The best communal solutions to the problems of living without are not necessarily expensive, but the demands for federal funds tied to homelessness and the appetite for that money seems to serve a powerful cross purpose. I think the essence of the problem is old news. Until the power of love exceeds the love of money, it will be a bit of a fight.

\*\*\*

## Nancy Holmes

Nancy Holmes is a homeless advocate currently living at the Dakota EcoGarden. Previously, she was homeless and lived at the Grain Silo encampment.

Rhodes: What have we learned over the last decade about what it is like to be homeless in Fresno?

Holmes: Well, I went from being a working person to a homeless person in two paychecks. I learned a lot on the street. I learned a total respect for the life out there. It was a life-and-death situation because you're at everyone's mercy. Who can you trust? Who do you dare trust out there? So I have learned a lot about the gravity of the whole situation. I almost died out there. It was hard, allowing someone's kindness or being afraid of someone's kindness as to what are they doing that for—do they have an ulterior motive? What do they want of mine? I think this project here (the Dakota EcoGarden) is a wonderful idea and a wonderful project, but it can only help, say, 13 people at a time. We need a lot more of these, and we need a lot more people thinking like Nancy Waidtlow [who donated the property for the Dakota EcoGarden]. You know that every little bit helps.

Rhodes: What is the City of Fresno's current policy on the homeless?

Holmes: I think it is cruel. I think it is an absolute cruelty to humanity to go in and bulldoze everything. They had a little area where they could keep track of and count the homeless, and I think they've made it much worse by bullying the people out there and scattering people everywhere. They're afraid too, when a car stops alongside of them, they take off because they don't know what's going to happen. I would say, hopefully with the new City Council in there that some of that changes. But I still think that the [FPD] task force for homelessness is a bully. A gang of bullies. Also, I don't think they have nearly the right count of how many people are homeless. How can you count them? They are everywhere. Who do you count twice? They are under every bush and every nook and cranny where they can be safe for a minute. I think Fresno is one of the worst communities that I have heard about so far for dealing with their homeless.

Rhodes: Have the policies of the City of Fresno helped or hurt the homeless?

Holmes: They are not helping the homeless at all; they are scattering them. I think it is atrocious the way they treat a homeless person like everyone is a drug addict. There are a lot of them out there that are homeless that are drug addicts and crooks but you find that everywhere, and it is hard to weed out good people from bad people. But they don't take the time and you can't just mow down someone's home and expect them to be okay.

Rhodes: If you were in charge of homeless policy in the City of Fresno, what would you do to improve homeless people's lives?

Holmes: Get rid of [Fresno Mayor] Ashley [Swearengin]. I was lucky that a place at the Dakota EcoGarden was offered to me, and I was smart enough to take it. I would take these abandoned buildings and send in my cleanup crew that usually bulldozes the encampments, and I would take these old buildings and refurbish them enough to where people could move into them. The city has enough property that they could donate a safe campground for these people. I would take a lot of the abandoned buildings and a lot of the abandoned properties and turn it over to a homeless advocate. You could charge people five dollars a month for rent. It could be just a tent city; it doesn't necessarily have to be a building because the city could provide a tent for each person and a toilet.

Rhodes: What would it take to end homelessness in Fresno?

Holmes: Like I said—donate property to them so they could have a safe camp. When I was at the Grain Silo encampment, I had a home. I did not feel homeless then, and it struck me that homelessness is desperation. When I was forced to live in a vacant field (after the city bulldozed the Grain Silo encampment), that was desperation. Maybe more doctors can get involved to help deal with those mental issues. Bulldozing them just creates more mental issues and it makes people so afraid.

\*\*\*

## Dixie Salazar

Dixie Salazar is an artist, poet, fiction writer and activist in Fresno. She is secretary and board member of the Eco-Village Project and a consultant and art therapist working with the Dakota EcoGarden in Fresno.

Rhodes: What have we learned over the last decade about what it is like to be homeless in Fresno?

Salazar: I have seen firsthand what a difference housing (with supportive services) can make in people's lives, especially at the Dakota EcoGarden. We have 13 residents presently, in a facility with most residing in tents, a few in rooms in the house on a half-acre property with organic gardening and utilizing green technology. The residents are flourishing—going to school, looking for jobs, becoming employed, stabilizing their lives. What we've learned is that it doesn't take millions to get people off the streets. It takes commitment and the will to do it. If churches, clubs, even individuals would commit to this, we could make a difference.

Rhodes: What is the City of Fresno's current policy on the homeless?

Salazar: I see their policy as a war on the homeless, as a way to drive them out. I have not seen true concern and willingness to really help people.

Rhodes: Have the policies of the City of Fresno helped or hurt the homeless?

Salazar: It has hurt them in many different ways. Bulldozing their dwellings without providing alternative housing was cruel to watch, and people actually died as a result of being exposed to the elements. There have been other proposed ordinances directed at the homeless such as putting restrictions on shopping carts, recycling and sleeping in public that appear to be the city's all-too-obvious way of making life so hard for them that they will leave or disappear. The Homeless Task Force, consisting of four police recruited specifically to follow, track and harass the homeless daily, seems like a complete waste of taxpayer money since they only harass and needlessly criminalize them. They publicly state that they help the homeless, but if you talk to actual homeless people, they will tell you they are constantly pushing them from one place to another, threatening to arrest them, stealing their property and do not offer assistance in finding housing.

Rhodes: If you were in charge of homeless policy in the City of Fresno, what would you do to improve homeless people's lives?

Salazar:
• I would change the General Plan to eliminate urban sprawl and really follow it, instead of just paying lip service to it.
• Appoint a task force that was working to identify the most vulnerable of the homeless and actually try to help them, rather than harass them and criminalize them.
• Institute a plan to educate the public as well as elected officials to the facts

around homeless needs and the savings that come from meeting those needs.

- Make funding emergency shelters a priority.
- Develop committees that include city officials, social service agencies, churches, homeless advocacy groups and homeless people themselves to hold meetings and workshops to find ways for all these groups to help the city develop policies that really help the homeless and provide housing.
- Appoint a homeless liaison adviser who would act as a go-between with the mayor, the City Council and the groups noted in the previous bullet point.
- Develop five- and 10-year plans with the aforementioned partners that have real working solutions modeled on those that have worked in other cities.
- Utilize empty public buildings and abandoned houses as housing for the homeless, making sure they are provided with needed complementary social services.
- At least consider temporary, safe, legal campgrounds if all other measures don't meet homeless needs.
- Partner with the university and various university programs that would encourage students to research, develop and institute innovative solutions to addressing homelessness.
- Provide seed money to groups who want to open group homes such as the Dakota EcoGarden.
- Revisit and redesign the city's current building codes and guidelines to make it easier for those who want to provide privately funded homeless solutions.
- Donate city property to groups such as the Eco-Village Project to use for green, self-sustaining homeless solutions.
- Work with the private sector to interface job components into homeless housing projects. There are models for this nationally.
- Provide homeless drop-in centers where they could get showers, wash clothes, receive mail, store property and use computers, etc., to look for jobs. These could hopefully be staffed by the homeless themselves.
- Create a homeless drop-in center focused on aesthetic needs of the homeless such as a place to get haircuts and other hygiene needs, clothing (donated), as well as a kiln, art studio, with classes in knitting and crochet, art and pottery, music. This could provide jobs and would help the homeless with self-esteem and overall personal development. There is such a place in San Francisco in the Tenderloin district.
- Develop housing for homeless families, partnering with groups such as Habitat for Humanity.
- Charge a homeless liaison advisor with also working with schools to identify homeless youth and work to help their families find housing.

Rhodes: What would it take to end homelessness in Fresno?

Salazar: I'm not sure it can be ended completely. But if even some of the solutions suggested above were being implemented, many lives could be saved, as well as a ton of money. I would love to see the city suddenly become enlightened and join with others in the community to tackle the homeless problem. Right now, this seems far away. I have not seen the will on the part of the mayor or anyone else in city government to really solve homelessness. So, for now, it seems like our best hope is for private groups, churches and others who care to chip away at the problem and hope for miracles.

\*\*\*

**Al Williams**
Al Williams is homeless and lives in the Roeding Park area. Williams was on the 10-Year Plan to End Chronic Homelessness committee.

Rhodes: What have we learned over the last decade about what it is like to be homeless in Fresno?

Williams: What I have learned over the past decade about being homeless in Fresno is that there is a huge number of residents in Fresno who are willing to help the less fortunate people. But if they do, the elected officials of Fresno, along with law enforcement, will issue them a citation (fine them). You may ask why? The answer is simple. Homelessness has been turned into a business by the officials of the city, the state, the country. Millions of dollars change hands over homeless issues. Much of that money goes to law enforcement, which to this day in December 2014 police still won't allow homeless people to sleep in peace.

Homeless people are chased from place to place, with nowhere to go. There aren't enough beds in the few shelters in Fresno to house the 20,000-plus homeless people Fresno has. In my opinion, the City of Fresno has no real desire to provide a safe place for homeless people to sleep. If the city had the desire to make life a little more livable for then homeless people, the City of Fresno would provide a piece of land so that Art Dyson (a local architect with a vision) could head the construction of an Eco-Village Project, which would be constructed with recycled material. The labor would be done by college students and homeless people working together. This has been tested with success. Fresno State students and homeless people worked together, side by side, and built six studio-type apartments within a week. This project would cost the City of Fresno and taxpayers virtually nothing. The City of Fresno said no. Today, there still aren't enough beds to accommodate the homeless people.

Rhodes: What is the City of Fresno's current policy on the homeless?

Williams: Fresno's current policy has, again [in] my opinion, gone back in time and is doing what Officer Rey Wallace did, which was handle the growing homeless issue by whatever means necessary. At this time, the City of Fresno is using the "Don't let them sleep tactic," which is against the [United Nations'] Universal Declaration of Human Rights, which obviously the City of Fresno does not recognize. The city, knowing there aren't enough beds to accommodate the number of homeless people in Fresno, still tells homeless people to move on somewhere else, in hopes that they will leave town.

Rhodes: Have the policies of the City of Fresno helped or hurt the homeless?

Williams: Today's policy definitely hurts homeless people. It only gives police something to do and makes the haters against homeless people happy.

Rhodes: If you were in charge of homeless policy in the City of Fresno, what would you do to improve homeless people's lives?

Williams: If I had the power to make life better for the less fortunate people (homeless people), I would first have all people on the city payroll spend a minimum of seven days living life as a homeless person. That would include the mayor, the city manager, the police chief and all police officers in command positions, and members of the City Council. These people for sure, before they make any decisions regarding the ways homeless people should be treated. Why? Simple. If you never flew an airplane, how can you tell me how to fly an airplane? If you have never been homeless, how can you dictate how it is supposed to be if you're homeless?

Next, put Art Dyson in charge because he has the desire to help rather than criminalize the homeless population of Fresno. Give him some land, let him use the students in our colleges, and allow the homeless people and college students to team up and work together. There are a huge number of ex-construction workers who are now homeless. This would give them a purpose again, plus take them off the streets. They could go across the country getting paid to teach others how to build housing for other homeless people across the country.

Rhodes: What would it take to end homelessness in Fresno?

Williams: And for ending homelessness, someone else can have that chore. Homeless people have been around since houses have been around. Also, the Eco-Village concept will work for only about 40% of the homeless population. The city or state should do the right thing for those with mental issues, not just an office waiting for them to walk in. You get paid to find them. Do your job, you get big bucks. Then we have homeless people who will be homeless people because they like it. This is America the land of the free, home of the brave, if they are brave enough give them a safe ground to be brave.

\*\*\*

## Beverly Fitzpatrick

Beverly Fitzpatrick is a mother, grandmother, retired teacher turned homeless advocate and social activist. She is also on the Board of Directors of the Fresno Eco-Village Project.

Rhodes: What have we learned over the last decade about what it is like to be homeless in Fresno?

## Fitzpatrick:

- Fresno's homeless population is a much larger number than the city or the county reports.
- Fresno has a high degree of poverty, thus a large number of homeless.
- No one "wants" to be homeless.
- Life choices within their control (e.g., drug use, relationships) or out of their control (e.g., loss of job, shelter) are the reasons for their homelessness.
- It is difficult to navigate the "system" once on the street, and the longer someone is homeless the harder it becomes to break that cycle.
- There is a stigma attached to homeless individuals that isn't always articulated, but it is felt by every person pushing their belongings or sitting on the sidewalk.
- Mental health issues increase the longer someone is homeless and they don't receive help.
- In Fresno, there aren't enough shelters beds for the thousands on the streets.
- Our homeless situation is known and the cause has been investigated on a national and international level.
- If a homeless person makes a connection with someone who cares and is there for support on a regular basis and receives some assistance, they can and do live productive lives.

- That after being among Fresno's homeless, I will never not be involved when I see an injustice.

Rhodes: What is the City of Fresno's current policy on the homeless?

Fitzpatrick: This is what I know: In 2010, the City of Fresno drafted a Memorandum of Understanding (MOU) with Fresno First Steps Home (a California non-profit corporation) regarding the city's 10-Year Plan to End Chronic Homelessness. After that MOU was drafted, the City of Fresno began a campaign to raise money for Fresno First Steps Home. Since becoming an advocate, it has been difficult to acquire a figure for the amount collected by the Fresno First Steps Home campaign.

At one time, the media announced that First Steps Home had collected $500,000. The funding was to be used to house a minimum of 20 homeless adults and provide wraparound services for up to a year.

The City will not allow encampments! The Homeless Police Task Force was established to enforce this policy.

The city bus system restricts what an individual can bring on the bus.

The Downtown Library also restricts what some individuals can bring into the library.

In 2014, an ordinance was passed that it was a crime to use a shopping cart to carry belongings.

In May 2014, the city joined the federally sponsored 25 Cities initiative on homelessness. The initiative seeks to end veteran and chronic homelessness by 2015. A leadership team was formed in Fresno consisting of the Fresno/Madera Continuum of Care, the VA, the Fresno Housing Authority, Fresno County and City Hall. The initiative attempts to house as many veterans and chronic homeless as possible in planned actions over a 100-day period.

Rhodes: Have the policies of the City of Fresno helped or hurt the homeless?

Fitzpatrick: The policies of the City of Fresno have hurt the homeless [by] continuing to disrupt the lives of individuals living on the street, in cars or in parks.

Since the evictions of four encampments in 2013, the city's Homeless Police Task Force has been the city's response to homelessness. The task force is visible in the early morning hours, rousting sleeping individuals from sidewalks around Poverello House and other parts of the city, making sure that they pack up all their belongings.

Because of the shopping cart ordinance (in effect for about one year), it is difficult for a homeless person to travel with her belongings and keep them safe, even if it is only in and around the streets where she sleeps. Many times along with the task force, there is a sanitation truck ready to bag and take personal belongings to a City Yard for storage for a period of 90 days. And if the individual has a shopping cart that is taken, a citation is issued.

The city continues to find ways to hurt the homeless. In the fall of 2014, the task force proudly announced that it was patrolling city parks to make sure no homeless person stayed (slept) in the park after the 10 o'clock closing time. The task force returns in the early morning hours making sure no one is there before six o'clock in the morning. If a homeless person is found sleeping in the park, he is issued a citation.

Instead of working on effective solutions, the City of Fresno is spending city money and time for trained police officers (the task force) to disrupt the lives of homeless individuals day and night.

What I have learned through my work in the homeless community is that the majority of homeless individuals are hurt by the actions of the City of Fresno, but the city likes to make the homeless out to be the ones who are hurting the city and its citizens.

Rhodes: If you were in charge of homeless policy in the City of Fresno, what would you do to improve homeless people's lives?

Fitzpatrick: I would not have a policy of the "haves and have nots." I believe that everyone has worth and should be treated with dignity. After all, the homeless person is a citizen of Fresno and the city should be there for all the citizens.

I would find ways to help each individual on a case-by-case basis. As a city, we should be involved in helping the homeless, not hurting them.

As a first step, I would set up organized camps with facilities and programs. In organized camps, agencies would be able to assist homeless individuals because they would be able to locate them. People would be sleeping in a tent, not on a sidewalk; they would have bathroom facilities and be located near a place that serves meals and has other services.

My next step would be to establish a 24-hour emergency shelter with services available onsite.

As a city, I would seek the support of the religious community, community groups, nonprofits and work with advocates.

I would have the city be a more active member of the Fresno/Madera Continuum of Care seeking out grants and money to assist individuals with immediate needs.

Rhodes: What would it take to end homelessness in Fresno?

Fitzpatrick: Elect city leaders who have what it takes to do serious work to help in the area of homelessness.

Personally, I want to think that ending homelessness is possible because it is a rather new phenomenon. A good model, in my eyes, is a socialist-type system with equality being most important and having a strong supportive welfare system.

However, working within our system of government, a good start would be to provide more support in the beginning for those individuals within California's welfare system with the most need. If the support was there before individuals lost everything, more could be done to help. The City of Fresno and Fresno County need to work together to devote more time to developing affordable housing and jobs where the pay allows for the necessities, food, shelter and healthcare.

No one wants to be homeless, but many times they are just helpless in a broken system.

\*\*\*

**Bill Simon**
Bill Simon has been active with several social justice organizations in Fresno, most recently including the Bishop John Steinbock Homeless Advocacy Committee and the Summit Conference on Homelessness for Fresno's Religious Leaders.

Rather than an interview, Simon sent me these reflections about homelessness:

I first worked with the homeless in 1968 on Clark Street, Chicago's second skid row. Almost all of the homeless on Clark Street were veterans of WWII and Korea. They were presumably all alcoholics, but all suffered from PTSD [post-traumatic stress disorder] many years before that disorder was defined. By today's standards, they weren't homeless at all. They could always panhandle enough or get a voucher to sleep in a seedy hotel or in a flophouse. I never saw a tent or a shopping cart. But now the flophouses are gone, and there aren't enough cheap, seedy hotels.

Since then, certainly in Fresno, the situation has become much worse. In addition to the alcoholic veterans, we have added the mentally ill, drug addicts, the poor, foster children turned 18 and those who have lost everything to the Great Recession. I can only remember meeting two homeless people in Fresno who said they came from anywhere but the Central Valley. So homelessness in Fresno largely stems from the poverty and its effects, which is so rampant in the Central Valley.

I first became involved with homelessness in Fresno in 2007 as chair of the Fresno Chapter of the ACLU, about the time the city lost a huge lawsuit the homeless had brought against the city for destroying personal property. I remember Taco Flats and New Jack City and the Hill [all homeless encampments] and the Street Church. With porta-potties, water and trash bins, they would have been barely tolerable places to live. But instead of supplying those minimal necessities, the City of Fresno destroyed those encampments because, the city always told me, no one should have to live that way. So the city put a few people in housing and left thousands to live in even worse circumstances.

The afternoon before the 2011 evictions, several of us met with the mayor, the city manager and others. One member of the clergy was in the group. Since then, I have never heard that clergy person say anything about the mayor except "She lies!" By 2013, the city had finally figured out how to evict the homeless legally. Not humanely, not intelligently, not helpfully, merely legally.

For some, the solution to their homelessness is simply to get a job, difficult to do when you don't have an address and the city has destroyed your ID. For most, it takes someone who will spend months or even years getting to know the homeless person and encouraging the person to get the help needed to live a better life.

Present city policy makes that impossible so the homeless problem will only become worse. The city's homeless task force now makes the homeless move every morning, never spending two nights in a row in the same place. If you can't find a person, you can't help him or her. I have had the Fresno Housing Authority call me to say they have housing for several people but can't find them. Do I know where they are?

There are some who say that, based on the last point-in-time count, the number of homeless in Fresno is dropping. They don't mention that it was raining one day of the count, which makes it more difficult to find the homeless. Nor do they mention that the city's "move every day policy" made it difficult to find the homeless. Nor do they mention that extensive "vulnerability index" interviews slowed the count. If you drive around Fresno and count every panhandler you see on a corner, you will probably come up with a larger number than the point-in-time count did. Of course, not every individual on a street corner with a sign is actually homeless. Rather than give money to corner beggars, it's better to contribute to people you know or to organizations.

Fresno is the largest city in the country that doesn't have an emergency homeless shelter. We must get that emergency walk-in homeless shelter with services available, but not forced, if we are to begin to deal with homelessness. The two most promising things I am aware of are that the Fresno Housing Authority is going to open an emergency shelter and that Wings Fresno is prepared to help people with housing vouchers to actually get into housing and give them the support they need to stay in housing.

Homelessness in Fresno and elsewhere can't be ended without a revolution. Unfortunately, it can't be a violent revolution. That would just leave people at odds with one another. It has to be a revolution by consensus. We have to decide that, as a society, everyone has to have access to a good education, to a decent job, to child care, to good healthcare, to food and shelter. Those who want more should be able to achieve more. But we have to get rid of the huge discrepancy in income between the super haves and everyone else. That revolution would solve homelessness and every other social ill. Can we do it? Probably not. But it's our only hope.

\*\*\*

## Rev. Dr. Floyd D. Harris, Jr.
Rev. Dr. Floyd D. Harris, Jr., is the international president of National Network in Action and the assistant pastor of New Light for New Life Church of God in Fre-

sno.

Rather than an interview, Rev. Harris sent me these reflections about homelessness:

I know everyone doesn't believe in God, and I respect how everyone feels. To be a Christian minister and to live my life by Christian values, it hurts my heart to see God's people be treated less than human. I love everything that breathes, but I believe the dog, cats, horses, etc., at the SPCA Fresno animal shelter get better treatment than homeless people in Fresno. The animals get three meals a day, fresh water, food, medical treatment and a bath. Our homeless community gets no public services. No food, no fresh water, no medical treatment, no bath. To be a pastor, it's my duty to stand for justice, equality and freedom once I see people being hurt by a government system that is supposed to help them.

Ephesians 6:12 says, "For we wrestle not against flesh and blood, but against principalities, against powers, against the rulers of the darkness of this world, against spiritual wickedness in high places."

I witness the wickedness and rulers in high places to see how they hurt those who don't have equal power to fight them back. I stood on the steps of Fresno City Hall with the homeless community to launch the first lawsuit to let the power structure understand we have rights too. My organization, National Network in Action, which is a civil and human rights organization, with the support of many other local organizations, did the first sleep-out on the steps of Fresno City Hall to bring national attention to the brutal treatment of homeless people. It really hit home when Big Sue died on the streets of Fresno, and she was a person who was an activist for homeless people. Big Sue's funeral drew more than 300 people who attended her services, and we walked to the Street Church for her services. I understand now we can't depend on the government to do for our people, but we must do for ourselves. We must build partnerships and do more education with each other and buy land to create our own system to empower our people for better equality of life. Poverty is big business in Mississippi Fresno to generate more money to keep Fresno City Hall operating. Fresno is a wicked town, and I believe God will not bless a town that hurts his people.

\*\*\*

**Brittani Fanciullo**
Brittani Fanciullo has been homeless in Parlier, Clovis and Fresno. She currently

lives in the Dakota EcoGarden and is studying alcohol and drug abuse counseling in college. In a couple of semesters, she expects to earn her certificate.

Rhodes: What have we learned over the last decade about what it is like to be homeless in Fresno?

Fanciullo: I don't know because when I was first homeless I was 19 and in Parlier, so it's a little different. I ended up homeless first because of an abusive relationship. The next time I was homeless, it was in Clovis. That was the worst because they come after you. Me and my boyfriend at that time, we were at a church getting food and clothes and were talking to these people at the church and here comes MAGIC [Multi-Agency Gang Enforcement Consortium], the gang enforcement agency. They knew our names, and they wanted to check us for drugs. The funny thing about it was is that they said they were interviewing all the transients to see where they're living. It is like, what you want an address? Were homeless! You're asking homeless people where they're living? That's crazy, yeah, they were really on us over there. I was homeless in Clovis for a year, and in Clovis we didn't have tents and all that. I didn't even know about the tent cities (in Fresno) at that time. We just slept on the doorsteps of churches to try to stay warm, so that was pretty bad over there.

I was in the H Street tent city in Fresno. On our street, it was okay because we had a little community. We took care of each other; we watched each other's backs. When we had an abundance of supplies we shared, and we watched out for each other. If you went to F Street, it was scary as hell! There were people fighting, setting each other's places on fire and that's right in front of the Poverello House. People treated us pretty good on H Street. A lot of people came and donated stuff and kept us going and helped us out. The porta-potties and the dumpsters were a huge help. People would bring us toilet paper and all kinds of stuff. Being there was good because the Poverello House was close. So those were our resources out there.

But once they bulldozed—I wasn't homeless a lot after they bulldozed, but it was enough to see what you do when it is so hard to find a place to put up the tent up for the night. You had to make sure that you set your alarm, if you had one, because you had to be out of there by 7 o'clock in the morning and what's sad about that is that you don't get to go and pop a tent up until midnight, at least. You don't get a good night's sleep; it's freezing.

Rhodes: What is the City of Fresno's current policy on the homeless?

Fanciullo: The city thinks they are making it better, but they're not. Because if they're trying to keep these quality-of-life ordinances where we don't have to look at the homeless, before they were all at least in one spot at least. You can keep track of what they're doing and they were not in everybody's neighborhood, but now they're spread out everywhere and they do have to sleep somewhere. I can only imagine they're breaking into certain places just to sleep. One good thing about the city's policy, although they were forced to do it, is that they now store people's property.

Rhodes: Have the policies of the City of Fresno helped or hurt the homeless?

Fanciullo: Hurt. They hurt them. The only help I think they give them is the storage, but they were forced to do that. There's nothing they are doing to help. If they're going to kick them out of places, they need to find someplace for them to go and what's really upsetting is when they say go to the [Rescue] Mission or go to the Poverello House. Those are not shelters! And there are only 25 beds in Naomi House, and Evangel Home is only for 28 days. The Evangel Home kicked me out because I came in after curfew because I had a job across town. So they're not as much help as people think.

Rhodes: If you were in charge of homeless policy in the City of Fresno, what would you do to improve homeless people's lives?

Fanciullo: There are so many old abandoned buildings. If they don't want to look at the homeless, stick them in there. Fixing them up would probably cost less than having to arrest homeless people all the time for sleeping places. And the Homeless Rights Act would be really good to pass. How come everyone else can picnic and take naps in the park except homeless people? How do you know the difference? Just because they're dirty and can't get a shower?

Rhodes: What would it take to end homelessness in Fresno?

Fanciullo: Places like the Dakota EcoGarden. Places that are not so exclusive and the homeless don't feel so trapped and restricted, like they almost feel that they're in jail. Using the old abandoned buildings and places like the Eco-Village that are more excepting and less judgmental and just stop treating homeless people like dogs. The Eco-Village is not judgmental, it's free, you can come and go as you please and there are resources like computers for people that want to look for jobs. It is a support system, and that's the most important part. It is a place where you can get on your feet that doesn't feel suffocating. That's huge for a homeless person and the people that like to be outside. You can go there, still be outside, but they're in a safe place.

\*\*\*

**Steven Ward**
Steven Ward was homeless but is now in an apartment, with assistance from the Fresno Housing Authority.

Rhodes: What have we learned over the last decade about what it is like to be homeless in Fresno?

Ward: When I first got there, I thought my life was over. Looking around and seeing the poverty. I learned that when you were out there homeless, it is like your life has been thrown away. I have learned that there are still people that do really care about human life. If you really want something in life, you have to do some work. You are not going to get it by somebody just handing it to you. You have to get it yourself. It took me a while.

I have slept on the sidewalk, I have slept in the rain, drenched, soaking wet, just trying to get warm and all bundled up. I have seen a lot of things. If it wasn't for that Poverello House, I don't know what I would've done because I wasn't in my right state of mind.

Rhodes: What is the City of Fresno's current policy on the homeless?

Ward: When you are homeless, what you have, that's all you have. It's not a house, it's not nothing big, but that is your stuff. That's your belongings. That's all you got in the whole world, and I would think a person would treasure that. For someone to come in and tamper with it, take it from you, that's wrong. That's really wrong. Because that is like you having a house and somebody comes in your house and takes it from you. What does that leave you? You are out in the cold and have a chance of getting sick and dying.

That is an indescribable feeling when somebody takes something from you and it's not even considered stealing. I can see if someone stole it from you. But somebody just comes and takes it from you! You feel that you're less than a man. How could you just come and take something from me and say it wasn't even stolen? That is a messed up feeling. I had that messed-up feeling for a while; you know, there were certain things that I treasure, I really treasured certain things that I had.

You know this settlement we had, that was all good, but that can't bring anything back. It is like somebody took a part of my body, and you could never get that back and that's how I feel. No money, well maybe money will help medical wise, but you can't get some things back. I feel the damage was done.

Rhodes: Have the policies of the City of Fresno helped or hurt the homeless?

Ward: I have nothing against the city. There are a lot of things that are dumped out there and so they have to clean that up. That is their job. I don't knock their job. But if you take something from a person that they really treasure, it leaves a hole. I still don't have anything against them because sometimes they came out there and did some cleanup stuff that really needs to be done. But it wasn't anybody's belongings. They can clean up the gutters, smelling dirty and everything, and they came and cleaned it and it was good, but when they can do that and don't take people's property, that's fine.

Rhodes: If you were in charge of homeless policy in the City of Fresno, what would you do to improve homeless people's lives?

Ward: I would set up some type of work program where a person can get their life back, get motivated and get their self-esteem back. Where you can give a person hope so that they know they're human so that they still have a life [and know] that this is not the end. Give people a push, some type of work program where they can really get involved get motivated because some people out there, they've given up on the work life. I'm not just saying responsibilities. I'm just saying they gave up. Nobody's going to hire me. That self-esteem just goes all the way down.

People that do have addiction problems, there are programs out there but you have to encourage a person and motivate them to get help. There needs to be a lot of counseling to bring the person back up to their standards where they understand that they're not too old.

Rhodes: What would it take to end homelessness in Fresno?

Ward: Get the people back into the work life. Get them motivated. Let them know that people still care about you and you're not an outcast. You're just down on your luck. Set up a center where someone can go and get counseling and not charge them a lot because a lot of people out there are dealing with a whole lot, and if they're dealing with a whole lot they are going to find a way to escape some way, whether it's drugs or whatever.

A roof is important because in order for you to really succeed and get a job you have to have stability. If you don't have stability, you have stuff here or other stuff there, it can't happen. Like you can keep your stuff in storage, but you have to have stability and a house.

\*\*\*

## Gerry Bill
Gerry Bill is emeritus professor of sociology and American studies at Fresno City College and is a founder and treasurer of the Eco-Village Project of Fresno, a project designed to provide transitional housing for the homeless. He is also co-director of the Dakota EcoGarden, a demonstration site for the Eco-Village Project.

Rhodes: What have we learned over the last decade about what it is like to be homeless in Fresno?

Bill: In the last 10 years, we have learned that it is not easy to be homeless in Fresno. There is a lot of harassment from the authorities, plus a lot of vulnerability to a criminal element that preys upon the homeless. On the upside, however, the climate in Fresno is a little bit milder than somewhere like North Dakota. Yet, despite that, we do have people who die from either extreme cold or extreme heat, which gets worse here than it does in coastal areas such as San Francisco.

Rhodes: What is the City of Fresno's current policy on the homeless?

Bill: The current policy of the city seems aimed at making life as uncomfortable as possible for the homeless—perhaps in an effort to drive them outside of the city limits into county territory. Life is made miserable for the homeless by forcing them to move around every day, taking only whatever belongings with them that they can carry. If they try to use a shopping cart to contain their belongings, the Fresno PD's Homeless Task Force is likely to dump the contents, confiscate the cart and cite the person pushing the cart. Possession of a shopping cart is a crime in Fresno, punishable by a fine—which, of course, the homeless cannot pay.

Rhodes: Have the policies of the City of Fresno helped or hurt the homeless?

Bill: The city, working with the Fresno Housing Authority, has housed a relatively small number of homeless people at an enormous cost. I guess those people, at least, have been helped. In my experience, the County of Fresno does more to help the homeless than does the city. I know of two cases in the last three months where county social workers have helped people obtain housing they can afford. That works with homeless who do have an income of some type. Still, it is a drop in the bucket. The city policies that hurt the homeless include the daily harassment mentioned above. It also includes the destruction of the property of homeless people, which is particularly obvious when the city comes around with its bulldozers to demolish the encampments.

Rhodes: If you were in charge of homeless policy in the City of Fresno, what would you do to improve homeless people's lives?

Bill: If I were in charge, I would use city resources, including city-owned land, to create safe and legal campgrounds for those homeless who can function in an environment like that. I believe that to be a significant portion of the homeless. We must recognize that no approach will work for 100% of the homeless. Safe and legal campgrounds could be operated at minimal cost to the city, certainly a tiny fraction of what it has taken to create a small number of apartments for the homeless under the Fresno Housing Authority's program. Safe and legal campgrounds would work pretty well in Fresno, given the climate here. They would not be without their problems, but problems will arise with any housing option. The Fresno Housing Authority's sites have serious problems, yet the city moves ahead with that approach anyway.

Rhodes: What would it take to end homelessness in Fresno?

Bill: To end homelessness in Fresno, or any U.S. city, would require a change on the national level. Homelessness is going to be a problem in any free-market capitalist society. To really end homelessness in the United States would require ending capitalism—something that is beyond the power of the officials in any one city to accomplish. I have seen a place without any significant homelessness—Cuba. Of course, Cuba is not a capitalist society—or at least was not when I made my eight trips there.

\*\*\*

There is a pattern in the responses above that gives me hope. Everyone seems to understand that in order to end homelessness, we need an economic and political system that provides adequate affordable housing and jobs. We also need social services for people with mental health problems or drug and alcohol addictions.

The challenge in front of us is to pressure elected officials to provide the resources needed to build enough affordable housing to end homelessness. At the same time, we have to convince people that homelessness is not a personal problem but the result of an economic and political system that is not meeting people's needs. While we are at it, we must fully fund a universal healthcare system and free education system (through college) and voila! We can now build that museum to show our children what homelessness was like.

By redirecting the funding being used to plan for future wars, ending the wars we are currently engaged in and stopping welfare to billionaires, we can end homelessness. We can live in a more peaceful world, a world with social and economic justice, a world where we treat everyone with dignity and respect.

\*\*\*

If you are interested in helping the homeless in Fresno, I encourage you to connect with the local Food Not Bombs group(s), Saint Benedict Catholic Workers Project or the Dakota EcoGarden. There you will find like minded homeless advocates doing good work locally.

A regional group, which I support and encourage you to help, is the

Western Regional Advocacy Project
2940 16th Street Suite 200-2
San Francisco Ca 94103
wrap@wraphome.org
(415) 621-2533

## ABOUT THE AUTHOR

Mike Rhodes is a journalist and former editor of the *Community Alliance* newspaper in Fresno, California. He is a photo journalist, was a news reporter for KFCF 88.1 FM and has produced many videos documenting politics in Fresno and the Central Valley. He is married, has two adult children, one grandchild, and lives in the community where he was born, Fresno. Politically a progressive, he is optimistic that a movement for social and economic justice will emerge and transform the world in which we live. A better world is possible!

CPSIA information can be obtained
at www.ICGtesting.com
Printed in the USA
FSHW022044070119
54888FS